GHANA'S FOREIGN POLICY 1957–1966

PEACE WITHOUT POWER: GHANA'S FOREIGN POLICY 1957–1966

KWESI ARMAH
Ghana's High Commissioner in London and later Minister of Foreign Trade in the last Cabinet of Dr. Kwame Nkrumah

GHANA UNIVERSITIES PRESS
ACCRA
2004

Published by
Ghana Universities Press
P. O. Box GP 4219
Accra, Ghana

Distributed in Europe and North America
by African Books Collective
The Jam Factory, 27 Park End Street
Oxford OX1 1HU, UK
Email: abc@dial.pipex.com
Website: www.africanbookscollective.com

© Kwesi Armah, 2004
ISBN: 9964–3–0300–9

PRODUCED IN GHANA
Typset by Ghana Universities Press, Accra, Ghana
Printed by Yamens Press Ltd., Accra

To

My wife, Esther and my children: Elizabeth, Charlotte, Esther, Hilda and John, as a token of my gratitude for the love and inspiration they have given me over the years.

CONTENTS

Foreword	xi
Preface	xiii
Abbreviations	xv

Chapter
1. INTRODUCTION ... 1
    Outline of the Problem ... 1
    Peace without Power ... 5
    Internal Cohesion and Foreign Policy: The Problem of Nation
        Building and the Pursuit of Foreign Policy ... 6
    Political Groups and Parties ... 7

Notes and References ... 12

2. THE FORMULATION AND EXECUTION OF POLICY ... 13
    The Status of the Former Colonial Boundary Treaties ... 13
    The Act of Independence, 1957 ... 15
    General Principles of Ghana's Foreign Policy ... 15
    The Ministry of Foreign Affairs ... 16
    African Affairs Centre ... 16
    Limitations on the Formulation of Policy ... 19
    The Portfolio of Minister of Foreign Affairs ... 20
    The African Affairs Secretariat ... 21
    The Bureau of African Affairs ... 22
    The Civil Service ... 23
    Inter-Departmental Rivalries ... 28
    Decision-Making and Foreign Policy ... 30
    The Decision-Makers and Administrators of Foreign Policy ... 35
    Foreign Policy and the Ghanaian Constitution ... 39
    Foreign Policy and the Armed Forces ... 40
    Execution of Foreign Policy ... 41

Notes and References ... 43

3. DE-COLONIZATION AND FOREIGN POLICY ... 45
    De-colonization and Federalism in Africa ... 46
    Ghanaian Policy of De-colonization and the United Nations ... 49
    De-colonization of the Congo ... 50
    Congolese Independence and the United Nations ... 51

All Africa Peoples Conference, 1958	57
International Corps of Volunteers	61
Direct Material Aid to Nationalists	63
Ghana's Foreign Policy in the Commonwealth	63
The Problem of the Republic of South Africa	68
The Obstacle of South African Economic and Military Power	74
International Pressure through International Action	75
Internal Confrontation of Apartheid in South Africa	76
Southern Rhodesia	78
Great Britain's Rights and Duties	79
Summary and Conclusion on Southern Africa	82
Ghana's Foreign Policy and the Institution of the British Monarchy	83
The Monarchy	84
British Commonwealth of Nations	86
The Commonwealth Secretariat	86
Notes and References	88
4. AFRICAN UNITY — THE ASPIRATION	90
The Ghanaian Approach	90
The 'Regional Arrangements'	92
The Continental Union of Africa	96
The Approach of the Brazzaville Group 1960	99
The Approach of the Casablanca Group	100
The Approach of the Monrovia Group 1961	101
The Legal Nature of the Union	105
Notes and References	109
5. THE ECONOMIC ASPECTS OF FOREIGN POLICY	110
The Colonial Economy	110
Post-independence Economic Policy Objectives	111
Domestic Factors which Influenced Foreign Economic Policy	114
Impediments to Industrialization	116
The Quest for Economic Independence and Foreign Policy	118
Attitude to International Aid	120
Foreign Investment	121
Capital Accumulation and Exchange Control	122
European Common Market and Africa	124
Intra-African Trade and Foreign Policy	129
Notes and References	130

6.	GHANA AND WORLD PEACE	132
	Ghana and the United Nations	132
	The World without the Bomb — Peace Plan of Ghana	136
	Positive Neutrality or Non-Violent Positive Action	139
	Cuban Missile Crisis	145
	Financing the United Nations Emergency Force	148
	Solution Based on Consensus	149
	Representation at the United Nations of the Peoples Republic of China	152

Notes and References — 156

7.	MAJOR ISSUES OF WORLD POLITICS	158
	The Problem of Refugees and Freedom Fighters	158
	Ghana and the Soviet Union	161
	The Will of the Electorate under Colonial Government	162
	Accusations of Communist Influence	163
	Misconception of the Extent of Communism in the Gold Coast	166
	Ghana-Soviet Trade Relations	169
	Ghana and the Peoples Republic of China	171
	General Disarmament	173
	The Sino-Indian Border Dispute	174
	The Peace Mission in India and China	175
	Ghana and the United States of America	180
	The US and the Volta Hydro-Electric Scheme of Ghana	181

Notes and References — 184

8.	CONCLUSIONS	187

Notes and References — 204

Appendices		205
1.	EXPORT OF DOMESTIC PRODUCE 1957–1966	205
2.	IMPORTS BY END USE	206
3.	NET FOREIGN EXCHANGE ASSETS OF THE BANKING SYSTEM	207
4.	GHANA'S MEDIUM TERM DEBT BURDEN	208
5.	DIRECTION OF TRADE (% SHARE)	209

Bibliography — 211
Index — 215

FOREWORD

This book is about the foreign policy of Ghana's first post-colonial government. It covers the period of the government of Kwame Nkrumah, (Founder of The Republic of Ghana) and first president of The Republic. This was a momentous period in Ghana's history, and indeed in the history of Africa.

As Ali Mazrui wrote:

> There are times in the history of nations when focusing on personalities is one effective way of capturing the dominant moods of the age. The age of Nkrumah in Africa was the age characterized by nationalist ambitions and self-conscious assertions. To examine the role of Nkrumah is thus, to examine more than one fundamental aspect of Africa in this time; it is to choose one broad perspective in the study of Political Africa as a whole during the period — (A. Mazrui, *Africa's International Relations — The Diplomacy of Dependency and Change*. London, 1977: p.41).

In a sense, therefore, this book is an account of the stewardship of Kwame Nkrumah on the world stage, where Ghana was the ultimate means for dramatizing the emergence of Africa in global diplomacy.

The book's main task is to explain why and how under Nkrumah, Ghana, a small country with few resources, and of the least strategic importance or interest in an ideologically divided world, could pursue an activist foreign policy. In particular, it explicates how Ghana's foreign policy could "arouse so many hopes" given the fact that this small country's pursuit of world peace was guided by the doctrine of positive neutrality. The book examines the determinants of this foreign policy, and how the country could succeed despite its obvious limitations and the global environment of aggressive, high power politics.

Towards this goal, the book covers an array of critical foreign policy issues in which the country played a surprisingly influential role. The issues include the formation of the OAU, the restructuring of the Commonwealth, the expulsion of apartheid South Africa from the Commonwealth, the problem of unilateral declaration of independence by Ian Smith's Rhodesia, the problem of disarmament and world peace (as shown in Nkrumah's holding of "The World Without The Bomb Conference" in Accra), his fateful trip to Vietnam and the imperative of China resuming its membership of the UN and its seat on the Security Council.

The author addresses the subject of the book with the obvious objective of setting the records straight, and clearing the myths and misconceptions surrounding Ghana's foreign policy in those momentous years. He succeeds admirably in this undertaking and does so in a very lucid and powerful style. In particular, he handles his subject with the rare advantage of direct experience, insight and intimate knowledge which very few can claim to have. It is very rare for Ghana's statesmen, retired diplomats, politicians and civil servants to write on the public issues, which once fell within their jurisdiction. Mr. Kwesi Armah is one of the few who have ventured to write what amounts to memoirs, and his book should illuminate Ghana's foreign policy of the period that has been obscured or misconceived to date.

Apart from Scott Thompson, whose work on Ghana's foreign policy Ambassador Kwasi Armah interrogates with intellectual vigour, and vehemently contradicts with a wealth of factual evidences as well as analytical rigour, there has not been any work remotely comparable in depth and breadth to the present book, which derives its strength from two sources. First, it is the result of carefully collated evidence, analyzed in the context of those historical moments, the motives, reasons and forces that shaped the country's foreign policy. Ambassador Armah achieves his purpose with a superb grasp of the interplay of all such complex, often mysterious, forces. Second, the book is based on both public and private archives, including the author's own collection from the years he served the country as a diplomat, minister and Nkrumah's special emissary. It is in this sense that this book attains immense significance and value, and, therefore, qualifies as an indispensable resource of reference book for Africa's diplomats, foreign ministers, foreign policy advisers, as well as university teachers and students.

PROFESSOR KWAME A. NINSIN
Executive Secretary,
African Association of Political Science
formerly Head, Department of Political
Science, University of Ghana, Legon

PREFACE

This book is a study of Ghana's foreign policy from 1957 to 1966. In writing it, I am bound to be influenced by the fact that I was a member of the Government of the First Republic of Ghana, first as High Commissioner to the court of St. James and later as Cabinet Minister. I have been able to draw on my experience of the conditions in which those who formed and executed the foreign policy of Ghana carried out their work, and of the nature of public opinion in Ghana concerning international affairs at the time. My experience is, in some aspects, at odds with some of what has been stated in the only major secondary work about this subject, and I believe it has provided useful insights in the preparation of this study.

The sources I have used include my own private papers and Ghana Government documents. I wish to record my gratitude to all the staff of the following institutions for their various assistance: The Royal Commonwealth Society and Chatham House, London; The African Library, Accra; and the Ministry of Foreign Affairs, Accra; The Bodleian and the Commonwealth Library, Queen Elizabeth's House, Oxford.

I must express my profound gratitude to Professor E. A. Badoe, the eminent Surgical Specialist at Korle-Bu Hospital and past President of the West African College of Surgeons, who was the first to see the need for this work, and urged me on in London to undertake this study at University.

I am also grateful to the following for their assistance while on field trip to Ghana: Mr. Fred Arkhurst, the former Supervising Principal Secretary, Ministry of Foreign Affairs, and later Ghana's Permanent Representative at the United Nations; Mr. Harry Amonoo, the former Supervising Principal Secretary, Ministry of Foreign Affairs and later Ghana's Ambassador to the United States, and Secretary to late President Nkrumah's African Affairs Political Committee; Mr. Sam Quarm, formerly Ghana's Ambassador to the United States and the Supervising Principal Secretary of the Ministry of Foreign Affairs, Accra. Their experience and insights into the operations of Ghana's foreign policy were most useful to me. Also the encouragement and interest of Professor Peter Armitage, Tutor for Graduates, St. Peter's College, Oxford, in this study were further sources of inspiration.

In addition, I would like to thank the late Asantehene, Otumfuo Opoku Ware II, for his advice on the impact of traditionalism and the concept of *Parens Patriae* on the functions of Government.

My greatest debt of gratitude goes to Professor Hedley Bull, my supervisor at Oxford. His helpful criticisms and guidance throughout my graduate studies were invaluable. But, of course, responsibility for the shortcomings of the book rests entirely with me.

Finally, I want to express my profound gratitude to my wife and children for the patience with which they bore my long hours of seclusion from them in the course of writing this book. Without their long suffering, forbearance and encouragement, I could not possibly have concluded this task.

September, 2000 KWESI ARMAH
Roman Ridge, Accra

ABBREVIATIONS

AAPC	All-African People's Conference
AAPSC	Afro-Asian People's Solidarity Conference
AEF	French Equitorial Africa
ASEAN	Association of South East Asian Nations
AYO	Anlo Youth Organization
CAO	Committe of African Organizations
CARICOM	Carribbean Community
CIAS	Conference of Independent African States
COMECON	Council for Mutual Economic Assistance
CPP	Convention Peoples Party
DFOCT	Development Fund for Overseas Countries and Territories
DSO	Distinguished Service Order
EACSO	East African Common Services Organization
ECM	European Common Market
EEC	European Economic Community
FLN	Front de Liberation Nationale (Algerian)
GAP	Ghana Action Party
GPRA	Gouverment Provisoire de la Repulique Algerienne
ICJ	International Court of Justice
IMF	International Monetary Fund
MAP	Muslims Association Party
NAM	Non-Aligned Movement
NATO	North Atlantic Treaty Organization
NCBWA	National Congress of British West Africa
NLM	National Liberation Movement
NPP	Northern Peoples Party
OAS	Organization of American States
OAU	Organization of African Unity
PFA	Parti de la Fereration African
PAFMECA	Pan-African Freedom Movement of East and Central Africa
QC	Queen's Counsel
RAF	Royal African Force
RDA	Rassemblement Democratique Africaine
SPF	South Pacific Forum
TANU	Tanganyikan African National Union
TC	Togoland Congress
TNC	Trans-National Corporation
UAM	Union of American States
UAR	United Arab Republic
UDI	Unilateral Declaration of Independence

UGCC	United Gold Coast Convention
UN	United Nations
UNCTD	United Nations Conference on Trade and Development
UNDF	United Nations Development Fund
UNEF	United Nations Emergency Fund
UNFP	Union Nationale des Forces Populaires (Moroccan)
UNO	United Nations Organization
UNOC	United Nations Operations Cost
UNTAF	United Nations Technical Assistance Fund
UP	United Party
USSR	Union of Soviet Socialist Republics
WANS	West African National Secretariat
WB	World Bank
ZANU	Zanzibar African National Union
ZAPU	Zanzibar African People's Union

Chapter 1

INTRODUCTION

Outline of the Problem

The conception of power politics, as is understood in Ghana and other developing states of the third world, involves political coercion under contemporary (and past colonial) conditions. Thus, the apparent aim of these countries after independence was the limitation of power in the international sphere and what Klaus Knorr called "non-power influence"[1]. By this is meant the ability of minor states to affect the behaviour of super powers without any adversary resort to superior strength, military or economic. Where such a situation prevails, it operates at least, to the advantage of the minor states of the third world in the sense that the latter are able to avoid clear identification with the opposing super power bloc, East or West, which powers have reached something of a balance of destructive forces with nuclear weapons and have, in order to gain their own policy ends, had to seek support of the smaller states. Indeed, the nuclear power stalemate has added greatly to the importance of the role of the minor and non-nuclear states. Their decision on which nuclear power to support on a particular issue before the United Nations or otherwise has become a matter of interest to the great powers. Had the nuclear powers not cancelled out each other's force through this nuclear balance, it would, in fact, have been largely irrelevant whether or not minor and developing states without power in the international community decided to adopt a detached foreign policy of non-alignment.

The First Republic of Ghana of 1960 emphasized that the foreign policy of Ghana was non-alignment. That did not mean that Ghana intended to remain in isolation. On the contrary, Ghana sought to maintain its policy of non-alignment with an independent foreign policy prompted by the necessity for the country to recognize its responsibilities for making its own contribution toward the preservation of international peace. A key element in that policy was the determination to help to prevent a third world war which the Ghana Government believed would only result in the extinction of human civilization by the nuclear bomb. It was for this reason that Dr. Nkrumah said that Ghana did not "choose to play the role of silent spectator in world affairs, or in matters which affect our country's vital interests and the destiny of the African peoples. Our policy of positive neutralism is not a passive or neutralist policy. It is a positive policy based upon our firm belief in positive action"[2].

Although Ghana is comparatively a small country in twentieth century

African politics — with a population of about six million at the time of its independence — it achieved independence in an atmosphere of goodwill towards all nations; and this spirit became amply evident, when a remarkable number of delegates from all parts of the world came to the independence celebrations. It was a time when the great powers were vying for the favour of small states. The interest other countries took in Ghana's internal affairs was great; this somehow gave a feeling that what Ghana did had significance far out of proportion to the size or strength of the country. The interests of the country in foreign relations were considerable.

Such international interest as was aroused by Ghana from 1957 to 1966 — from independence (1957) to the first military coup d'etat (1966) — deserves a comprehensive and systematic analysis especially with reference to super power competition. The available works on the subject appear to be coloured by the predilections of the writers. Far too many works have been compounded chiefly of irritation and pique, mystification and bewilderment, suspicion and mistrust of Nkrumah.[3] Indeed, the account given by many commentators of Ghanaian neutralism in this period consisted largely of cliches, stereotypes, erroneous value judgements, and plain factual errors. Furthermore, the unevenness both in quality and scope of the earlier works on Ghanaian foreign policy has been due to lack of practical examination of the problem as it affected the international community at large, and Ghanaians who were involved in it.

The purpose of the present study is to conduct a practical examination of the problem by a Ghanaian who found himself involved in the issues reported on the period under review. It is hoped to make the problem more intelligible and to provide a more satisfactory basis for appraising the issues involved than mere dislike of Nkrumah or the Government of Ghana under him.

Ghana commands or stands in no strategically important place in terms of sea or land communications and is, therefore, of no importance as a military or naval base for any world power. Moreover, economically, with the exception of supplying about one-third of the world's cocoa, its role in the global economic structure is negligible. And yet, "every figure who appeared on its (Ghana's) stage was magnified and distorted, almost beyond recognition"[4]. People took interest because they saw exemplified in Ghana, the struggle for the freedom of the African continent. This was because many pioneers ranging from the late Kwegyir Aggrey and Casely Hayford to Nnamdi Azikiwe, Kwame Nkrumah and others, whose Pan-African views had been dimmed by colonialism, were given a foothold in African soil to propagate their ideals. Thus, in a public letter to Dr. Nkrumah at the convention of the government of eight independent African states in Accra, Dr. Du Bois could write as follows:

> I hereby put into your hands, Mr. Prime Minister, my empty but still significant title

of President of the Pan-African Congress to be bestowed on my duly elected successor who will preside over a Pan-African Congress due, I trust to meet soon and for the first time on African soil, at the call of the independent state of Ghana".[5]

As a result, Ghana became the vortex of African nationalism. Moreover, unlike Liberia and Ethiopia, Ghana also had the Commonwealth framework through which it could wield influence at the time of independence. The writer agrees with Scott Thompson that Ghana's foreign policy is intrinsically important during the years covered; and that as the first sub-Saharan colony to gain independence, Ghana played a larger role in African and international affairs in its nine years of independence than might be expected from a small country. In fact, excluding India, none of the successor states in the post colonial era aroused so many hopes as Ghana; and none came to independence with so extensive a commitment to the development of a forceful foreign policy.[6]

There is no doubt that one of the reasons for the unique position which Ghana held during this period within the African independence movement, was the country's foreign policy, particularly its African policy: the policy outside Africa calculated to shield Ghana from ideological conflict, since the country was born into a world torn and divided in its political relationships. Ghana feared that as a small country, if it aligned itself with the great powers, it would lose in its independence and ability to act for peace. The second reason was Dr. Nkrumah's own dominant influence and character. He had several moods and attitudes: he was affable, sympathetic, patient, humorous, open to compromise on one hand, and on the other hand ambitious, extroverted and yet rigid. He artfully and dexterously permuted and combined the use of these qualities with very little effort. It is generally accepted that Nkrumah possessed the gifts of magnetic charm which endeared him to all who came into his presence: he doubtlessly utilized this charm to the full and at quite a number of conferences his presence and mood proved to be influential. It seemed that in 1959 the whole business of government, in so far as Ghana's external relations were concerned, centred around his movements. Nkrumah's official visits to India, the United Arab Republic, Nigeria, the Cameroons, in 1959 were a practical demonstration of Ghana's neutrality in the context of non-alignment.

As Ali Mazrui has written of Nkrumah's period:

> There are times in history of nations when focusing on personalities is one effective way of capturing the dominant moods of the age. The age of Nkrumah in Africa was the age characterized by nationalist ambitions and self conscious assertion. To examine the role of Nkrumah is to examine more than one fundamental aspect of Africa in this time: it is to choose one broad perspective in the study of Political Africa as a whole during the period[7].

Ali Mazrui was quite correct in stating that the personality of Nkrumah stood out firmly as a symbol of political inspiration for Africa. Nkrumah made an inestimable contribution in awakening the spirit of national consciousness — the undaunting spirit — and dogged resistance among African states still under colonial rule. And he had the courage and dynamism to face the odds in those early days of nascent nationalism when political leadership was intractable and badly fraught with danger of persecution and imprisonment.

When on March 6, 1957, Nkrumah announced the independence of Ghana, he also set out programmatically what the immediate foreign policy concerns of Ghana would be: *The independence of Ghana is meaningless,* he announced, *unless it is linked with the total liberation of Africa*.[8] No other African leader insisted more on an international perspective, when confronted with an African problem, than did Nkrumah.

But why should Nkrumah have been particularly concerned with the independence of the other African countries to the point of defining Ghana's independence as bound up with theirs? As we have said, Nkrumah's thinking was characteristically historical. "Ghana" had lost her independence not as an isolated stroke of historical bad luck but as an integrated link in a chain of events which came to be projected as the European 'scramble for Africa'. Ghana's independence could, therefore, only be said to have been recovered in the context of a liberated Africa.

In their limited sovereignties, the African states counted for little on the international stage. At home, they remained poor in the midst of plenty and, therefore, exercised little autonomy in their historical destiny. United, however, there would be power. And to achieve continental unity, they had first to attain their independence. This was the central theme of the first All African People's Conference in Accra in 1958.

Dr. Nkrumah was also historically minded. It appears, therefore, that when we review his foreign relations, we also adopt a comparative and historical approach. What then was the historical conjuncture in which Ghana achieved its independence and Nkrumah uttered the memorable proclamation we have quoted above?

This independence was achieved in the context of the overall colonial debacle which followed the Second World War. It is often said that wars provide the motor for historical change. But in the history of the colonized peoples of the world, the changes in their national destinies inaugurated by this war were simply seismic. Within two or three years after 1945, India wrested its independence from Britain, to be followed immediately by Ceylon, Burma, Indonesia and Philippines. Elsewhere, in Indochina, France, the other major colonial power, was locked in a war, doomed to failure, to preserve its colonial possessions. The process of de-colonization had started and could not be reversed. The movement for, and ultimate achievement of independence for Ghana, belonged to this order of events.

Peace without Power

It follows from what has been said that, the policies which Ghana pursued and implemented were calculated to bring peace in Ghana and the other parts of Africa; it was hoped that through this process a modest contribution to world peace might ensue. What then is the meaning of "peace without power" within the context of Ghana's foreign policy? This is a legitimate question because peace has a distinct connotation in Ghana's foreign policy. For instance, in the period 1945-1960, Africa was engaged in a struggle for political liberation. Consequently, peace within that period meant primarily de-colonization. The conflict between colonialism and anti-colonialism was looked upon as the foremost threat that could lead to a conflict of major proportion.

Arnold Wolfers saw the dangers involved in such a situation; this led him to observe that, only agreement and co-operation among the great powers would provide a framework within which all nations could live in peace, but the existence of small states imposed self-restraint and patience on the mightier countries.[9]

If small nations were to remain dependent territories, they would exercise no influence on conflicts among the super powers. For the small states to be able to interpose between East and West and make any contribution to peace, they had to be free and independent, and to achieve this meant there had to be a process of de-colonization. It is this process which made Ghana's de-colonization policy an instrument for peace. Ghana's policy, therefore, was directed towards the creation and encouragement of independent states whose existence could impose restraint on the great powers in the interest of peace. After political independence, peace meant primarily the realization of social and economic benefits for the newly independent nation. Indeed, as Nkrumah said:

> The only kind of war we seek is the good old fight against man's ancient enemies.... Poverty, disease, hunger and illiteracy.[10]

So, the peace to be won would be the one that ensured food, clothing and shelter for everybody. As the Ghana Government indicated, there were enough resources to go round. What was lacking was organization. An important aspect of this organization is removal of trade barriers and harmonization of trade between primary producers and the great industrial nations. The problem of currency liquidity and restrictions impose difficulties upon the economies of the developing countries, especially Africa. The new organization will help to resolve this problem, more especially that the world is now a global village and its prosperity is indivisible. It is, therefore, vital that, based on this organization, the trading companies of the world could act together to prevent crises from creating depressive conditions for world trade. It can be argued that Ghana's foreign policy was a contribution to bring about this new organization of the world that would eliminate poverty and foster peace.

Another meaning of peace within the said context is accord between the Great Powers so that developing countries including Ghana could carry out their economic development. Thus, Ghana did not align itself with any particular bloc or group of powers: the reason was to retain its independence, and thus be able, where possible, to act in concert with other states as a restraining influence for peace.

However, in modern times, quite apart from the Security Council, economics and military power are the most important ingredients for exercising influence in the international scene. Developing countries which lack such power are at a serious disadvantage in influencing the policies of the developed countries. Nevertheless, the emergence of many small states on the international scene has created a different situation. This is especially so at the UN and its Agencies, where the developing countries have dominant voting power, and can use it to influence discussions in the world today.

Although the developing countries possessed little military or economic power, yet in the first nine years after Ghana's independence, several of them had sufficient political influence to forge a new pattern of international relations between the super powers. Thus, in 1958, Nkrumah said that force alone is no longer a decisive factor in world affairs; he visualized a distinctive African contribution to international discussion and the achievement of world peace.

The other side of the coin relates to where there is conflict between the great powers in respect of specific issues in Africa. In fact, wherever there is a state of instability in Africa, the Great Powers are tempted to intervene; such a situation intensifies their rivalry in Africa, and has at times led to confrontation between the two nuclear super powers. This was illustrated by the Congo crisis which sparked off a direct confrontation: the struggle between the Soviet and Western Powers in the Congo increased the options available to the Congolese Government. It pursued its foreign policy objectives not through available power or strength based on military might, but rather through its ability to exploit the competition between the great powers.

Similarly, although the absence of intrinsic power was a great handicap, Ghana and other African states were able to take advantage of their bargaining position in prosecuting meaningful diplomatic activities.

Internal Cohesion and Foreign Policy: The Problem of Nation Building and the Pursuit of Foreign Policy

For a new state, internal strife and divisions could weaken the nation's ability to conduct a useful foreign policy. Divisions in a society where tribalism has deep roots, could engender diverse interests which may not necessarily conform to the national interests which, in the final analysis are the basis of every country's foreign policy. Ghana inherited the colonial problems of local rural and urban councils on the British model on one hand, and on the other, the intricacies of chieftaincy and the old colonial administrative network which still existed. These factors had to be harmonized if there was to be one nation. Party divisions aggravated the situation and brought about a struggle between the old and the new, a struggle on one hand to adopt the Western Parliamentary democratic system, and on the other, to revert to, or adapt, traditional institutions. The nation had to seek methods by which the old and the new could be blended. Ghana could only make her contributions significant if she succeeded in showing how an African society could be transformed without losing its essentially-African character. Consequently, the Nkrumah Government introduced a new system of local government in which the old native authorities were abolished, and new local, district and urban councils composed mostly of elected members were set up. In the elections to the councils, Nkrumah's Party, the Convention People's Party (CPP), swept the polls, and the youth and school leavers replaced the chiefs in the field of local government.

Political Groups and Parties

It was also necessary to infuse national consciousness into political parties whose activities were confined to regional or tribal objectives. This awakened ethnic sentiments and loyalties, and divided the nation; for instance, the Northern Peoples Party (NPP) was recognized as a regionalist party whose aims were duly limited to political and social development of the Northern Region, the Muslims Association Party (MAP) was confined mostly to people of the Muslim faith. The Togoland Congress (TC) was centred only on people who advocated the unification of French with British Togoland, while the Anlo Youth Organization (AYO) advocated unification of all Ewe people in French Togoland, British Togoland and the Trans-Volta Region, the Ghana Action Party (GAP) was merely a one-man party; at the 1954 general election, it fielded only one candidate, Dr. Ansah Koi, the founder of the party and the National Liberation Movement (NLM) was seen to be essentially an Asante national movement. In fact, but for the activities of the NLM which advocated a federal form of government, and the old Togoland question, Ghana would probably have gained its independence from Britain soon after the 1954 elections.

Politically, the activities of these regional parties represented a spirit of regional separation — keeping ethnic groups split and separate from one another. The aim, it was claimed, was to mobilize regional support, which would enable the regional leaders to have some influence on Central Government for purposes of regional development; but in reality regional political organization involves playing on people's fears and suspicions, stirring up animosity between tribes in order to manipulate and undermine the authority of the Central Government. The danger these tribal and political divisions posed to the unity of the country was considerable. Only firm action was able to bring cohesion in the society. Thus, Geoffrey Bing observed that:

> The political danger of politics becoming tribalist had been obvious from the start and the Nkrumah Government attempted to meet it, at first, by imposing by legislation the British Political system. In effect, the two-party system was introduced by law. The Avoidance of Discrimination Act, 1957, made illegal all tribal, '... and regional parties and thus forced the opposition which had hitherto consisted of four or five separate elements, to come together in one so-called 'United Party'".[11]

Here the possibilities which Pan-Africanism as an integrating force presented were recognized and vigorously implemented. Consequently, dissipation of energy gave way to fusion of talents for the purposes of nation-building. The Nkrumah Government was able to demonstrate its ability beyond all doubt to cope with the complex problems connected with governing and developing a young nation. Thus, Pan-Africanism was seen to act as the binding force which enabled African states to heal the wounds of the past, and open up vistas of new hope for the future.

Ghana's Pan African policy was based on the ideas of Black pride, Black identity, African emancipation and unity. **Black pride** is a concept originating in the belief in African achievements in the past, in Africa as the forerunner of modern civilization, as the originator of mathematics, medicine, astrology, religion and architecture. That Africa has given a lot to the world and can do so again given the chance. **Black identity** involves the togetherness of all Africans, where ever they may be and that, Africa is their common home-land. **African emancipation** deals with the possibility of the African regaining his freedom and dignity. And **African unity** concerns the possibility of the African uniting under one government in the best interest of the continent and its people.

Nkrumah realized that the factors militating against the achievement of black pride, black identity, African emancipation and unity were colonialism and domination. He saw colonialism as the policy by which the colonial power, the mother country, binds her colonies with political ties, with the primary objective of promoting her own economic advantage. And he saw domination as the policy of creating, organizing and maintaining an empire.

To pave the way for the realization of African pride and dignity, the continent had to be liberated. So, on attaining independence in 1957, Ghana plunged into the struggle for the de-colonization of Africa. And by 1960, about 30 African countries had been liberated.

The de-colonization of Africa was necessary for the self-determination of the African, for determination of his political and economic policies unfettered by any power in the world. However, de-colonization per se was insufficient for the realization of African aspirations unless it was linked with the unity of the continent. This will enable Africa to utilize its vast resources in the interest of all its people.

Nkrumah's arguments for African unity were that, if Africa were not united, the continent will be competing with itself instead of utilizing its immense resources for the optimum advantage of each member state.

In terms of defence, it will be safer and cheaper to belong to a united family than to remain outside it, as it will be more daunting and costly to attack a united Africa than a balkanized one. It will also yield enormous savings for economic development.

Also diplomatically, it will be better for one voice to speak and represent the whole Africa instead of many hostile voices opposed to one another in the councils of the world. A unified diplomatic representation will also yield enormous savings for economic development.

Ghana looked upon African unity as a potent and rational formula for solving the intricate and urgent problems facing Africa. It is "an inescapable desideratum for creating a modern society which will give our people the opportunity to enjoy a full and satisfying life".[12]

Nkrumah's concept of African unity has a wider connotation. Where men of history like Napoleon of France, Garibaldi of Italy and Gamel Ataturk of Turkey sought unity because of the state power and military grandeur it conferred, Nkrumah sought African unity for the political and economic benefits it would confer on the African peoples and mankind, as a whole. As Nkrumah put it, "it is only when the artificial boundaries that divide her are broken down so as to provide for viable economic units, and ultimately, a single African unit, that Africa will be able to develop industrially, for her own sake, and ultimately for the sake of healthy world economy".[13]

But the major obstacles to the realization of the dream of African unity is neo-colonialism, according to which the state subject to it is in theory independent and has all the outward trappings of international sovereignty, but in reality, its economic policies are dictated from outside.

Nkrumah's radical Pan-African policy can only be understood by reference to the times in which he lived. Nkrumah's world was a world ravaged by colonialism. Africa had been conquered and divided up among the colonial powers. It was also an age witnessed by two world wars and revolutions in Asia and Eastern Europe. No doubt, these nationalist and revolutionary currents co-mingled to form in Nkrumah a strong belief in the possibility of liberating and uniting Africa into a political and economic block to pursue a progressive path of development.

Pan-Africanism as an integrating force has two facets: internal cohesion giving rise to national unity, and the political unification of the continent; but economic reconstruction is a vital ingredient of both facets. Thus, Ghana's foreign policy flourished within the confines of internal cohesion and national unity. Ghana's foreign policy, especially the Pan-African policy, had, therefore, a nation-building function: it was intended to unite Ghanaians in a feeling of nationhood and to create a spirit of dignity and a mental emancipation supplanting the colonial past. This situation kindled the enthusiasm of Ghanaians and enabled the country to make the efforts and sacrifices which made development possible. It did, in fact, serve to control Ghana's disparate tendencies and to facilitate the task of building a nation fostering those feelings of identity which made independence a reality.

This is not to say that Ghana's foreign relations during the period were without impediments. Ghana did experience certain criticisms in its pursuit of its Pan-African policy. For example, Ghana's opposition to the political federation of East Africa generated considerable tension. Ghana opposed this on the grounds that it would delay the wider unity of the continent. Greater tension, however, revealed itself as a result of the concept of "assimilation" which closely associated French West Africans with France. The critics of assimilation argued that, it is a concept which appears to militate against African unity and this adversely affected the relations between Ghana and the French African states. It was also argued by these critics that, there were two apparent contradictions in Ghana's foreign policy. The first contradiction, they alleged, was that, although she fervently pursued a policy of African unity, Ghana, in fact, obstructed such unity in the sense that for the purposes of exercising her newly found sovereignty, she quit or resigned from many of the common African institutions in which she had been associated with other British colonies — for example, the West African Frontier Force and the West African Currency Board. These moves were justified in terms of national interest, but, it was said, conflicted with professions of commitment to African unity.[14] According to non-British African states, a second contradiction was Ghana's becoming a member of the Commonwealth.

However, what these critics failed to realize was that, the unity of Africa would provide the continent with an historic opportunity to pull resources together, diversify and develop more quickly than otherwise. Moreover, if Ghana had continued her membership of the common African institutions with other colonial states, this would have inhibited a rapid adaptation of policy and would have restricted Ghana's freedom of action. As regards their criticism of Ghana's membership of the Commonwealth, there is no denial that Commonwealth amity became one of the pillars of Ghana's foreign policy; and Nkrumah justified this, not simply because of the economic advantages such as technical assistance and trading preferences which it offered, but because of its lack of formal organization and the complete equality of status among members.[15]

The Ghana Government also felt that inter-racial co-operation, which characterizes the activities of the Commonwealth, is an important factor in creating understanding between the developing countries of the Third World and the developed countries.

The theme of the book can, therefore, be summarized as: (1) total liberation and de-colonization of Africa; (2) the political and economic unity of Africa; (3) active participation in the Organization of African Unity (OAU) after 1963 and commitment to its objectives; (4) active participation in the UN and (5) attachment to the Commonwealth of Nations.

Ghana's policy outside Africa was calculated to shield Ghana from the ideological conflicts of both East and West. This stand gave great impetus to Ghana's quest for peace in the international arena; it enabled the Ghana Government to organize the "World Without The Bomb Conference" which was held in Accra in June, 1962. Eminent scientists from all over the world attended this Conference and views were expressed which gave hope to Ghana's efforts to promote peaceful co-existence among nations.

This study is intended to examine the foregoing developments in detail. The study of Ghana's foreign policy has devoted little attention to the theme of a thrust for peace, or to the institutional changes which laid the foundation for the state power and authority to conduct meaningful foreign policy.

There is the need to throw light on the dominant textures of Ghana's foreign policy as the attempt to bring about a more comprehensive and all-embracing balance of power by persuading China to join the UN and open formal relations with the United States; a Sino-Indian policy which contributed to and helped to bring about the Colombo Peace Talks; a policy of Commonwealth amity which led to Ghana's proposal and the establishment of the Commonwealth Secretariat, and the establishment of the OAU. Moreover, it is necessary to examine the foreign policy moves which made Ghana a meeting place where people from the Third World, from the West and from the Socialist countries, were able to exchange ideas in a climate of cordiality. It can be argued that, the commanding position which Ghana held during the period was derived especially from the role between 1957 and 1966 of Dr. Nkrumah, a leader who was armed with an ideal — African liberation and unity. This instantly recalls a well-known formulation that people who have a message only win when armed. In the chapters which follow we shall endeavour to elucidate the ideal and the weapons with which the Ghana Government tried to pursue its objectives.

NOTES AND REFERENCES

1. Knorr, Klaus 1975. *The Power of Nations: The Political Economy of International Relations.* New York: 310–319.
2. *Africa Digest.* VII, February, 1960, p.132.
3. Schlesinger Jr., Arthur, M. 1965. *A Thousand Days (John F. Kennedy in the White House).* London: 498–9.
4. Bing, Geoffrey 1968. *Reap the Whirlwind.* London: 11.
5. Wallerstein, Immanuel, 1967. *Africa: The Politics of Unity.* London: 26.
6. Thompson, Scott, 1969. *Ghana's Foreign Policy, 1957–1966.* Princeton: xvii.
7. Mazrui, Ali 1977. *Africa's International Relations. The Diplomacy of Dependency and Change.* London: 41.
8. Nkrumah, Kwame, 1957. Announcement of Ghana's Independence. Speech at Polo Grounds (Accra), March 6th 1957.
9. Wolfers, Arnold 1944. In defence of small countries. *Yale Review*, Winter 1944, pp. 201–202.
10. Bing, *op. cit.*, p.23.
11. *Ibid.*
12. Nkrumah, Kwame 1963. *Africa Must Unite*, Heinemann Edition. London: 221.
13. Nkrumah, Kwame 1965. *Neocolonialism, the Last Stage of Imperialism.* London: 25.
14. Coldicott, T. 1964. *Post-Graduate Seminar. Paper on Ghana's External Relations.* London: 1.
15. Nkrumah, Kwame 1973. *I Speak of Freedom* (Panaf Edition). London: 100–101.

Chater 2

THE FORMULATION AND EXECUTION OF POLICY

Assuming that a reasonable and effective overall plan, including the formulation and execution of foreign policy, can be worked out and agreed upon, very little can be gained unless that plan proves acceptable to the public and can be put into operation. In an authoritarian or dictatorial regime, there is no such problem, because the chief of the government usually knows — or thinks he knows — what he wants, and because any policy, once approved by him, will be carried out regardless of the opinion of others — officials, parties or individuals. This, of course, makes it possible for such regimes to act more quickly and often more consistently than democratic or constitutional regimes, such as that which existed in Ghana during the first democratic republic led by Dr. Kwame Nkrumah. Of course, in the long run, the advantage of the dictator is offset by rigidity. No one is permitted to criticize policy, let alone change it, once the dictator is set upon its execution, disastrous though it may be, for the country concerned.

The Status of the Former Colonial Boundary Treaties

The complexities of colonial ambition produced a type of treaty agreement made, typically, directly between metropolitan colonial powers in respect of their respective colonial territories. For example, (1) On July 1, 1890, an agreement had been negotiated between Britain and Germany with regard to their respective spheres of influence in East, West and South Africa. The boundary line was drawn between the British Gold Coast and the German Protectorate of Togoland within the Gulf of Guinea; (2) On July 12, 1883, an arrangement was entered into between Great Britain and France for the delimitation of a boundary between British and French possessions on the Gold Coast; (3) On February 24, 1894, a convention was concluded between Great Britain and Germany which established a customs union between the Gold Coast east of the Volta and Togoland. The effect of such an agreement was that, these possessions formed a single custom territory, the same rate of customs duty was levied within them and goods could be imported into each other's territory without additional payment.[1]

Finally, throughout the nineteenth century, Ghana (then the Gold Coast Colony), the Gambia, Nigeria and Sierra Leone were brought together as united settlements under one governor-in-chief, seated in Sierra Leone.

It was no doubt common enough for such colonial boundary agreements as between Ghana (then Gold Coast) and the neighbouring territories to be negotiated and discussed by colonial administrative officials. However, these agreements having been negotiated in such fashion, were signed by agents of Great Britain and the Party concerned in the form of inter-state treaties. Indeed, the vast increase of inter-colonial business on the West Coast of Africa in this period led to the practice of allowing such agreements to be concluded directly at the respective metropolitan headquarters. With regard to such colonial boundary treaties, a genuine difficulty arises. The Gold Coast Government had no control over them. In fact, the relation between Ghana (then Gold Coast) and the above-mentioned neighbouring territories was considered an international affair between the metropolitan powers on behalf of their respective territories which had no personality in international law. The competence to make such agreements must, in the last resort, depend on the public internal law of the metropolitan states concerned. But the laws of most states are silent on the subject, and historically it seems that such colonial boundary agreements were the deliberate creation of colonial practice, which the constitutional texts merely recognized.

In many cases, the source of these colonial agreements can be traced directly to the negotiation between the two powers in the traditional form. In such cases, the subject matter was considered of a technical character similar to the questions that dealt with by delegated legislation in the modern democratic state. Consequently, these colonial boundary agreements relating to Ghana and the neighbouring states can be placed no higher than municipal agreements analogous to British Orders in Council made under a Principal Act. These agreements conferred no international status on the Gold Coast which had no power to dabble in the foreign affairs conducted by Great Britain. She was no more than a colony and she remained as such until 1957. Even after 1957, when the colony had achieved independence in practice, and Kwame Nkrumah had been appointed as Prime Minister, the policy of the majority of the leadership of the United Gold Coast Convention (UGCC) which, up till 1951, it was assumed would come to power, was simply that colonization should be continued in an Africanized form.

The policy of the CPP had, after their electoral victory of 1951, been one of securing independence by agreement — Self Government Now — and this meant, in practice, never forcing an issue such as the appointment of outside experts which Dr. Nkrumah had tried to secure in 1953. On the political independence issue alone, was the CPP prepared to make a stand. Speaking in the National Assembly in November 1956 when he announced that the British Government had agreed on March 6, 1957 as a firm date of self rule, Nkrumah admitted that:

> When I first became Prime Minister I determined that I would compromise, if necessary, on every issue except one — the Independence of this country. In consequence I have had from time to time, to give way on this or that point and even to persuade my

party to accept half measures which we all know in our hearts were basically unsatisfactory. This policy of which I, at times, had grave doubts, has proved successful.[2]

The result was that, Ghana was declared fully competent to act in international affairs, but it was governed by the Governor in partnership with Kwame Nkrumah and the CPP under the latent powers of the metropolitan power — Great Britain. Thus, the period between 1957 and 1961 saw the functioning of the Governor-General, representing the Queen, as Head of State, and the Prime Minister, as head of government. Consequently, Ambassadors-designate nominated by their governments for service in Ghana were technically accredited to the Court of St. James and could not, as such, be accredited without the Queen's approval. Moreover, appointment of Heads of Missions, in practice, had to be submitted to the Queen for approval. They were never reversed; and administratively, the procedure involved very little delay; but the political implications were among the factors which impelled the Nkrumah Government to work for the establishment of a Republic.

The Act of Independence, 1957

The above situation dramatically changed with the enactment of the Ghana Independence Act, 1957, by the United Kingdom Parliament. In providing for the Legislative Powers of the Government of Ghana, it stated *inter alia* that, the Colonial Laws Validity Act, 1865 was no longer applicable to any laws made on or after the appointed day by the Parliament of Ghana. No law or provisions of any law made on or after the appointed day by the Parliament of Ghana was void or considered in-operative on the ground that it was repugnant to the laws of England. The Parliament of Ghana was endowed with power after the appointed date to repeal or amend any UK Act, Order, rule or regulation insofar as it was part of the law of Ghana. Furthermore, the Parliament of Ghana was endowed with full powers to make laws with extra-territorial operation. Thus, Ghana acquired full capacity in the conduct of her external relations.

General Principles of Ghana's Foreign Policy

Ghanaian foreign policy was, on the whole, directed by the following fundamental principles: the campaign against colonialism and neo-colonialism; the advocacy of African Unity with the adoption of a common foreign policy; the creation of a Joint African High Command; an African Common Market; an overall continental economic planning including more equitable system of international trade; there was, however, complete acceptance of a mixed economy. There was the belief in Non-Alignment, a 'Third Force' comprising Non-aligned states which would not depend on east or west and which would yet have a definite and concerted policy of its own. There was, at the United Nations and elsewhere, an assertion of international equality. Finally, Ghana strenuously worked for co-operation between the industrialized nations and the poorer states who comprise the great bulk of mankind.

However, in the first democratic republic of Ghana — in-built with every kind of constitutional limitation on the formulators of foreign policy — the difficulty was to get a foreign policy accepted, and once accepted, to apply it consistently. The obstacles to acceptance were those which arose from profound differences between the party in power and the party in opposition; between those in charge of the five influential and related departments of government, namely the Ministry of Foreign Affairs, the Bureau of African Affairs, the African Affairs Secretariat, the African Affairs Centre and the Civil Service; between the government and public opinion; and between the politicians and the soldiers.

Thus, within an accepted overall policy, there occurred major differences of approach. It is instructive to examine some of these differences.

The Ministry of Foreign Affairs

Making policy and portraying one's country abroad are the twin charges of a Foreign Minister. The Foreign Minister, as the political head of the Foreign Ministry expounds the foreign policy that arises from the objectives of the ruling political party, in the case of Ghana, the Convention People's Party (CPP). This Ministry carried out what would properly be called staff functions, but a staff in the conduct of foreign policy was not as yet organized. The membership of the office, however, was drawn from the cream of the general civil service. Attempts were made to keep the supplementary external services or service groups as a nucleus foreign policy staff. However, this idea was found impractical, and the Bureau of African Affairs and personnel were established by the President, as a separate department. The staff functions of the Foreign Ministry were thus linked together with some aspects of 'policy formulation' and a great deal of routine work.

African Affairs Centre

Most of the Senior Freedom Fighters did not stay at the Centre and were housed in government bungalows. Persons such as S. G. Ikoku from Nigeria, T. R. Makonenn from Ethiopia, Harry Basner from South Africa, Habib Ntiang from Senegal, Djibo Bakari from Niger and the King of Sanwi tried to interfere with official policies. They had easy and direct access to Nkrumah and tried to influence decisions, but for the vigilance of senior officials at the Flagstaff

House and the Castle. For example, Nkrumah did agree to send away all freedom fighters at the Bamako Summit on the eve of the OAU Summit Conference in Accra. Kojo Botsio, Chairman and Harry Amonoo, Secretary of the Ghana's Planning Committee of the Conference made all arrangements to despatch the freedom fighters. At the last minute, Nkrumah summoned Dei-Anang and Harry Amonoo to his office at the Castle (Nkrumah did operate 6 months at the Flagstaff House and 6 months at the Castle after 1964) at 10 pm to complain that the freedom fighters were not to leave Accra. Nkrumah was reminded that, without their departure there would be no quorum for the OAU Summit Conference. Nkrumah finally agreed when he was told that all the freedom fighters had been given return tickets to Accra after the Conference. Harry Basner of South Africa had a very hot argument at the Castle with Harry Amonoo concerning the publication of Nkrumah's new book, *Neo-Colonialism — The Last Stage of Imperialism*. Harry Basner wanted the book to be published and launched before the Accra Conference, as the draft of the book criticized so many African leaders who were going to attend the Accra Conference. Dei-Anang and Harry Amonoo vehemently opposed the publication of the book before the Conference. Harry Basner lost the argument and the book was only published after the Accra Conference.

Some time during November, 1965 when Harry Amonoo was in charge of the African Affairs Secretariat with Dei-Anang on leave, the freedom fighters supported by the militant media reported Harry Amonoo to Nkrumah at the Cabinet room of the Flagstaff House. They wanted the Secretariat to release a building, an annex, for their use as a Club House — a meeting place — with modern communication equipment. Nkrumah therefore summoned Harry Amonoo to the Cabinet room to confront the freedom fighters. But Harry Amonoo was not cowed. He told Nkrumah that he had refused their request on grounds that Nkrumah also needed the building to communicate with his brother Heads of State and Government. The African Affairs Secretariat and the African Affairs Committee were directly under Osagyefo Dr. Kwame Nkrumah and doing equally important jobs for African Unity as the freedom fighters. Nkrumah was impressed by the arguments of Harry Amonoo and dismissed the pleas of the freedom fighters.

The Principal Secretary of the Foreign Ministry and other top most officials had the normal responsibility of advising the Foreign Minister over the whole range of his official duties. This advice was not only on the formulation of policy, but also on the execution and effect of any proposed policy. But the choice between alternative proposals rested with the Foreign Minister, and once he made his final decisions, it was the duty of the Foreign Service officials to implement them in the best possible manner, as if the decisions had been made by the officials themselves.[3]

The Government's view was that sooner or later African foreign offices everywhere on the continent would be provided with staff in exactly the same manner as military commanders rely on the assistance of their general staff. This development was inevitable because old-style diplomatic channels were not equipped to gather and evaluate all the necessary information relating to such topics as, for example, the assessment and analysis of the innumerable facts which must be known to the modern policy maker. For instance, if African governments before the crisis in the Congo in 1960, had evaluated the situation not simply on the basis of ambassadorial reports but on the basis of an exhaustive analysis of comparative literature and reports by persons trained in the observation of movements and tactics within the territory, a more effective policy might have been devised, both in the respective individual states and collectively at the United Nations, before the crisis became unavoidable. That this was not done was not the fault of this or that diplomat, although many of the foreign representatives in the Congo erred, but of organizational shortcomings. There were no instrumentalities for the collection of the really-pertinent information, let alone for the selection of appropriate tactics and their execution. Significantly, the UN Representative in the Congo, Dr. Conor C. O'Brien, in retrospect made a similar criticism.[3]

The area where Ghana's Ambassadors and Foreign Ministry Officials made great contribution was in respect of adaptation of policy in accordance with changing circumstances on the international scene. In this connection, there were five ways in which the Foreign Ministry helped in the formulation of policy:

1. There was interaction between the Ministry and Heads of Missions of Foreign Embassies in Ghana. As a result, the main Foreign Ministry in Accra gathered information by holding discussions with the Diplomatic Corps in Accra; it also tapped information by having contacts with Home Ministries including the Flagstaff House or the seat of government. These data were processed and, where they were relevant, used to assist in the formulation of policy.

2. The despatches from Ghana Missions Overseas were of great importance in the formulation of policy. The Foreign Ministry received various reports from Ghana's Foreign Missions, especially from Heads of Missions who were accredited representatives of the President.

3. The management of the Foreign Ministry, that is the Principal Secretary and his team, carried out preparations of 'position papers' on policy formulation. This was done after a careful consideration of all available data on government policy.

4. The Foreign Ministry also engaged in long range research and planning based upon the international scene, the needs of the country and necessary foreign policy considerations and assessment of Envoys and Foreign Office officials. This approach enormously assisted in the formulation of policy, especially the assessment of the various departments or desks such as the UN Desk or the African Affairs Desk.

5. The Foreign Ministry also obtained reports through international Conferences such as the United Nations, the Commonwealth, Afro-Asian and the Non-aligned meetings; the gathering of information was also done through regional bodies such as the Organization of African Unity, the Ghana-Guinea-Mali Union, and the Casablanca Group, the 'Monrovia' and the 'Brazzaville' Groups of States. All these reports were processed and made available to the Foreign Minister and the President for purposes of decision-making and the adaptation and direction of policy; in certain circumstances they also helped in the policy-making process.

Limitations on the Formulation of Policy

Formulation of policy owe so much to the expositions of intellectuals, such as lawyers, journalists, learned doctors, professors and lecturers. In other countries such as United States, Britain and France, the contribution of intellectuals in helping to formulate policy is immense. They are in a position to expose the flaws in government policy, to analyze action according to their causes and motives and often to draw attention to hidden intentions. And above all, intellectuals in these countries, by their training, are able to seek the truth lying behind the veil of distortion and misrepresentation of policy; all these help their governments to adjust policies.

In no way can one speak of Ghana at this time in comparable terms. Accra reflected the country's social and economic structure in microcosm. So far as foreign policy analysis was concerned, the country's professional classes had their sights not further beyond Ghana, although in other fields such as education, law or medicine, their eminence was internationally recognized. Another source of impediment in the formulation of foreign policy was the role of the Press. When Ghana became independent, it is true that the tradition of a vigorous press dating from the nineteenth century in Cape Coast still existed.[5] But leading Ghanaian papers such as the *Daily Graphic* and *The Ghanaian Times* did not have the influence and the weight of newspapers in most European and American countries, such as the *Times* in Britain, *Le Monde* in France, *The New York Times* in the United States and *Corriere della Sera* in Italy. The reason for the importance of these newspapers lies in their independence, the wealth of information and funds they have at their disposal, and the lively interests they take in foreign news with experts analyzing various issues to the benefit of the public and their governments. The absence of comparable organs in Ghana, and indeed Africa generally, gravely handicapped foreign policy initiative within the period under review.

The Portfolio of Minister of Foreign Affairs

Despite the fact that the Prime Minister, Dr. Nkrumah, was very busy, he took over the foreign relations portfolio when the new Ministry of Foreign Affairs was set up in 1957. In other words, he retained to himself the portfolio of the External Ministry in the initial stage of our Independence. He organized the First Conference of Independent African states in April, 1958 and the All African People's Conference for Freedom Fighters in December, 1958. He made De-colonization and African Unity the cornerstones of Ghana's foreign policy.

Nkrumah's aim was to lay down a firm policy of Pan-Africanism which Ghana would follow in international affairs. And he retained the External Affairs portfolio for over a year; after he had ensured that a firm policy formulation had been laid, he handed the Ministry to Kojo Botsio, who was perceptive and competent political administrator; Nkrumah and Botsio played major roles in the formulation of Ghana's de-colonization policy. Botsio held the Foreign Affairs portfolio from November, 1958 to April, 1959; then Ako Adjei, one of Ghana's early lawyers, took over as Foreign Minister from 1959 to August 1962. Ako Adjei presented a very sober image of Ghana and powerfully presented Ghana's stand to the UN and other international conferences. The burning question of African Unity saw Botsio back as Foreign Minister from March 1963 to June 1965; the leadership and the inspiration Botsio gave to the staff of the Foreign Ministry and to Ghana delegations to international conferences including the OAU summits, were great. Tactically, to make Nkrumah's views on African Unity properly understood, a political decision was taken for the Foreign Minister, Kojo Botsio and the High Commissioner in London, to launch Nkrumah's book *Africa Must Unite*. Botsio's timing for the launching of the book was impeccable. He did this on the eve of the African Heads of State Conference in Addis Ababa, preceding the formation of the OAU Ethiopia's radio and newspapers carried the report the following day. The result was electric. Later, the writer carried out the launching of *Africa Must Unite* in London and in Paris. Thus, Nkrumah's message on African Unity was transmitted forcefully to Africans, the French and English speaking peoples of the world at large. The last Foreign Minister during the period was a career diplomat, Alex Quaison-Sackey, who had served with distinction as Ghana's UN Representative and as President of the 19th Session of the UN General Assembly. As Foreign Minister, Quaison-Sackey had to contend with two factors. First was the seniority of Dei-Anang, who at one time had been Quaison-Sackey's boss as Principal Secretary and Secretary-General of the Foreign Office, and under whom he served as Foreign Service officer. Dei-Anang had become Head of the African Affairs Secretariat in the President's office with direct access to the President. Secondly, some of Quaison-Sackey's contemporaries, with whom he had joined the foreign service, were now the senior officials in charge of the Foreign Ministry. These factors did not make things easy for Quaison-Sackey; but he had a grasp of the work and was able to ride the storms and discharge his duties.

Until the establishment of the African Affairs Secretariat in 1961, the Foreign Minister was in principle the overseer of all foreign affairs; he reported to the President directly or through the Cabinet to the Government. He and his team at the Foreign Ministry prepared memoranda and advised on various issues which demanded urgent attention. In most cases, the memoranda submitted by the Foreign Ministry to the Cabinet influenced the foreign policy decision-making processes. This was especially so when the President and Foreign Minister agreed on the policy objectives. Indeed, the Foreign Minister and President co-ordinated the activities of the Foreign Ministry, the African Affairs Secretariat and the Bureau of African Affairs. They were advised by the three departments on foreign policy. They also co-ordinated their activities with other aspects of external relations, for example, international economic and financial matters, including international trade formulated by the technical missions and departments of Ghana overseas.

The African Affairs Secretariat

The African Affairs Secretariat undertook a role similar to that of the Ministry of Foreign Affairs, but its activities were in theory almost solely connected with African countries. The Secretariat was created in 1961 as part of the President's office; and Michael Dei-Anang with the rank of an Ambassador, the head of the Secretariat, K. B. Asante and Harry Amonoo acted as Senior Assistants to the President. Dei-Anang and his team handled formulation of Ghana's African policy, especially the unification policy. The diplomatic reports of Ghana's African Heads of Missions were processed by the Secretariat and were used for formulation of policy. These despatches also assisted the Government in decision-making and the execution of policy.

The divisions of African thought essential to European stability in the previous century was frowned upon by Nkrumah who challenged a continuation of the old practice. In the 1880s balkanization in Africa was conceived as a stabilizing policy; balkanization in Europe, three decades later, provoked the First World War. Perhaps, Nkrumah saw more clearly than any other statesman of his period, that African fragmentation contained within itself equally-dangerous elements. He understood, and did not hesitate to point out, that the national tensions which on the surface had provoked the First World War, were only capable of doing so because the external pressures of the developed world were projected into Balkan politics. Thus, Nkrumah saw that, world peace and African Unity were linked; the one was impossible without the other. The African Affairs Secretariat formed an essential part of this thinking. To buttress this policy or thinking, Nkrumah established an African Affairs Committee at the Flagstaff House with himself as Chairman. Other members included the Minister of Foreign Affairs, the Minister of Defence, the Secretary to the Cabinet, the Head of the African Affairs Secretariat, the Director of the Bureau of African Affairs and Harry Amonoo who was Secretary, played a great role in the work of the Committee. It was an action-orientated Committee and dealt with issues such as Ghana's relations with China, the Soviet Union and Afro-Asian affairs. In fact, Nkrumah's own brief to Vietnam was prepared under the aegis of the Committee. The year, 1965, was also extremely busy for the African Affairs Secretariat which supervised all preparations for the OAU Conference of Heads of State and Government during October that year. Several trips were undertaken by delegations to other Heads of State to convince them to accept Osagyefo's proposals for a Continental Union Government and Joint African High Command. Finally, Nkrumah was persuaded to drop his proposals and accept instead the creation of an OAU Executive Committee of a few Heads of State.

The Bureau of African Affairs

The Bureau of African Affairs exclusively handled contacts with freedom fighters in dependent territories. Ghana played host to many freedom fighters from all parts of Africa including those from Mozambique and South Africa. They organized their affairs in Ghana, but such matters were not the concern of Ghana alone, but also other African countries because of decisions taken at the OAU Conference of African Heads of State and Government. It was paramount to Nkrumah that a state of affairs in Ghana which interfered with the effectiveness, or even the psychological comfort of these Freedom Fighters and Movements was the concern of the whole of Africa. It was also part of the Bureau's responsibility to organize seminars, conferences and workshops for the freedom fighters. Such activities offered them opportunities for political education and training. Exchange of ideas with various freedom fighters helped the co-ordination, formulation and direction of strategy of the Liberation Movements. Successful operations of the Bureau owed much to the contacts of its Director, A. K. Barden, with Freedom Fighters in their respective centres of operation; and the assistance of various politicians in the independent African

States. Barden and David Bosomtwe-Sam, the Secretary of the Bureau, put to a very good use the Bureau's compilation of background history of political parties and their leading members from independent states and liberation movements in dependent African territories. This action helped the Government to seek the advice of certain politicians in the independent African states, and also identify and select the most effective liberation movements which should be given recognition and support. This assistance took many forms: it ranged from supplying them with material and financial aid, including medicine and clothing, to arranging educational facilities for them in Ghana and other high institutions of learning in foreign countries; in addition to providing them with legal aid and constitutional experts during constitutional conferences when negotiations took place for peaceful transition to independence. An example was the appointment of Professor Ekow Daniels, who later became Dean of the Law Faculty, University of Ghana, as Constitutional Adviser to Jomo Kenyatta in 1961 during Kenya's Constitutional Conference in London.

Moreover, in certain cases, such as the East African countries, the Bureau's representatives were attached to the regular Ghana Diplomatic Missions or Legations. In their work, these representatives were placed at vantage points and were able to have easy contact with freedom fighters from Southern Africa and the Portuguese colonies in particular. The Bureau became a centre for checking information, ascertaining the needs of freedom fighters and communicating them to base. The Bureau's emissaries were sent to make on-the-spot investigations and check on the veracity of the information received in Accra. These reports were then summarized and presented to the President with the Bureau's comments. De-colonization policies were enhanced and revised on the basis of these reports. Thus, the Bureau of African Affairs acted as a catalyst and helped in moulding government policies in respect of dependent African states.

The Civil Service

The most fundamental shortcoming of Ghana's policy was the preoccupation of the Civil Service with achieving the entrenchment of its establishment in the Constitution. One would have expected to find a reference to the fact that the structure of the Civil Service might have to be altered after Independence, so as to provide for development. The reason was that the expatriates had all along occupied the more responsible positions and their knowledge, skill and experience were not readily replaceable from local sources. The policy was to use the machinery of the Colonial Office and the Crown Agents to fill posts in the senior administrative, professional and the supervising grades. The Civil Service was, therefore, unable to respond to the national aspirations that eventually led to Ghana's independence. The main problem after independence was to transform the Civil Service not only from the colonial pattern to a nationally orientated service, but also from being mainly controlled by expatriate senior staff to an indigenously based one.[6] The object of creating the Public Service Commission was to preserve the old administration and bring it under indirect control of the Secretary of State for the Colonies. A machine had, therefore, it seemed, to be created to perpetuate, if not his authority, at least the system by which he had worked:

> As power is steadily transferred from British to local hands, the preface explains, "the role of the Secretary of State in Public Service matters diminishes and finally comes to an end." At the same time, the Public Service Commission is built up to assume increasing responsibilities for the Public Service and ultimately to be an independent executive body fully responsible for the appointments and careers of individual members of the Public Service.[7]

The significance of this passage is the insight which it gives into Colonial Office thinking. Although under-developed states could pursue any appropriate policy, the supervision of the people carrying out this policy must be taken out of the hands of the politicians. Supporters of this point of view went further to suggest that foreign policy be left to expert civil servants who should direct its course because of a sub-conscious belief in division of labour and the specialization of functions as the basis of modern organization.

Scott Thompson powerfully supported this view and observed:

> ... the calibre of the purely political appointees was such as to justify concern. Few Services are without their political appointees but a young country does well to err on the side of caution in these affairs and trust its trained men.[8]

It appears that the absence in his book of an authoritative distinction between the 'Decision-making' and the 'Administration' of foreign policy during 1957–1966, clouded his assessment and obviously resulted in wrong conclusions; moreover, politics, especially foreign policy, is not a science but an art, hence the quality of the product depends largely on the ability of the artist. Some foresight is an essential part of political ability which is not shared by the mass of the people or by most civil servants, the politician and/or statesman will always have to cope with the difficulty of enlisting support for measures the necessity for which is not being understood by the civil servant. If the advice of Scott Thompson on this matter was adopted, it would mean that (1) policy decisions would be responsibility of civil servants instead of Cabinet and/or Ministers; (2) the bar placed on civil servants not to reply to public criticisms would be removed, and they would assume the voice and authority of a Minister.[9] (3) Collective responsibility of the Cabinet would thus be extended to be applicable to civil servants. It is difficult for any government to function under these circumstances. Mr. A. H. M. Kirk-Greene has advised against hasty and premature conclusions on this matter. He suggests caution because not enough is known on the decision making process in African ministries of external affairs — and indeed to what extent Missions abroad are genuinely policy-influencing as well as patently policy-explicative organs. How useful or influential is the African Desk in the Ministry? How far does the Cabinet heed advice from its professional advisers on foreign affairs? And, within the Cabinet, how influential are the views of individuals whose portfolio is not external affairs?[10]

The Civil Service from the top-most downwards was opposed to any constitutional changes which might imperil the existing structures of power in its hands. This point can be illustrated by the conflict between the Ghana Government and the University of Ghana, then the University College of the Gold Coast. For some time, the bodies appointed to prepare policy to put before the Faculty in general meeting (Congregation) or the Academic Board (Senate) was not composed of the most senior or representative senior members of the University, but of elected representatives of the academic staff. Staff curriculum and standards of admission were all decided in this way without reference even to the Council. After independence, in proportion to its per capita national income, Ghana was spending ten times as much on education as Spain, and yet under the pretext of academic freedom, the Government was excluded from any say in how the University should be run. This was tantamount to the imposition of a mechanism of rule, not sanctioned by Ghanaian Law, nor even approved of by the outgoing Colonial Administration.

A clash over the University's relationship with Government was inevitable, and a report made in April, 1959 of the University's finances by a committee composed largely of expatriate experts proved the point. The experts had reviewed various extravagances in the administration of the University, and in particular the excessive costs of providing allowances to senior members of the College to go on leave by first-class air passages every year. The cost of providing these passages was more than £100,000 per year. Kwame Nkrumah's office referred the report to the University and the latter was not amused. What the University staff were asserting was not the right of individual dissent, the essence of academic freedom as understood in industrial countries, but the right to determine education policy.

This situation led A. L. Adu to observe that, another effect of the colonial structure of the Civil Service is the distortion of the educational policies of the various states.[11] Thus, when Ghana achieved internal self-government in 1951, it became necessary to change the educational policy for development purposes. Scholarship schemes were also instituted. Consequently, the Minister of Education, Kojo Botsio, introduced a policy of universal primary education in the shortest possible time; and ordered that this should be implemented with immediate effect. This policy was vehemently opposed by the Ministry of Education staff. It advised that the policy was sound as long-term objective but that obstacles might make it impracticable in terms of immediate implementation. These obstacles included the financial burden of an accelerated programme, a shortage of qualified teachers and the dangers of dilution, the shortage of classrooms, the inability of some parents to meet the cost of educating their children, and the danger in lowering standards. These reasons were rejected and the Minister, Kojo Botsio, confirmed that it was the Government's firm determination to go ahead with the policy. Consequently, an accelerated education plan on national basis was prepared. The ruling party took advantage of every possible improvization — temporary classrooms, emergency teacher training colleges, week-end classes for untrained teachers, modifications and streamlining of curriculum; thus a national grid system of supervision of schools and teachers provided built-in safeguards for preventing dangerous falls in standards. A most progressive and imaginative programming was evolved which laid the foundation for primary and higher education in Ghana. This is now providing standards of education which at least compare favourably with the pre-1951 standards and with standards in neighbouring countries.

As regards to awards of scholarships, the Cocoa Marketing Board (CMB) Scholarship was first introduced and awarded by the CMB Board of Directors; then the Registrar of Scholarships under the direction of the Minister of Education, awarded scholarships. In 1961, a Scholarship Secretariat was established as one of the presidential secretariats. Its functions came under the direct supervision of the President. The power of awarding scholarships was later vested in the High Commissioner of London; although in certain circumstances where the scholarships awarded were numerous, approval from the President was necessary. An example is the award of scholarships to Ghanaian students in America.[12]

The Civil Service in Ghana, as indeed in the rest of Commonwealth Africa, was a carbon copy of the Colonial Civil Service. And as a carbon copy, it tended to magnify the defects of the original. The full effect of such a carbon copy of the old Civil Service was to produce a machine which, like its colonial predecessor, acquired a momentum of its own. The long standing tradition in Britain where civil servants are said or held to be apolitical means that, they are neutral in matters of a partisan nature. Where the matter at issue related to Britain's interests abroad, the British civil servant, if he differed with the Minister or Prime Minister at all, did so not about the objective but about the means. And in a country that operates without a written constitution it may well be that what is important is not what is said or written but what is left unsaid and unwritten. And one may do well to listen for the silences. This was precisely what the elite of the Ghanaian Civil Service failed to appreciate.

They enthusiastically practised the British tradition of civil service apoliticism with abandon: in the Civil Service environment, the tradition was consecrated into an ironcast principle which insisted that in matters political, the civil service remained *virgo intacta*. Another important example in this connection was the case of Bureau of African Affairs. The Permanent Secretary for Foreign Affairs, A. L. Adu, opposed the appointment of George Padmore as Adviser to Dr. Kwame Nkrumah on African Affairs. George Padmore, a West Indian author and journalist, was educated at Howard University in the States. He had dedicated his life to the anti-colonial struggle during a long stay in Britain. At the fifth Pan-African Congress, held in Manchester in 1945 under the chairmanship of Dr. W. E. B. du Bois, Padmore and Nkrumah acted as joint secretaries to the Congress. Moreover, one of Padmore's books — *The Gold Coast Revolution* — was widely acclaimed in Ghana and other parts of the Commonwealth. Padmore was to head the Bureau of African Affairs. In effect Adu opposed the establishment of the Bureau of African Affairs, and justified this on the grounds that Padmore was not competent to advise on African affairs because 'he had never lived in Africa'. Here, Dei-Anang disagreed with Adu as follows:

> perhaps it can be said that at the time of Adu's opposition he had inadequate information about Padmore's background. Obviously the fact that Padmore had never lived in Africa was irrelevant. He was already known as an anti-colonial fighter.[13]

Dr. Nkrumah responded by establishing the Bureau of African Affairs outside the orthodox government machinery. The significance of this was not easily realized at that time because in 1957, when Ghana became independent, none of the most senior civil servants had any Pan African experience. It was in fact a completely new field for even A. L. Adu, the first Principal Secretary of the Ministry of Foreign Affairs, who later became Secretary to the Cabinet. His celebrated opposition to the Bureau of African Affairs, is to my mind, emblematic of the essentially thorny problem of a refusal to exercise imaginative adaptation on the part of the high reaches of the Civil Service at that time. Thus, the Pan African policy of de-colonization was put outside the control and direction of the Foreign Ministry. This weakened the authority of the Ministry in African affairs, and gave the Director of Bureau of African Affairs autonomy over the policy of de-colonization making him responsible not to the Foreign Minister but to the Prime Minister or the President. Thus, a strong difference of outlook between the first Foreign Minister and Dr. Nkrumah and his Foreign Service became evident at the very beginning. This culminated in giving the Bureau of African Affairs a legal status in 1959, after the death of George Padmore.

Part of the reason for such behaviour was that the Civil Service in its early stages was not required to deal with the complex responsibilities of the modern-day administrations in political economic and social sphere.[14] Moreover, local senior officers did not start holding high-level policy advising and directing positions until 1951, when internal self-government brought in Ghanaian Ministers. Consequently, the expert knowledge and experience that existed among Ghana's Civil Servants at Independence in 1957, could not be said to be as rich as in the older countries. In truth, the policy begun in 1901 of closing the civil service even to qualified Africans had only been hesitatingly and grudgingly reversed. There was thus during the preparatory period for independence no hard core of experienced African civil servants. The new recruits were mainly those who came from the university. As a result, knowledge in professional, technical and specialist fields was borrowed under technical assistance arrangements or purchased by contracting with individuals. Under such circumstances, it was difficult to establish the convention which exists in Britain, that Ministers seek the advice of their staff on all policy matters. But even in Britain experienced Ministers do not necessarily turn to official advisers, but make their own decisions on major issues.

Inter-Departmental Rivalries

With the exception of formulation and execution of de-colonization policy which was handled by the Bureau of African Affairs and operated outside the orthodox government machinery, the Foreign Ministry was in full control of foreign affairs, including the other aspect of the Government's Pan-African policy — the unification of the continent. But the Congo crisis of 1960 brought about the setting up of 'A Special Congo Co-ordinating Committee' at the President's office, under the chairmanship of Kwaku Boateng, the Minister of Information. Other members of the Committee were Geoffrey Bing, then Attorney-General, Eric Otoo, who subsequently became Head of the Special Service, Major-General Alexander, the Chief of Defence Staff who was an expert on logistics. The Foreign Ministry suffered a setback in this exercise in the sense that its Principal Secretary, Michael Dei-Anang was released from routine work and sent to Congo to assist in the setting up of a new Ghana office in the Congo. The Deputy Principal Secretary of the Ministry, Richard Quarshie, a shrewd operator and one of the most competent officials, was also appointed as Secretary to the Congo Co-ordinating Committee. In this way, the Foreign Ministry was not only partially dismembered, but also immobilized and virtually deprived of the opportunity of direct participation in the problems of the Congo.[15]

The Congo experience brought about the formation of the African Affairs Secretariat in the President's office. Dei-Anang was appointed as head of the

Secretariat and handled its affairs from its inception in April 1961 to the end of Nkrumah's government in February 1966. The Foreign Ministry suffered another blow — the African Affairs Division in the Foreign Ministry was moved to the Flagstaff House as the staff of the newly established African Affairs Secretariat. Prominent among the staff of the Secretariat were K. B. Asante, Harry Amonoo and E. P. K. Seddoh; all of them were later appointed as Ambassadors. The Bureau of African Affairs also had its prominent ambassadorial appointment in the person of David Bosomtwi-Sam, an efficient Secretary of the Bureau, who became Ghana's High Commissioner in Kenya and the Dean of the Diplomatic Corps.

However, after 1961, Ghana Ambassadors in Africa ceased to be under the administrative control of the Foreign Ministry. Their reports were sent direct to the African Affairs Secretariat. As a result of these arrangements, by 1961, there were virtually two independent official heads in charge of foreign affairs at the Foreign Ministry and at the African Affairs Secretariat. As for the Bureau of African Affairs, it often worked through the Ghana Missions in Africa; it employed a separate code for communication with its headquarters in Accra. The Bureau was also able to use the diplomatic bag for transmission of messages and supplies, but under a separate seal. Consequently, with the Secretariat also acting separately, there was no major system of reporting in Africa. This lack of essential co-ordination at the centre made the work of the Foreign Ministry extremely difficult. The effect was that, the position of the Foreign Minister at the time the African Affairs Secretariat was set up was greatly reduced in influence.

However, the emergence of Kojo Botsio for the second time as Foreign Minister[16] gave the Foreign Ministry some control of Ghana's Pan African policy. Obviously Botsio was not prepared to take any dictation from the African Affairs Secretariat. Tension between the Foreign Ministry and the Secretariat became more and more evident. Nkrumah called a meeting of Botsio, Dei-Anang, Barden and Kwesi Armah, the writer, to find a solution to the problem. Botsio made his position quite clear that, he could not run the Foreign Ministry properly without having control over African affairs; Dei-Anang defended his actions and described them as legitimate in the circumstances; and Barden stuck to his independent control of the Bureau of African Affairs as necessary for his operations. Botsio partially conceded the case of the Bureau because of its unorthodox methods in respect of de-colonization policy, but stood very firmly against the operations of the Secretariat. Nkrumah turned to the writer at the meeting and asked for his independent assessment or opinion: the advice given was that the Government could not develop policy on Africa without making an impact on the interests of non-African countries; therefore, the Government had to take account of the policy inter-connections; and here, the Government simply had to rely on the inputs of the Foreign Ministry.

The Foreign Minister had to take broader charge of foreign affairs and African policy in international conferences and other forums. Consequently broad strategy should also be dictated by the Foreign Ministry. Pertaining to Africa itself, while the Foreign Minister led the delegation to the meetings of the OAU Council of Ministers, diplomatic reports of Ghana's Heads of Missions accredited to African states were sent to the African Affairs Secretariat. Yet, quick access to and reading of diplomatic despatches were very important to the Foreign Minister. They facilitated and encouraged a learning process by government so that foreign policy could be adopted, modified, or, if necessary, made more congruent with reality in the operation environment. For instance, a change of position by another country and an Ambassador's consultations or telex reporting it could make a world of difference in adaptation of policy and decision-making. In these matters, time was always the essence, but the African Affairs Secretariat was very distant from the Ministry of Foreign Affairs; moreover, the Secretariat had the advantage of working at the President's elbow, so a clear attempt to influence policy decisions to reflect the dynamics and importance of the African Affairs Secretariat was being resisted by the Foreign Ministry. The Foreign Ministry was resisting on grounds that, in the final analysis, the broad implementation of foreign policy, including the Pan-African policy, was its responsibility. This was supported by the fact that at OAU Conference, although the Head of African Affairs Secretariat and other senior officials played an important role, the chain of command was that, the High Commissioner in London came next after the Foreign Minister. This was very unpalatable to the Head of the Secretariat and his team who, at times, saw their briefs completely ignored. The fate of the African Affairs Secretariat seemed to be in the balance at the end of that meeting. This led to the comment in Dei-Anang's book that 'Nkrumah was equivocal . . . at one time, he requested Botsio who was Foreign Minister to arrange for the merger of the Secretariat and the Foreign Ministry.'[17] As an indication of his influence on Foreign policy, Kojo Botsio, then in charge of State Planning and Minister for African Affairs, was appointed Chairman of the Ghanaian delegation to the Accra OAU Conference in 1965, although Quaison-Sackey was the Foreign Minister at that time.[18]

Decision Making and Foreign Policy

If the Foreign Minister is the political head of the Foreign Ministry, the Prime Minister or the President is the supreme political head of all Ministries, including the Foreign Ministry. He must know all that is going on; his duty requires familiarity with and understanding of the problems of every department and every part of the country. More than that, the price of an Administration's continuance and success is eternal vigilance. A Prime Minister or a President must find time enough to stand back and think about the problems of the Administration, its purpose, its co-ordination and its longer term strategy.[19] No Prime Minister or President has authority to intervene in any Department or Ministry in order to make decisions which could either change policy or initiate new policy in accordance with his perceptions and judgement. Thus, in order to force decisions or hasten changes of direction in policy, British Prime Ministers since World War II have been inclined to play a personal role in foreign policy. An example is Britain's controversial decision to seek entry to the European Common Market. Public opinion was uncertain; the Labour Party was skeptical and there was uneasiness running to hostility and open resistance from within the ranks of the Conservative Party. Nevertheless, the then Prime Minister, Harold Macmillan acted firmly and was able to decide quietly and announce suddenly that the United Kingdom would negotiate for membership of the Common Market.[20] Macmillan's decision was so significant that Edward Heath, who was appointed as principal negotiator, and later became Prime Minister, observed that the decision to 'pool sovereignty', is as momentous as any decision government is called upon to make.[21]

In Ghana too, Nkrumah had the authority to make dramatic decisions in foreign policy. As the first Foreign Minister of Ghana, Nkrumah initiated major political changes in Ghana's foreign policy. As *parent patriae*, he was able to use his authority to sanction or advance policies. Nkrumah set out the problems, suggested the kind of solutions that might be expected, and directed what action might be taken.

But though Nkrumah could, at times, behave like a British Prime Minister in policy-making and decision-making, the procedure adopted by his Government in arriving at foreign policy decisions was similar to that which operates in the partial cabinet system of Britain. A partial cabinet is different from the inner cabinet in the sense that, it is a standing or *ad hoc* committee presided over by the Prime Minister, which may — in matters of great moment and secrecy — prepare policies in detail and sometimes take decisions without prior consultation with the cabinet as a whole. The cabinet is in due course informed and consulted. A partial cabinet is the very opposite of prime ministerial government. It pre-supposes that the prime minister carries influential cabinet colleagues with him.[22]

In Ghana, the concept of partial cabinet powerfully operated in foreign policy decision making. The President, the Foreign Minister, and the High Commissioner in London[23] (in his capacity as the official representative of the CPP overseas) took the decisions on foreign policy. The operation of foreign policy on the basis of partial cabinet system in the proper circumstances was necessary and generally accepted by the cabinet as a whole. For example, the partial cabinet decision was taken to make Accra the venue of the 1965 OAU Heads of State Conference.[24]

Nkrumah's knowledge of foreign affairs and influence on policy acted as his insurance against opposition when he happened to make any policy decision. But despite this, Nkrumah did not make any important foreign policy decision without consultation with the partial cabinet. Nkrumah frequently held meetings with his political advisers. These included the Minister of Foreign Affairs, the Minister of Finance, the Minister of Defence, the Minister of Interior, the High Commissioner in London who was also CPP official representative overseas and the Secretary-General of the TUC. The importance of the London Mission was demonstrated by three things:

1. At independence in 1957, one of the most senior and competent cabinet ministers, Sir Edward Asafu-Adjaye, was appointed as the first High Commissioner. Sir Edward's flashpoint was the Congo crisis of 1960, his tour of duty ended by July, 1961.

2. When President Kennedy died in 1963, it was the High Commissioner in London who deputized for President Nkrumah and led a delegation which included Alex Quaison-Sackey, Ghana's UN Representative, and Michael Ribero, Ghana's Ambassador to US — to the funeral, and signed the Book of Condolence at the White House on behalf of the President.

3. The dominant position which the High Commissioner in London occupied in the making of foreign policy and his influence as the CPP official representative overseas over and above other envoys of Ghana. In Party political matters, the reports of all Ghana's Ambassadors and High Commissioners were sent to the High Commissioner in London as their head. Politically, the High Commissioner in London as CPP official representative overseas, was directly responsible to President Nkrumah as General Secretary of the CPP.

On domestic matters, Nkrumah's political advisers changed from time to time in accordance with the issues under discussion, and the relative influence exercised by these advisers in the ruling Convention People's Party. However, on matters of foreign policy decision making, the views of the President, the Foreign Minister and the High Commissioner in London prevailed. For instance, the decision about the appointment of Ambassadors were taken by the Foreign Minister or the President, but in 1965, after the High Commissioner in London had been appointed a Cabinet Minister, Dr. Bossman, the Ambassador in France and Fred Arkhurst, the Principal Secretary of the Foreign Ministry, were appointed as High Commissioner in London and UN Representative respectively, on the advice of the outgoing High Commissioner.

Ghana's foreign policy, in broad terms, was remarkably stable during the period under review. This was due to the consistency of the Government's policies. It was characterized by pragmatism rather than ideological orientation. At international conferences, the spokesman of the Government seemed always at ease to decide on the spot when to press their argument, to propose a compromise or to resign themselves to accepting either minority or majority view. However, the greater concern of the President and the partial cabinet, was the question of self-preservation, the territorial integrity of Ghana and its people; to this all else tended to be subordinated. Protection of Ghana against foreign interference in her internal affairs and freedom to express and implement an independent viewpoint on foreign or external affairs was other vital foreign policy principles Nkrumah would not sacrifice.

After 1961, there existed no groups, associations, lobbies or interest groups that were influential in the area of foreign policy decision-making. The only objective internal constraints which adversely affected government's control of foreign policy were the limitations of the country's economic position and development. These factors compelled Scott Thompson to observe that, Ghana's foreign policy was Nkrumah's, and a reflection of his moods and ambitions.

As indicated earlier, the powers which Nkrumah and the partial cabinet possessed in foreign policy decision-making were similar to the authority of the British Prime Minister and his partial cabinet.[25] According to a very senior British Cabinet Minister, Richard Crossman, the concentration of power in the Prime Minister was so great that he, in effect, displaced the Cabinet. The 'point of decision' passed upward to the Prime Minister; the reality of the constitution was now that Cabinet Government had given way to the Prime Ministerial Government.[26]

Crossman's argument rests on two main points: firstly, that the Prime Minister's control over the Party machine inside and outside Parliament has raised him to unassailable supremacy; secondly, that Atlee decided to make the Atom Bomb and Eden to invade Suez without consulting the Cabinet.[27]

This situation led to a former Conservative Member of Parliament, Humphrey Barceley, to observe:

> I accept that we are now operating a presidential system; to do otherwise would be unrealistic. Let us concede the Prime Minister Presidential Powers and equip ourselves with safeguards.[28]

In consequence, P.W.G. Benemy asserted that ". . . the Prime Minister is sovereign — that is to say, he governs with absolute authority."[29]

But in the case of Ghana, if the President occupied a strong position in foreign policy decision-making, his political advisers had sufficient influence to make him change his mind on any major issue even after he had taken a unilateral decision. An example was where the Ghana Government contemplated withdrawing from the Commonwealth over the Rhodesian question.[30]

In October, 1965, the OAU unanimously decided at a Summit Conference to re-appraise among other things, their diplomatic relations with the United Kingdom if the proposed Rhodesian Unilateral Declaration of Independence (UDI) was not stopped. Smith eventually carried out his UDI, and at an emergency meeting of the OAU Council of Ministers at Addis Ababa, it was unanimously decided that all the member states of the OAU should break off diplomatic relations with Britain. Nkrumah went further, and took steps to effect Ghana's complete withdrawal from the Commonwealth. President Nkrumah sent a delegation to London with a letter to the then British Prime Minster, Mr. Harold Wilson, announcing Ghana's intention to withdraw completely from the Commonwealth. The delegation comprised Michael Dei-Anang, Ambassador Plenipotentiary in charge of the African Affairs Secretariat in the office of the President; Enoch Okoh, the Secretary to the Cabinet, and Albert Adomako, the Governor of the Bank of Ghana. There was also a message from the President instructing the then Ghana High Commissioner in Britain to lead the delegation to the British Premier. The then High Commissioner was able to stop Ghana's complete withdrawal from the Commonwealth. This happened by means of asking Ghana's former Ambassador to France, Kwame Jantuah, to fly to Accra with a letter from the then High Commissioner to the President appealing to him to reconsider his stand and take into account the arguments advanced against the proposed action.[31] Kwame Jantuah succeeded to buttress the implications of the withdrawal as contained in the letter to the President. Nkrumah's positive response to the letter as expressed in the recision of his original decision to withdraw Ghana completely from the Commonwealth, was proof of his flexibility, tolerance and ability to change his mind when he was proved wrong.

However, Nkrumah did finally implement the OAU resolution on Rhodesia on 16th December 1965. According to Amonoo:

> few OAU members had taken the lead in breaking off diplomatic relations with Britain. It was becoming very embarrassing for Ghana. Some officials back home were wondering whether Nkrumah's membership of the Privy Council in Britain, the visit of the British Prime Minister, Mr. Harold Wilson, to Accra, one week before UDI or the influence of the Ghana High Commissioner in London had made Nkrumah delay in breaking relations with Britain. In fact, only the British High Commissioner to Ghana was withdrawn. The note verbal was handed over to the British High Commissioner at the Flagstaff House by Harry Amonoo as Alex Quaison-Sackey, the Foreign Minister, was reluctant to take action.

Nkrumah's acceptance not to withdraw completely from the Commonwealth

but to take a limited action by breaking diplomatic relations with Britain, and later restore relations when Rhodesia's Unilateral Declaration of Independence (UDI) was resolved was commendable.

Moreover, the growing diversification of Ghana's foreign relations, combined with many technical facets of present day diplomacy such as international finance, the law of the sea, north-south dialogue on economic affairs and UN Peace Keeping calls for some degree of independent action by the Foreign Ministry and African Affairs Secretariat. A reasonable degree of authority and institutionalization of decision-making process was imperative if the efficiency and quality of Ghana's diplomacy were to be maintained. But the President and his political advisers took decisions on major foreign policy issues. This situation led Dei-Anang, the Head of African Affairs Secretariat to observe: "In my job, I was constantly required to confirm with the President that he instructed Barden, the Director of Bureau of African Affairs, to undertake activities in independent Africa about which I had heard from other sources".[32] Clearly, a policy decision had been taken without his knowledge and in the course of its implementation, he got to know through the Ambassador in the country concerned or from the Government with whom Ghana was dealing. No official had greater influence in the Government than Michael Dei-Anang. But if he as 'Chief Administrator' and Head of the African Affairs Secretariat was in the dark about major foreign policy decisions, it would perhaps not be unreasonable to say that, "the President and his political advisers played the cards very close to their chests. It was this which led Dei-Anang to the conclusion that 'the President became almost the sole initiator of policy and it was impossible for Administrators to argue demarcation of responsibilities which would have restricted any particular Agency to an agreed role."[33] While Dei-Anang's observations was true, it is important to state that, the method, the President and the CPP political advisers adopted in handling foreign policy decision-making was informed by the CPP inner-party democracy according to which every major decision was furiously debated; but once a decision was made Party discipline was imposed to enforce it.[34]

The Decision-Makers and Administrators of Foreign Policy

In order to forestall the ill-effects of the domestic power competition between the civil service machinery and the political machinery of the Cabinet and/or Ministers of the Government, President Nkrumah made it clear from the outset that, top career civil servants were to administer the ministries and advise the ministers. These functionaries, called in some countries Permanent Secretary, in others Secretary General, and in others Under Secretary, are as a rule appointed from the service for the purpose of advising the Minister. Indeed, at Independence Dr. Nkrumah asserted that the duty of civil servants or foreign service officers was (1) to advise the Government, and (2) to execute the policies of the Government in accordance with instructions.[35] This is supported by Mr. A. L. Adu, Permanent Secretary for Foreign Affairs. He writes:

> the minister's responsibility is to lay down political policy, and it is the duty of the Permanent Secretary and the heads of the Divisions in the Ministry to execute this policy and translate it into action.[36]

Of course, the Civil Service also has the responsibility to interpret to its staff the precise nature of the Minister's policies. Yet in practice, certain civil servants deliberately turned this principle of Dr. Nkrumah upside down in the sense that they, on occasions, made policy decisions. In fact, there were deliberate attempts at turning the very principle of Parliamentary Government upside down. For example, under Section 44 of the 1954 Constitution, it was provided as follows:

> ... if the Governor shall consider that it is expedient in the interests of public order, public faith or good government ... that any Bill introduced, or any motion proposed, in the Assembly should have effect, then if the Assembly fail to pass such a Bill or motion within such reasonable time ... the Governor at any time which he shall think fit, may ... declare that such Bill or motion shall have effect as if it had been passed by the Assembly ...[37]

These provisions ensured that, immediate pre-independence Legislative Assembly of the Gold Coast was made responsible not to the electorate but to the Governor. The Governor was to exercise his powers under Section 44 if he had the approval of the Cabinet or, if the Cabinet did not approve, with the concurrence of the Secretary of State for the Colonies. A situation was thus created that, if the Cabinet and the Governor agreed, they could ignore the Legislature which remained just as much a façade as it had been in the old days of the Burns Constitution. If the Cabinet and the Governor disagreed, the Governor could go over their heads to the Secretary of State. In consequence, far from the Cabinet being responsible to the Legislature, as the Constitution formally stated, in practice they were responsible to the Governor, and the Legislative Assembly was, in its turn, responsible to them both.

In the circumstances, it was only fair for the President to set the records right. Decision-making was carried out at the highest level, where no civil servant and/or career diplomat from the Foreign Office or the African Affairs Secretariat was present. The role of the Foreign Affairs senior officials was to prepare 'position papers' on clear instructions and to execute policy on direction. This does not deny the fact that they were very competent in the administration of policy. Perhaps the most striking example that officials knew nothing about the decision-making of policy was the holding of the OAU Heads of State Conference in Accra, 1965. This was the climax of Ghana's unification policy and second in importance only to the formation of the OAU in Addis Ababa, 1963. And yet the most important career diplomat, Michael Dei-Anang, whom Scott Thompson had described as the 'Chief Administrator', did not know about Ghana's decision to host the Conference in Accra until the last moment. Supported by K. B. Asante, one of the Principal Secretaries, Dei-Anang made a great play of this in his personal memoir. He writes:

> It would not be correct to state that the 1964 Conference in Cairo had agreed to hold the 1965 meeting in Accra. In fairness to Dr. Nkrumah, it should be indicated that he did not originate the idea of inviting the conference to Accra. Notes that I made at that time indicate that, it was some of his enthusiastic followers who advanced the idea and he reluctantly agreed. These enthusiasts ignored official advice that no invitation should be issued until Ghana was in possession of the appropriate facilities. In fact, it was Nkrumah who, confronted with the *fait accompli*, came down to earth and initiated consideration of the question of facilities.[38]

The holding of the OAU Heads of State Conference in Accra was one of the major policy decisions throughout the whole period of Dr. Nkrumah's administration. It cost a considerable amount of money in terms of expenditure on the delegates and the construction of an adequate Conference Hall. Ghana completed on the grounds of the State House, a magnificent complex consisting of a twelve storey building of 60 self-contained suites carefully arranged to give maximum comfort. There was also an up-to-date Conference Hall which could contain one thousand people, and a Banquet Hall capable of seating nearly two thousand guests near this residence, both of which were linked by a series of covered ways to the residential edifice. This complex of building were all centrally-air-conditioned. On the same grounds, provision was made for garages which accommodated up to forty cars for the Heads of State and parking area for over seven hundred and fifty cars. Two large fountains operated by seventy-two jets with multi-coloured interplay of lights, and rising to a height of sixty feet when fully turned on, had been installed. The scale and nature of these buildings show the great importance which the Government of Ghana attached to the Conference of the OAU. In an issue of such magnitude, nobody in the Government could have presented Dr. Nkrumah with *a fait accompli* and I do not share Dei-Anang's opinion on this point. The truth of the matter was of that the decision to host the OAU Conference in Accra in 1965, like all the others which were political, were all taken by the partial cabinet which included President Nkrumah, the Foreign Minister Kojo Botsio and Kwesi Armah, the then High Commissioner in London. The card was played very close to the chest until the last moment. This caused a great deal of irritation and Dei-Anang's response is not surprising.

In fact, when the President eventually raised the issue in Cairo, only one person, Ambassador David Bosomtwi-Sam, who was the Dean of Diplomatic Corp in Kenya, supported the position of the partial cabinet that the OAU Conference should be hosted in Accra in 1965. The experience of Ambassador Bosomtwi-Sam, who had previously worked as Secretary of the Bureau of African Affairs, was highly respected, and his support of the partial cabinet's decision was very heartening.

Actually, except for the fact that the decision of the partial cabinet came as a surprise to Dei-Anang, there were really no grounds whatsoever for his criticism; for this was a policy matter; for when even it came to the question of reviewing Ghana's African policy preparatory to the OAU Conference in Accra, 1965, three members of the partial cabinet delivered the keynote addresses at a Conference held purposely to review that policy; they were President Nkrumah, Foreign Minister Kojo Botsio and Higher Commissioner to Britain, Kwesi Armah. Michael Dei-Anang was completely excluded from it; and this annoyed him.

It is important to state for purposes of clarity that, in terms of decision-making, there was the institutions of the Civil and Foreign Services. But Nkrumah did not rely on them, because he perceived them to be "subservient to colonial interests". So, he created the African Affairs Secretariat and the Bureau of African Affairs under his personal control to facilitate the implementation of Ghana's Pan-African objectives. As Professor Bretton argued, this was a "personalized policy-and decision-making".[39] But, according to Professor Frankel, leaders who are "confronted with problems of exceptional magnitude usually take full charge of Foreign Policy."[40]

Nkrumah was, however, subject to influences by both the radical and conservative elements in his Party and Cabinet. Influences also came from sympathizers such as the late English Philosopher Bertrand Russell, George Padmore, William Du Bois, C. L. R. James and Lord Ferner Brockway, to name only a few. But in the final analysis, Nkrumah fashioned his own foreign policy and dominated the decision-making process.[41]

However, based on my own experience as Ambassador and Cabinet Minister, it could not be said that civil and foreign service officers were "subservient to colonial interests". Rather by the nature of their training and positions they serve, they are not responsible for any failure of policy.

It is interesting that Dei-Anang confined his personal memoir to the "Administration of Ghana's Foreign Relations." In the administrative field, Dei-Anang excelled and made great contribution to the implementation of Ghana's foreign policy. Dei-Anang possessed a lucid mind and a facile pen and the foreign service officials who served under him benefited immensely from his wide knowledge and experience.

Foreign Policy and the Ghanaian Constitution

It is proper to give attention to the difficult and vexatious problem that constantly plagues and sometimes obstructs Ghanaian foreign policy, namely the constitutional problem. The First Republic Constitution remained silent on the formulation and/or execution of foreign policy. However, it contained a broad and general outline of the principles which govern Ghanaian politics — although it did not determine how those principles were to be implemented. The Lennox-Boyd Constitution was unworkable from the start and had in any event to be replaced by the Republican Constitution. By 1959, the demands of the time were such that it would have been difficult to secure acceptance of another monarchical constitution to replace it. In fact, an executive presidential type of government was almost dictated by the nature of the civil machine left behind by the departing British imperial authorities. Even to the last, the Gold Coast civil service administration had been centred around the Governor. From 1951 onwards, it is true, civil servants were distributed in theory to ministries but this was nominal rather than real. A centralized system of government was the colonial legacy.

    The Convention People's Party election victory, following the introduction of a modified form of the Coussey Constitution, transformed the 1946 Colony — Ashanti Legislative Council into a parliamentary system along party lines. But the CPP was not yet fully in control. It had a majority in the reconstituted Executive Council and a substantial minority of the seats in the Assembly but still had to serve a period of apprenticeship under official control. In February, 1951, Kwame Nkrumah became Leader of Government Business, appointed by the governor and confirmed by the votes of the Assembly members.[42] It would, therefore, be seen that what Ghana was in practice capable of doing when it adopted the Republican Constitution was affected and limited not only by what had happened in the Gold Coast before Independence, but by the conditions under which that independence came about. Under colonial rule, every political development was based on the imperial power of the colonial Governor. Thus, the establishment of the Republic in July 1960 was not, as it is often represented to have been, a first step to build an autocracy on colonial foundations. On the contrary, it was the last planned effort to establish a western type democracy.

    With the emergence of the First Republic, it was obvious that the structure of the new Republican Constitution would have to conform, at least in appearance, to the requirements of the time. The new constitutional order was bound to be influenced by the character of the existing government, and Ghana's government in this period was, frankly and deliberately, government of the CPP and ex-colonial officials. The investment of the President with the powers of hitherto external sovereignty did not depend upon the affirmative grants of the Parliament and/or National Assembly. The power to make treaties and to maintain diplomatic relations with other states were vested in the President as necessary concomitants of his special powers under Article 55 of the Constitution. According to Article 55(2), the Parliament had no power to regulate the foreign policy formulation and implementation of the President. On the contrary, it was affirmed that, whenever the President considered it to be in the national interest to do so, he could give directions by legislative instrument.

Foreign Policy and the Armed Forces

Article 54(1) of the Constitution provided that, subject to the provisions of any enactment for the time being in force, the powers of the President as Commander-in-Chief of the Armed Forces should include the powers to commission persons as officers in the said Forces and to order any of the said Forces to engage in operations for the defence of Ghana, for the preservation of public order, for relief in cases of emergency or for any other purpose appearing to the Commander-in-Chief to be expedient. And in terms of the Armed Forces Act 1962, the President could call out any Reserve, or volunteer Force for any of the purposes noted above, or in addition for the preservation of public order. Thus, the President could, in exercising his powers as Commander-in-Chief, order an armed force to engage in military operations against another state should the need arise.

This Constitutional provision was, however, criticized in the sense that the army, like the university, should be a sovereign entity that must be entitled to determine for itself who would or would not exercise command. In his book, *The Ghana Coup*, A. A. Afrifa, elaborately advocates this 'martial freedom' and condemns the despatch of Ghanaian troops to the Congo, though he himself admits that the reason for his disapproval was not clear to him. That army was, according to Afrifa, apparently terrified of being committed to action in Rhodesia. Geoffrey Bing, the then Attorney General and legal Adviser to the President was at a loss as to how such a rumour spread in the army. He claimed that the despatch of Ghanaian troops to Rhodesia was never discussed at any of the many staff talks which were solely concerned with the question of how effective a force could be mounted by the African states acting as a unit in the event of the United Nations authorizing military action.[43]

By virtue of being Commander-in-Chief, the President was able to send the Armed Forces of Ghana wherever he pleased. Parliament, however, was of the opinion that in certain circumstances, its approval of the President's decision to call out the Armed Forces for external military operations was necessary. The then Minister of Foreign Affairs said that the President "is constitutionally entitled to commit these forces to offensive military action. It was, however, far better that, whenever it was possible, the National Assembly be consulted and asked to approve the use of Armed Forces for offensive purposes."[44] It was obvious that such a power of the National Assembly, though not a constitutional provision, to approve presidential decisions to commit the Armed Forces of Ghana to offensive military actions outside of Ghana was a limiting factor on the latent powers of the President in the conduct of foreign affairs. This was reinforced by the fact that, in some way or the other the actions of the president had to be financed; and the President did not risk the National Assembly passing laws which might invalidate his agreements. However, all that the President needed was a simple majority to carry through his actions and nothing more.

During the Congo crisis, where the declaration of support for the United Nations action in the Congo became an inescapable formality, it was considered by some members of Parliament that Ghana needed the scarce resources of the nation at that time for development. It was feared that the Congo operation might involve the nation in a vast expenditure and economic development of the nation might suffer. Consequently, it was felt by some members of Parliament that the Congo operations must not take precedence over the nation's development. Moreover, the critics of the Ghanaian policy in the Congo affairs insisted on a precise declaration of war as a condition of legality for foreign military operations. The Foreign Office and the Bureau of African Affairs insisted that, there was no such rigid requirement in the Constitution, while those criticizing Ghana's support of the United Nations action in the Congo insisted that Parliament was to check presidential prerogative where it was considered wrong. In their arguments the Bureau of African Affairs and the Foreign Office stressed the Commander-in-Chief provision in the Constitution, and drew from it an inherent power in the President's constitutional authority. This stand is reminiscent of the power of the colonial governors of the Gold Coast to commit territorial forces of that colony to foreign operations without explicit approval of the colonial legislature. Although record of the precise basis for the decisions of the colonial governors reveals influence from the Colonial Office in London in each case, some of those involvements were subject to authorization by the Legislative Council, while in yet others the Governor acted on his inherent authority as Governor of the territory.

Execution of Foreign Policy

"The art of diplomacy", ran a British White Paper, "consists in making the policy, whatever it may be, understood and, if possible accepted by other countries."[45] In this regard, the management of the Foreign Ministry and its diplomats did a good job. As part of the machinery of the executive branch of government, the duty of the foreign service officials was to put into effect the policies of the Government. In fact, the effectiveness of Ghana's foreign policy during the period (1957–1966) was partly due to the efficiency of foreign service officials and their ability to respond, in practical terms, to policy decisions taken by the Government.

Execution of policy was carried out through (1) the Ghana Embassies abroad; (2) co-operation between the Foreign Ministry and the Foreign Missions in Ghana; and (3) by means of conferences and delegations. Here there was a great deal of flexibility in the exercise of discretion in handling implementation of policy. Adaptations and changes involved in carrying out the execution of policy were within the province or control of the Foreign Ministry, the African Affairs Secretariat and the Bureau of African Affairs. The three Agencies of the Government exercised complete discretion regarding Field Reports reaching each Agency; and these despatches were vital to policy implementation. In the case of the Bureau, the President intervened from time to time. The Director of the Bureau of African Affairs, A. K. Barden, carried out the President's personal instructions which were not conveyed to other parts of the civil service machine.[46]

In the case of the Foreign Ministry, directions to officials pertaining to implementation of policy were given by the Principal Secretary who had the rank of an Ambassador. From 1957 to 1966, the post of Principal Secretary was held by A. L. Adu, M. F. Dei-Anang, Richard Quarshie, A. B. Kofi, Richard M. Akwei, Henry Amonoo and Fred Arkhurst. Of the post 1966 Principal Secretaries of the Foreign Ministry, Ambassador Sam Quarm was one of the most brilliant and outstanding. His record as Ambassador to various countries including the United States of America, was simply exquisite. The competence, skill and flexibility, with which these Principal Secretaries carried out their functions at the Foreign Ministry, were remarkable. Their guidance to foreign service officers regarding execution of policy was almost always comprehensive. The Government considered it preferable to use Ghana's envoys abroad in the execution of policy because, as personal representatives of the President, they had access to the highest echelon of the government to which they had been accredited. In certain circumstances, they did not even go through the Ministry of Foreign Affairs in their respective countries of accreditation. They first booked appointment to see the Prime Minister, the President or the Minister of Trade in accordance with the nature of mission or assignment to be performed. The Government found it more advantageous to use its own envoys abroad to deliver messages and carry out other diplomatic assignments. This method of implementing policy was more useful than relying on foreign envoys accredited to Ghana, who because they were far away, sent their communications to their governments through the normal diplomatic channels.

However, in modern times the world is becoming smaller and smaller because of telecommunications, telephones, satellites, telexes, etc. Ministries want to meet and exchange ideas and information with their counterparts in other countries. More and more, internal affairs are attracting foreign interests. Heads of governments telephone one another and take decisions. The question, therefore, arises as to whether it is still necessary to have ministries of foreign affairs and Diplomats. In spite of all these developments, it is still necessary to have diplomats and maintain the Ministry of Foreign Affairs including diplomatic missions abroad. The reason is that diplomats are trained personnel. More cautious, they have greater power of assessment: moreover, the diplomatic missions abroad could report more accurately on matters of supreme interest to the sending states. They could also make representation to the receiving state. Although the electric telegraph and the aeroplane have technically boosted diplomacy, they have not totally eliminated the role of the diplomat.

NOTES AND REFERENCES

1. Hartslet, Sir Edward. 1896. *Map of Africa by Treaty*. London: 661.
2. Armah, K. 1981. *The Persuit of Peace without Power: Ghana's Foreign Policy 1957–1966*. M. Lit. Thesis submitted to St. Peter's College. Oxford: 18.
3. Adu, A. L. 1965. *The Civil Service in New African States*. London: 27.
4. O'Brien, Conor Cruise 1962. *To Katanga and Back: A UN Case History, passim*. London.
5. Jones-Quartey, K. A. B., 1974. *A Summary of History of the Ghana Press, 1822–1960*. Accra
6. Adu, *op. cit.*, 11–12. (Adu became Secretary to the Cabinet after Independence).
7. Mulhall, J. A. 1962. *Note for the Guidance of Members of the Public Service Commissions in Overseas Territories*. London.
8. Thompson, Scott W., 1969. *Ghana's Foreign Policy, 1957–66*. Princeton: 104.
9. Adu, *op. cit.*, p.26.
10. Kirk-Greene, A. H. M., 1974. *The Formation of Foreign Service Cadres in Nigeria, Kenya and Uganda, Institute of Commonwealth* Studies Series, No.81. London: 16.
11. Adu, *op. cit.*, p.19.
12. Secretary of the Cabinet to the High Commissioner in London: SCR-0325 of April, 15, 1965.
13. Dei-Anang, M. F., 1975. *The Administration of Ghana's Foreign Relations, 1957–1965: A Personal Memoir*. London: 13.
14. Adu, *op. cit.*, p.16.
15. Dei-Anang, *op. cit.*
16. *Ibid.*
17. *Ibid.*
18. Thompson, *op. cit.*, p.364.
19. Wilson, Harold 1976. *The Governance of Britain*. London: pp.x–xi.

20. Waltz, Kenneth N. 1967. *Foreign Policy and Democratic Politics*. 136,225. London: 136, 225.
21. House of Commons Parliamentary Debates, Vol.645 (August 3, 1961, Col.1670–1689).
22. Walker, Patrick Gordon 1970. *The Cabinet* (Jonathan Cape Edition). London: 88, 91.
23. Mazrui, Ali 1969. *Towards a Pax Africana, A Study of Ideology and Ambition*. London: 73.
24. *Ibid.*
25. Walker, *op. cit.*, p.91.
26. Crossman, R. H. S. 1963. Introduction to Bagehot *The English Constitution* (new ed.). London: 48–52.
27. Walker, *op. cit.*, pp.85–66.
28. Mckintosh John 1962. *The Listener,* 25 August 1966: *The British Cabinet,* virtually *passim* asserts this thesis. London.
29. Benemy, F. W. G. 1965. *The Elected Monarch — The Development of the Powers of the Prime Minister*. London: 245.
30. Aluko, Olajide 1976. *Ghana and Nigeria 1957–70 — Study in Inter-African Discord*. London: 175.
31. Armah, Kwesi 1974. *Ghana: Nkrumah's Legacy*. London: 157–159.
32. Dei-Anang, *op. cit*, p.30.
33. *Ibid.*
34. Colin Legum in The Observer, November, 22, 1959.
35. Nkrumah, K. 1957. *Ghana's policy at home and abroad,* Speech to Parliament, Accra. August 29, 1957.
36. Adu, *op. cit*, p.183.
37. Section 44 of the 1954 Constitution (of the Gold Coast).
38. Dei-Anang, *op. cit*, Note 3.
39. Bretton, H. L. 1966. *The Rise and Fall of Kwame Nkrumah*. London: 112.
40. Frankel, Joseph 1963. *The Making of Foreign Policy: An Analysis of Decision-Making*. Oxford: 23.
41. Krafona, Kwesi 1986. *The Pan-African Movement: Ghana's Contribution*. London: 24.
42. Gold Coast, Legislative Assembly Debates, February 26, 1951.
43. Bing, Geoffrey, 1968. *Op. cit.,* p.425.
44. *Parliamentary Debates Ghana* Vol. 20, No.18, p.676, Col. 1.
45. Proposals for the Reform of the Foreign Service CMD, 6420 (1943), p.2.
46. Dei-Anang, *op. cit,* p.30.

Chapter 3

DE-COLONIZATION AND FOREIGN POLICY

In most of the former colonial and then newly independent territories of the Continent of Africa, pronounced ethnic differences existed among the indigenous peoples. This affected the pattern of de-colonization in Africa. While the great majority desired independence, they did not feel themselves to be a single community. The anti-colonial leadership was thus faced with three options: (1) the establishment of a multi-national state; (2) the imposition of a unitary state in which the strongest group would use authoritarian forms of government to suppress the political aspirations of the smaller national groups; and (3) the establishment of ethnic-based independent states in each territory.

One of the fundamental principles of Ghanaian Foreign Policy was relentless opposition to colonization anywhere on the African continent or indeed in any other part of the world. Ghana, like other African countries, had a stake in the end of colonial rule. The persistence anywhere in the world of colonial hegemony outraged African conscience. Ghana, under Kwame Nkrumah, was interested in seeing that old relationships by which certain countries remained producers of raw materials for the benefit of highly-industrialized countries, come to an end. Ghana's anti-colonial leadership recognized that, colonialism also imposed completely distorted economic, social and cultural patterns whose effect extended beyond their own territorial limits. Economically, it diverted the foreign trade of the colonial territory from its natural direction, i.e., to neighbouring African states almost invariably to the metropolis. Nkrumah frequently attacked or criticized colonialism's policy on inter-African communication. There was little or no rail or road connection between the former British and French colonial territories in Africa. Postal and telecommunication services were still largely based upon the old colonial pattern, which retained the imperial power as a nerve-centre of communications through which all mail, telephonic and telegraphic communications were routed.

This lack of inter-communication between African countries was, for Ghana, one of the greatest obstacles to inter-continental development. That obstacle was only capable of being removed, Nkrumah argued, when independent African states were able to plan their communication systems in concert. And this would only be possible after colonial withdrawal, for as long as colonialism still existed in any part of the African continent it would be impossible either to plan African development on a continental basis, or make the fullest use of African resources for the benefit of the people. To ensure rapid economic development of the continent, Africa had to develop modern physical infra-structure. In fact, all her commercial relationships, for far too long, had lacked a home-based logic. These and other reasons informed the

CPP Government's struggle for the liberation of Africa. Freedom, for Nkrumah, was indivisible. For example, his Government supported the fight of the Algerian people against colonial rule and considered their seven-year struggle as part of a wider struggle. An imperial power seldom, if ever, voluntarily grants freedom. Freedom is attained only as a consequence of pressures from an organized indigenous and militant movement in a colonial territory.

De-colonization and Federalism in Africa

The conditions accompanying the break-up of colonial empires in Africa raised fundamental issues and real concern with respect to the nature of the units that might succeed these empires. Colonial territories were often merely the product of administrative convenience, historical accident, ignorance, or worse — the scramble for empire! As a result, colonial political boundaries rarely even related to the pre-existing racial, linguistic, national or religious communities, or to mutual economic, geographical and historical interests. In most cases, not only were widely dissimilar peoples grouped under a single administrative system and set of communications, but people and nations were split between different administrative provinces and even imperial powers. Consequently with the ending of colonial rule, there were pressures for the erection of new political units that were more closely representative of the economic, historical, and cultural affinities and diversities of the peoples of Africa.

But the creators of newly independent states were at once faced with conflicting demands for both territorial integration and for balkanization. They had to reconcile the need, on the one hand, for relatively-large economic and political units (in order to facilitate rapid economic development and sustenance of genuine political independence), with, on the other hand, the desire of the smaller units to enjoy some degree of autonomy associated with traditional allegiances and ethnic, linguistic and religious communities. These opposing pressures were confounded by the legacy of colonial rule, which created within the artificial units of colonial administration, new loyalties and interests cutting across those of pre-existing cultural and traditional communities. This situation brought about conflicting demands for unification and separation. The tensions between these pressures appeared both in nationalist movements and the approach of colonial administration. The struggle for political independence in Africa thus divided peoples as well as united them. Based on multi-ethnic demand for self-government, nationalism was an integrative force. As a provincial and ethnic force, it was divisive.

In such situations, where the forces for integration and for separation had been at odds one with another, a federal constitutional solution proved a popular formula in Africa. It made possible large political and economic units comprising various peoples and cultures in which smaller groups were assured of some measure of autonomy. In some cases, new federal governments started life either imposed by the imperial power or developed by a process of negotiation between nationalists and the imperial government, e.g., the Rhodesia and Nyasaland in 1953; the Nigeria federation in 1954. The East Africa High Commission in 1947 decided to administer common services in the British territories in that region, later on known as the East African Common Services Organization (EACSO).[1] The attempt of the French Equatorial Africa (AEF) was another example. After the French colonial federations in Africa disintegrated, they were succeeded by the Mali Federation (1959) and the Union of Central African Republics (1960). Both collapsed almost immediately after their establishment. Many of these colonial federations shattered at a most critical time, just before or after the withdrawal of the imperial power. It was not only the federations established by the imperial powers that disintegrated quickly; the Mali Federation, the Union of Central African Republic, and the Union between Egypt and Libya fell apart almost as soon as they had been agreed upon.

In Ghana, despite the urgent advocacy of a federal political structure by certain groups, unitary government, right from the onset, was the choice of Kwame Nkrumah. Viewed against the broad background of the general character of politics in newly-independent states in Africa, neither the failure of many of those federations nor the seeming rejection of federal government in other instances — e.g., the Sudan and the former Belgian Congo — surprised Nkrumah. Indeed, the apparently predominant trend against liberal democratic institutions, the propensity for active presidential forms of government, one-party systems or military rule; the emphasis upon rapid economic growth and national solidarity, and the shortage of trained civil servants to manage complex systems of administration, all appeared to provide a generally-unfavourable climate for federal systems of government. In his speech to the National Assembly on 18th April, 1961, Kwame Nkrumah tried to explain to the world why he had chosen a unitary structure of government for Ghana and why Ghanaians, in the main, believed that such a unitary structure of government was more suited to African conditions and the conditions of newly-independent states in general, than other constitutions based upon the historical patterns of certain older nations. Federalism, he maintained, was falsely believed by some people to be a cure for all the economic and political ills of the African continent. Outside nations almost invariably approached the problems of Africa from the quite contradictory standpoints. In the first place, they all recognized the need for strong government (developing states are still told that foreign investment can only be made in an atmosphere of internal stability) but equally, world public opinion recognized that progress was impossible unless there was the widest possible area of economic co-operation and free trade. On the other hand, when actual political suggestions were invited with regard to the form of government suitable for Africa, outside thinking remained dominated by the political and historical ideas of an eighteenth century world.

The basic idea behind the United States Constitution, for example, was that, all government was bad and should only be tolerated as a necessary evil. There should, therefore, be a series of checks and balances in which some powers of government should be exercised by the basic units of the states whilst other powers should be exercised by a federal government. In that way, neither could be all-powerful. The authority of Congress was limited, but so too was the authority of the President. Moreover, the Supreme Court was established to ensure that, neither the Federal Government nor the States over-stepped limits assigned to them in the Constitution. Neither Congress nor the President exercised powers not expressly granted to them. In the historical conditions in which the United States was established, it is almost undoubtedly true that the only union which could have been set up with the consent of the people was one based upon these principles. It does not necessarily follow, however, that because a constitution of checks and balances was suitable in the United States in the eighteenth century, that it would also be automatically suitable in Africa or in other parts of the world in the second half of the twentieth century. Indeed, Nkrumah firmly advised that, the people of Ghana had decisively rejected a federal form of constitution at the General Election of 1956, and that their reasons for so doing was instructive.

One of the worst legacies of colonialism was the absence of a trained body of African technocrats and administrators. A federal form of government automatically meant that it was impossible to concentrate the limited manpower available in the central government machine. It had to be dispersed in regional and the federal governments and would hence be very thin on the ground. Even more serious than this, was the power vacuum created by federal forms of government. Once institutions started laying down what powers a federal government would have, a vast area of doubt was at once created. It might well not be clear whether this or that particular matter fell within the power of the federal government or of the regional government. Nothing could be done by either until the courts had pronounced one way or another as to where power lies. And appeals could be more time-consuming. In consequence, just at a time when a strong government was necessary, federalism might slow down the process of governmental action and introduce an element of paralysis into the machinery of state. It would be a luxury which Africa, and particularly Ghana, could not afford. This was typically argued as follows:

> The Congo, indeed, provides a striking example of how federation can be used as a cloak to conceal new colonialism. In fact this type of federalism is not federation at all; it is separation. It does not unit, it balkanises.[2]

In all African communities there was a natural and reasonable tendency for ethnic groups to come together and seek to reorganize themselves, both politically and economically, so as to restore their cultural and traditional ways of life, much suppressed under colonialism. It was necessary that Africans understand and appreciate the force of this entirely praiseworthy motive; Nkrumah after some time warned them against its exploitation by those who might wish to restore colonialism in a new guise on the continent of Africa. The whole history of colonial penetration in Africa is the history of colonial powers supporting one ethnic group against another and taking advantage of African differences so that, in the end all might succumb to the colonial yoke.

The solution, therefore, suggested by Nkrumah was a broad form of political organization which allowed expression to all ethnic groups and yet maintain that essential unity which is a pre-requisite of true independence. He did not believe that such a political orgnization would be difficult to evolve, given the will of African states.

He defined the nature of such a government or political unit as follows:

> I mean an African Continental Government — a single continent, which would develop a feeling of one community among the peoples of Africa and work for the economic, technological, social, scientific and cultural development of Africa. Notwithstanding all notions to the contrary, I firmly believe that such an African Continental Government is both essential and necessary.[3]

Ghanaian Policy of De-colonization and the United Nations

Although the tensions and conflicts associated with the so-called 'cold war' had taken the headlines and undoubtedly were of major importance in shaping the course of world politics and the functioning and role of the United Nations during the period of Kwame Nkrumah's governance of Ghana, the emergence of organized nationalist movements in Africa and Asia constituted a phenomenon which in the long run acquired equal, or even greater significance. Before the second world war, the world was largely dominated by the culture and political influence of the West — i.e., Western Europe and the countries of the Western Hemisphere. With few but sometimes important exceptions, the peoples of Africa and Asia were either subordinated within empires or under state governments, which, while theoretically independent, were subject to important practical limitations on their sovereignty. The war served as a powerful stimulant to nationalism and to demands for independence.

Having been subject but recently to foreign rule, that experience, as described above, was paramount. Hence, Ghanaians were primarily concerned with making their own independence secure, improving their living conditions, and with seeking and obtaining for similarly situated dependent African states, independence, the like of which they themselves so greatly prized. With these interests and attitudes, in her foreign policy, Ghana was unwilling to align herself closely with either East or West but insisted on following an independent course, in order to further her own and her pan-African interests. Kwame Nkrumah ardently believed that, the United Nations could, in this respect, do much to contribute to the peace that the international community desired.

Ghana, therefore, strongly supported the United Nations and was active in promoting it as the most important instrument in the international community for the preservation of peace and for orderly and vital change in the fortunes of newly independent African states. Indeed, Nkrumah often emphasized that, it was the duty of the United Nations to ensure that change takes place in an orderly and peaceful manner and he considered that the United Nations would fail if it ever became a body for enforcing the status quo. He vehemently opposed any tendency for it to be converted into an 'Holy Alliance' of the early nineteenth century type, playing the role of preserver of arbitrary frontiers and maintaining intact existing colonial relationships. The United Nations must, indeed, effect the complete and final liquidation of colonialism by peaceful means. Nkrumah vigorously argued that, the continued existence of colonialism constituted a serious threat to world peace and security. Thus, Ghana's diplomats were not inclined, in the General Assembly or the Security Council, as were the colonial powers, to stress the role of the United Nations as a guarantor of the status quo against violent change or even as an enforcer of law and order, at least as they were envisaged by colonial powers in colonial territories. As a result of the influence of Ghana and other Afro-Asian states, the United Nations came to accept the role of assisting the transition of dependent states from dependence to independence, a role several metropolitan powers viewed with less enthusiasm.

De-colonization of the Congo

It is true that, the major motives for decolonization may be varied, but common to nearly all movements to attain freedom from colonial domination is the desire for genuine political independece and international influence. This was vividly illustrated when the Congo crisis became a test case in the pan-African struggle for genuine political independence. It has been argued that, the determination of the Ghanaian government to rid the African continent of alien domination, and to overthrow the colonial governments which persisted in Africa, was the most obvious consistent and all-embracing common denominator of Ghanaian foreign policy during the period under review. Independence for the Congo was thus much more than a national affair. Indeed, it was part of the world ideological struggle. But it was particularly an African affair and to Africans everywhere, the movement was part of the general drive towards the freedom from colonial domination of the entire African continent. At the very moment of independence, Kwame Nkrumah had made his seminal declaration that "the independence of Ghana is meaningless unless it is linked with the total liberation of Africa."[4] This in part explains why Ghana became a vigorous partner of progressive Congolese at the time of initiation of their nation and crisis which immediately ensued.

Ghana-Congo solidarity began with the All-African People's Conference held at Accra in December, 1958. Among the hundreds of delegates who attended the Conference was Patrice Lumumba — who became the President of the Congolese National Movement Party — and two party associates. This memorable Conference was for them a baptism of fire in the struggle for Africa's liberation. On returning home to Congo, a mass meeting was convened on January 3, 1959 at which Lumumba announced with fiery outcry the need for immediate and total independence for his country. The new year was to be one of new resolutions. On January 4, some 30,000 demonstrators, mainly unemployed workers, marched through the streets and publicly demanded independence. The spontaneity of this event and its impact nation-wide were tremendous. The All-African People's Conference in Ghana thus made an immediate and dramatic impact on the Congolese political scene. And there was no turning back. Like the CPP of Ghana, Lumumba's Party was the first Congolese political organization to recognize the need for a national leader and national movement to express the principles of Pan-Africanism.

The kind of divisions which beset political parties in the Congo soon after the Brussels Conference were not new to Ghanaians. The experience of the national movements in both countries, though different in points of detail, had certain basic characteristics in common; their struggle for national independence involved, to some extent, a struggle between the new nationalism and local ethnicity or tribalism, and disagreement about a unitary system of government and federation.

Congolese Independence and the United Nations

On 10th May, 1960, the Belgian Senate passed *La Loi Fondamentale sur les Structures de Congo*, which was signed by King Baudouin the following day. This Basic Law, which may be compared with the Ghana Independence Act of 1957, provided the constitution of the new Republic of the Congo. There were to be a Head of State, a Government directed by a Prime Minister, a Parliament consisting of a Chamber of Representatives and a Senate. Each province was to have a provincial government directed by a president and provincial assembly. In the 259 Articles of the Law, the powers of the various organs of government were clearly stated and provisions were laid down for the division of powers between the central and provincial authorities. But in spite of all this elaborate division of powers, the constitution essentially envisaged a unitary government for the Congo. Thus, Article 6 of the Basic Law provided that the Congo, within its present boundaries, is an indivisible and democratic state. This appears to have been a deliberate attempt, on the part of the framers of the constitution, to incorporate unitary and federal features within the single political system of the Congo at the same time. It was to prove particularly difficult during the attempted secession of Katanga province from the Republic of the Congo.

On June 29, 1960, the day before independence was officially proclaimed, a Belgian-Congolese treaty of friendship was signed. It stated that Belgian metropolitan troops stationed in bases in the Congo could only be used within the Congo at the request of the Congolese Minister of Defence. Along with Article 6 of the Basic Law, this provision was soon to be violated. Within two weeks of independence, mutinies and riots occurred in various parts of the Congolese Army in support of demands for improvement in the pay and conditions of service for the troops. Panic-stricken Europeans began to leave the country as Belgian troops intervened, seizing Matadi and Leopoldville airports. Then Katanga announced its secession. This was followed on July 12, by the appeal of the Congolese Government for United Nations military assistance against the return to the Congo of Belgian troops:

> The Government of the Republic of the Congo requests urgent dispatch by the United Nations of military assistance. This request is justified by the dispatch to the Congo of metropolitan Belgian troops in violation of the treaty of friendship signed between Belgium and the Republic of the Congo on June 29, 1960. Under the terms of that treaty, Belgian troops may only intervene on the express request of the Congolese Government. No such request was ever made by the Government of the Republic of the Congo, and we therefore regard the unsolicited Belgian action as an act of aggression against the country.
>
> The real cause of most of the disturbances can be found in colonialist machinations. We accuse the Belgian Government of having carefully prepared the secession of Katanga with a view to maintaining a hold of our country. The Government, supported by the Congolese people, refuses to accept a *fait accompli* resulting from a conspiracy between Belgian imperialists and a small group of Katanga Leaders. The overwhelming majority of the Katanga population is opposed to secession, which means the disguised perpetuation of the colonialist regime. The essential purpose of the requested military aid is to protect the national territory of the Congo against the present external aggression which is a threat to international peace. We strongly stress the extremely urgent need for the despatch of United Nations troops to the Congo.[5]

This request was signed jointly by Joseph Kasavubu (President of the Republic of the Congo and Supreme Commander of the National Army) and Patrice Lumumba (Prime Minister and Minister of National Defence, of the Congo). The President and the Prime Minister emphasized, in a following telegram to the Secretary General of the United Nations, that they wanted military assistance not because of the internal situation in the Congo, but rather to protect the national territory against acts of aggression committed by troops from metropolitan Belgium.

When this matter was first placed before the United Nations, the only African member of the Security Council was Tunisia. Tunisia had, however, agreed to act as the agent of the African Group, whose work had just commenced and whose existence was reaffirmed at the Addis Ababa Conference of Independent African States. The collective African point of view, as interposed by Mongi Slim, Tunisia's delegate, was very influential at this point. When, in the following month, relations between the Lumumba Government and the United Nations forces seriously deteriorated, it was to the collective African powers that Lumumba turned to strengthen his position. He toured various African countries and called for a summit conference to be held in Leopoldville (subsequently Kinshasa). Because of the friendly and close personal relations between Patrice Lumumba and Kwame Nkrumah and in view of the importance of the Congo to the rest of Africa, Ghana decided to do all it could to help resolve the difficulties being experienced by the Republic of Congo. In a letter dated July 13, 1960 Nkrumah declared to Lumumba the willingness of Ghana to help the Congo in any way possible, including the despatch of a battalion of the Ghanaian Army as a part of the United Nations Organization force in the Congo — always provided that, the Government of the Congo deemed it necessary. Moreover, he eschewed the participation of non-African powers.

> That the present difficulties in the Congo should be solved primarily through the efforts of the independent African states within the framework of the United Nations machinery. Intervention by Powers from outside the African continent, in the view of the Government of Ghana, is likely to increase rather than lessen tension.
>
> The Government of Ghana has made this statement in the belief that, the present situation in the Congo is one capable of peaceful and quick solution provided that rival outside powers do not interfere as a means of serving their particular interests."

Nkrumah informed the Secretary General of the United Nations, Dag Hammarskjold, by telephone, that the Congolese Government had asked Ghana for military aid and that Ghana as an African state was ready and willing to send troops. The same evening, July 13, 1960, the Security Council met and passed the resolution authorizing the despatch of United Nations forces to the Congo. Mr. Hammarskjold agreed to make it a predominantly-African operation, although Sweden and Ireland, both unquestionably neutral, were also asked to send troops. The great powers, excluded from the United Nations military force, provided air transport. On July 15, 1960, the first Tunisian soldiers, closely followed by Ghanaians, landed in the Congo. By then more Belgian soldiers had arrived in the Congo and on July 14, Lumumba and Kasavubu broke off diplomatic relations with Belgium.

Ghana's efforts to help find a solution to Congolese crisis was in accordance with her non-aligned policy. In effect, the Ghanaian policy to the Congo crisis of 1960 was to support the United Nations totally till the end of the crisis though Ghana was determined to become highly critical of the United Nations actions. At no time were Ghanaian armed forces employed other than in strict accordance with United Nations orders, although this involved, on occasions, issues such as the prevention of Patrice Lumumha from using Leopoldville radio to explain his position when he had been removed as Prime Minister by Kasavubu. Though, under considerable pressure from the more radical African states, the Ghana Government refused to withdraw Ghanaian troops as other states had done and throughout, Dr. Nkrumah insisted on a solution being found within the framework of the United Nations. If there is any criticism to be made of the Ghana Government's policy it was that, it put too much trust in the United Nations ability — and will — to solve the crisis.

Ghana was soon placed in a most embarrassing and invidious situation *vis-à-vis* the legitimate government. She had originally landed troops in the Congo under the umbrella of the United Nations Organization to aid the legitimate Lumumba Government. Subsequent development, however, perverted the original objective and seriously undermined Ghana's position in the eyes of the legitimate Government of the Congo Republic in that Ghana's troops were used as a cat's paw against Lumumba, to the extent of even preventing him from using his own radio station. At the same time, Radio Brazzaville, which was controlled by France, a permanent member of the Security Council, indulged in the most violent propaganda against the legitimate Lumumba Government. Radio Elizabethville, which in effect was under Belgian control, was also allowed to indulge in similar propaganda. Thus, Ghana was used virtually to tie Lumumba's hands behind him while a permanent member of the Security Council was allowed to whip him. In the circumstances, it is hardly surprising that the Ghana Government decided that:

> if Lumumba is not allowed to use his own radio station at Leopoldville for keeping the Congolese populace informed of the critical situation and thus mobilizing support for the legitimate Government of the Congo Republic of which he is head, Ghana would withdraw her troops forthwith from the United Nations command and reserves the right to place her troops in the Congo Republic entirely at the disposal of the legitimate Lumumba Government of the Congo Republic.[7]

At the same time, a preparatory conference at ministerial level of African states was held from August 25, 1960, in Leopoldville. The delegations that came were, for the most part, those that had been at the Conference of Independent African States at Addis Ababa. They were Cameroon, Congo

(L), Ethiopia, Ghana, Gouverment Provisoire de la Republique Algerienne (GPRA), Guinea, Liberia, Mali, Morocco, Somalia, Sudan, Togo, Tunisia and the United Arab Republic. Lumumba had hoped to get this group of states to endorse his idea of direct African military aid to the Congo, but the response of the majority was cautious. The assembled delegates did affirm support for the unity of the Congo and did recommend that a conference of heads of state be convened before the opening of the United Nations General Assembly, the meeting was nevertheless a letdown for Lumumba and presaged his imminent fall from power.

Already at this point, it was evident that, the African states were divided into three admittedly somewhat fluid camps — the 'revolutionaries', the 'moderates' (who did not attend this Leopoldville meeting, and the 'neutrals'. When Lumumba was deposed by Kasavubu in September, Lumumba contested the legality of the action. Since Kasavubu was in fact given support both by the United Nations Command and, from October on, by those elements of the Congolese army controlled by Mobutu, Kasavubu held *de facto* control of the capital. Nonetheless, Lumumba still claimed that his was the legal government and some of his supporters, led by Antoine Gizenga, established *de facto* control over the northeast of the country by November of the same year.

Early in November 1960, the struggle for power between Ksavubu and Lumumba turned strongly in favour of Kasavubu when he flew to America to address the United Nations General Assembly. There were then two Congolese delegations in New York, one accredited by Kasavubu and the other by Lumumba. The Credentials Committee, on November, recommended the seating of the Kasavubu delegation and on the 22nd their recommendation was accepted by the General Assembly by 53 votes to 24 with 19 abstentions. Belgium, France, South Africa, the United Kingdom and the United States of America were among those who voted in favour of the Kasavubu delegation.

President Nkrumah agreed with President Sekou Toure of Guinea that in view of the gloomy situation in the Congo, and particlularly in Leopoldville, where the army of Mobutu was carrying out a reign of terror against the defenceless civil population by day and night, some definite action must be taken by the Heads of African States in an endeavour to restore law and order. Nkrumah, therefore, wrote to President Nasser suggesting that, the time had come to get together a few officers to form such a Command. Whether the African High Command was to be stationed in Cairo, Accra or Conakry was, to his mind, immaterial but the important thing was its formation and eventual use in Leopoldville to help maintain law and order.

The idea of forming an African High Command was not new to the thinking of the Ghanaian Government. The latter had urged this step to other African states several times. The Government believed that, such a Command was essential if the independent African states were to intervene effectively to save the Congo. Dr. Nkrumah realized that the independent African states did not have the military strength to exercise any real weight in international politics. With a united force, their views could not be ignored. He believed that, it was only by firm measures that the independent African states would impress the colonial powers that there was a new African who was no longer prepared to accept their persistent efforts to deprive him of his legitimate rights and aspirations. In breaking diplomatic relations within Belgium he observed that:

> As for the African stooges of colonialism who are content to become willing marionettes in the exploitation of their own country, one can only be sorry for them, for the trend of events in Africa indicates that their days are numbered. Their successes must therefore be regarded as short-lived and ephemeral.[8]

Most of the African states that had troops in the United Nations Command in the Congo voted at the United Nations against the seating of the Kasavubu delegation. The continued crisis led to the request of King Mohammed V of Morocco for a conference in Casablanca primarily to discuss the Congo. This conference took place on 3rd–7th January, 1961, and was attended by the Heads of State of Morocco, the United Arab Republic (UAR), Ghana, Guinea, Mali, the Foreign Minister of Libya, and the GPRA, and an observer from Ceylon. The grouping was a mixed one. The Conference helped the King of Morocco steal the thunder from his left opposition by adopting a strong pro-Lumumba stance. For the UAR, joining the Casablanca group represented its first commitment to a deep involvement in pan-African affairs. Tunisia did not come, in part because it was beginning to sharply differentiate its position from that of its old allies in the African Group, and partly because its relations with the host country, Morocco restrained as a result of Tunisia's recognition of Mauritania. (Ghana had in fact also recognized Mauritania shortly before the Conference). There was some uncertainty as to whether or not Tunisia had been invited. Others say they were not. An official invitation list has never been made public.

While all the participants at this Conference supported Lumumba, there was division of tactics *vis-à-vis* the United Nations. Guinea and Mali had withdrawn their troops from the Congo because they rejected the use made of these troops by the United Nations Command. Morocco shared this view and the UAR leaned in the same direction. They argued that, Ghana's reluctance to follow suit was jeopardizing the solid support African troops could give directly to the Lumumba regime installed in Stanleyville. Ghana argued, on the contrary, that removal of African troops only left the field open to the opponents of Lumumba and that, behind a façade of militancy, this suggestion was in fact a major concession. In fact, Nkrumah convinced Nasser on this point. The conference decided to give the United Nations a last chance, failing which troops would be withdrawn.

Shortly after the Casablanca meeting on 17th January, 1961, Lumumba was murdered. With graphic detail on the 'murder of Lumumba', Nkrumah[9] explained that, Lumumba and his two companions were flown to Elizabethville in circumstances which shocked even the Belgian pilot and his crew. According to the pilot's evidence, the three prisoners had been roped together and were beaten continuously throughout the flight. The crew were so sickened at the sight of the savage punishment inflicted on the prisoners that they shut themselves up in the front cabin. At Elizabethville airport, eye-witnesses reported that, the prisoners showed obvious signs of ill-treatment; they were further manhandled by troops and police as they were pushed quickly into a waiting jeep at the airport from where they were transported to a house on the outskirts of Elizabethville, where in the presence of Tshombe and Munongo and possibly others, they were cruelly murdered.

The removal of Lumumba from the scene was followed a few days later by the inauguration of President Kennedy. United States and United Nations policy in the Congo soon began to change markedly. Reconciliation of the Leopoldville (Kasavubu) and Stanleyville (Gizenga-Lumumbist) forces, under the leadership of the former, and at the expense of Tshombe was not vigorously pursued. One key element in this reconciliation was the resolution of the United Nations Security Council, introduced by Ceylon, Liberia, and the UAR, and adopted on February 21, 1961 which gave authority to the United Nations Command for the "use of force, if necessary, as a last resort".[10] It was necessary, and it was eventually used against Tshombe. The new alignment of forces was in fact consummated in August 1961 with the installation of Cyrille Adoula as Prime Minister of the Congo. Adoula was elected by a reunited Parliament. His election ended, for the moment, the Leopoldville-Stanleyville duality.

When in late December of 1962 the United Nations Command finally occupied Katanga, the last major obstacle to African reconciliation was removed. The ending of the Katanga secession had been one of the principal demands of the Casablanca powers and the Lumumbists in the Congo. Adoula unfortunately removed the Lumumbists from his national government. But the fall of Tshombe in Katanga counterbalanced this, i.e., in terms of correlation of interested forces in and out of the Congo. Finally, on March 11, 1963, the Ghana Government suspended its demand that the Security Council pursue its investigation into the death of Lumumba. The way was now paved for a conference of all Africa.

All Africa Peoples Conference, 1958

After Ghana achieved Independence in 1957, there began a rapid succession of events which tremendously attracted international attention. There were two most significant events which sparked off the process: (1) Conference of Independent African States held in Accra in April 1958, and (2) the All African People's Conference of December 1958 held in Accra. At the time of the former Conference, there were only eight independent states (Ethiopia, Ghana, Liberia, Libya, Morocco, Tunisia, Sudan and Egypt). The purpose of the meeting was to (1) discuss questions of mutual interest, (2) explore ways and means of consolidating and safeguarding independence, (3) strengthen the economic and cultural ties between the independent states and (4) find ways of helping Africans still oppressed under colonial rule. The African leaders in attendance were resolutely and unanimously anti-imperialist, and agreed to co-ordinate diplomacy mainly at the United Nations level.

The All African People's Conference held in Accra in December 1958 was the true successor to the Pan-African Congress of Manchester in 1945 (attended by indigenous Africans such as I.T.A. Wallace-Johnson and Jomo Kenyetta). The aim of the All African People's Conference was to encourage African nationalist political movements in colonial areas in their struggle for freedom. Though the preparatory committee of the Conference had been composed only of representatives from eight independent African states (i.e. Ghana, Ethiopia, Libya, Tunisia, Morocco, Egypt, Liberia and Sudan), delegates from twenty-eight African countries and sixty-two nationalist organizations, most of them from colonies attended the Conference. None represented a government as such. The participants were representatives of two kinds of groups: political parties or movements, and trade unions. It was at this Confeence that the dangers of neo-colonialism were thoroughly examined. After Dr. Nkrumah's opening address, Tom Mboya of Kenya was elected Chairman, partly to emphasize the participation of other than West and North Africans and partly to pay tribute to the active Kenyan struggle for independence. J. K. Tetteh of Ghana and F. S. McEwan of Nigeria were elected joint secretaries. The achievement of independence was clearly the primary problem the delegates addressed. Mboya said: "The problem is not to know if we want independence, but how to get it". In principle, the organizers had hoped to attract all of Africa's nationalist movements. They did rather well, though the governing political parties in the French community states which had just become autonomous did not come, except that of Senegal.

The impact of this and subsequent All Africa People's conferences or meetings on political awareness in Africa was tremendous. It brought many African nationalist leaders north and south of the Sahara desert into contact for the first time on African soil. They realized that it was in their mutual interest to preserve the independence and unity of Africa. The All African People's Conferences had become the meeting grounds of three groups: (1) African nationalists in non-independent countries; (2) Leaders of the so-called revolutionary African states and (3) Leftist African nationalist opposition movements in independent states, which states were considered by these opposition movements as clients or 'puppets' of the West.

The latter group (which included the Union des Populations du Cameroon — French Cameroon — which must not be confused with the Uganda People's Congress, the Sawaba of Niger led by Djibo Bakary, the Moroccan Union Nationale des Forces Poulaires (UNFP) represented by Mehdi Ben Barka) was perhaps the most genuinely and the most persistently militant. It also had the least real power; therefore, while this third group often dominated the conferences and gave the tone to the resolutions, it was the second group (the governments) that held the purse strings and therefore had over-arching influence. Although the third All African People's Conference formally decided that a fourth meeting was to be held in February 1962 in Bamako, Mali, the meeting in Cairo in 1964 was in fact the last one ever held. The Casablanca governments were content to let the All African People's Conference disappear quietly in their attempt to come to terms with the other African governments.

One of the central issues of the Cairo meeting was the legitimacy and desirability of using violence. This question was put before the Conference by the Algerian Front de Liberation Nationale (FLN), still engaged in armed struggle for independence. This problem (which had bedevilled Pan-African movements in the past) was indicative of the ideological conflict between the militant tactics of radical nationalists who pressed for immediate freedom, unity and development throughout Africa, and reformists who were mildly critical of colonialism and even believed in co-operation between colonially-exploited and their exploiters and masters. Indeed, the latter preferred the gradualist approach to independence and self-government. The militants, on the contrary, were thoroughly dedicated to radical agitation for independence, self-government and African unity. These differences were apparent in the discussions of the Pan-African Conferences of 1921 and 1945, the former in Brussels and the latter in Manchester.

At the Congress held from 30th August to 2nd September, 1921 in the Palais Mondial in Brussels, M. Blaise Diagne (a Senegalese Deputy and Commissioner General during the War of 1914, in charge of the recruitment of black troops, vehemently attacked Du Bois's London Declaration which encouraged radicalism and separatism). The Afro-Americans, he said, were "*animes des sentiments plutot dangereux*" whereas French and Belgian negroes believed in co-operation between whites and blacks. Even though the Afro-Americans and English-speaking Africans formed the majority, Diagne refused categorically to submit the London Declaration to the vote of the Congress, on account of its 'Communist' connotation adding that the Negro race belonged to no party.[11] The suggestion that the controversial Declaration should be submitted to a special Committee which would examine it and report to the Paris session of the Congress, found no support. Diagne boldly pressed his challenge and, though outnumbered, imposed his will on the Congress.

At the Manchester Congress in 1945, Du Bois addressed the problem again. Although he agreed on the necessity of self-government for Africans, he warned the militants that such forms of government demanded experience and practice.

> A great many of us want to say that we can govern ourselves now and govern ourselves well; that may not be true. Government is a matter of experience and long experiences.[12]

The dichotomy between the 1921 Brussels Congress and 1945 Manchester Congress is revealed by the fact that the Congress's Declaration to the Colonial Powers written by Du Bois, affirmed its belief in peace and in the principles of the Atlantic Charter, but warned that 'as a last resort' force might be used in the struggle for independence. This difference was revealed among the groups which revived the national Congress of British West Africa whose objective was the liberation of West Africa and the formation of West African Unity. This was a more moderate group of middle-class nationalists who had also drawn their inspiration from the Manchester Congress of 1945. In the Gold Coast, the Accra intelligentsia led by men like Dr. F. V. Nanka-Bruce, the Hon. G. E. Moore, the Hon. Akilagkpa Sawyerr, K. B. Ateko, W. E. C. Sekhi, J. B. Danquah, and A. M. Akiwumi met at the Rodger Club on 18th December 1945 to revived the National Congress of British West Africa. Their enthusiasm, however, did not last. Organization was poor and by 1946, their movement sank into oblivion. Their group was different in political outlook from Kwame Nkrumah's West African National Secretariat group. The National Congress of British West Africa (NCBWA) represented by the men mentioned above was reformist, legalistic and elitist, seeing itself as the natural successor of the colonial regime; indeed the potential heir to the colonial regime. Dr. Nkrumah and his West African National Secretariat (WANS), on the other hand, thought in terms of mass politics, boycotts, and strikes as the quickest means of seizing power. From the point of view of the colonial élite, then, Nkrumah was an impostor and disruptive force.

Nkrumah's tendency therefore, to see himself and the West Africa National Secretariat as a revolutionary version of the NCBWA seems understandable. According to Peter Abrahams, the West African National Secretariat was:

> the deliberate creation of Dr. Kwame Nkrumah and other militants such as Wallace-Johnson who designed to seize power as quickly as possible. He (Nkrumah) was one of the members of the inner circle of the Pan-African Movement until he broke away to find his own West African National Secretariat. I thought then, and still think, that he was the most practical politician of the lot of us. We were concerned with ideas, with the enunciation of great principles. He was concerned with one thing only, getting power and getting it quickly.[13]

For Nkrumah, the only road to power lay in the organization of the masses, and the West African National Secretariat was designed to facilitate such organization of the masses.

It is not, therefore, surprising that in his address to the All African People's Conference in December, 1958, in his capacity as life chairman of the Convention People's Party (CPP), Nkrumah said that, never before has it been possible for so representative a gathering of African freedom fighters to assemble in a free independent African state for the purpose of planning for a final assault upon imperialism and colonialism. Declaring that the assembly marked the opening of a new epoch in African history, he called on the delegates to remember always that before the final objective of Pan-Africanism could be achieved, three stages had to occur, namely, the attainment of freedom and independence; the creation of unity and community between African states; and the economic and social reconstruction of Africa. He reminded the delegates that, the liberation of Africa was the task of all Africans, and in conclusion he said that fighters for African freedom should be resolved and re-dedicated to the task of forming among the political parties in their respective countries a broad united front, based upon one common fundamental aim and object, namely, the speedy liberation of their territories.

Apart from the presence of so many major African political parties, the Conference itself was significant in many ways. On the central issue of the legitimacy and desirability of using violence to obtain colonial freedom, the Conference agreed that there were and would continue to be colonial situations in which it must be used. This would remain the position of most African leaders and movements throughout future developments of Pan-Africanism. Algeria once again came in for special attention, and full support was given to the then proclaimed Gouvernment Provisoire de la Republique Algerienne (GPRA). The Conference called for the establishment of various all-African organizations, such as trade unions and youth groups. This task too would be of extreme importance. It also called for setting up of a Bureau of Liberatory Movements. A permanent secretariat was established with headquarters in Accra, Ghana. The first Secretary-General was George Padmore, a Ghanaian by adoption. When he died the following year, he was succeeded by Guinea's Resident Minister in Ghana, Abdoulaye Diallo.

International Corps of Volunteers

The most revolutionary proposal at the All Africa Peoples Conference, 1958 was that of the Algerians and Moroccans for an "international corps of volunteers" to go to the aid of the Algerians (in the manner of the International Brigade in Spain which helped the anti-France forces in the Spanish civil war in the 1930s). The proposal for such a corps was adopted in principle. But although its use was to be strictly limited to Algeria, President Bourghuiba of Tunisia denounced the proposal as propaganda and indicated that such a corps would not be permitted on Tunisian soil. Bourghuiba's reaction, symptomatic of the tactical ambivalence indicated above, was a major factor in the African liberation struggle. The independent border states of a country fighting a colonial revolution have had more power to affect tactics than any pan-African structure, however, strong. And border states have been prudent, since they pay the price of imprudence most immediately. The self-interest of the sovereign African states led inevitably to moderating revolutionary action. Thus, when the Conference proclaimed the 'irrevocable character of the movement towards African independence, liberty and unity', there was no assurance that for everyone present it meant the same kind of independence, liberty and unity.

Finally, the Conference agreed to:

1. work actively for a final assault on colonialism and imperialism;

2. use non-violent means to achieve political freedom, but to be prepared to resist violence if the colonial powers resorted to force;

3. set up a permanent Secretariat to co-ordinate the efforts of all nationalist movements in Africa for the achievement of freedom;

4. condemn racialism and tribalism wherever they exist and work for their eradication, and in particular to condemn the apartheid policy of the South African Government;

5. work for the ultimate achievement of a Union or Commonwealth of African states.[14]

These have remained the basic objectives of African freedom fighter organizations, though equally important is their determination to end all forms of exploitation. The most powerful force that determined the course of Ghana's foreign policy in the period under review was the need to preserve the ideals and goals of the Pan-African revolution. Ghana and the countries which shared her ideology of revolution repeatedly proclaimed that the struggle would not be complete until the entire continent of Africa was free of colonial control and all African territories attained majority rule.

Fulfilment of the goals of the revolution also required, in their opinion, a commitment to a form of system which, through an equal sharing of the products of economic development, would ultimately replace the exploitation of the colonial system. Nkrumah observed that only with the attainment of the goals of the revolution would the true independence of Africa be realized. "One of the cardinal tenets of our policy is to see all Africa free from foreign rule, for we believe that freedom for Africans on their native continent of Africa is essential for world peace."[15] The Conference was not the forum to argue the validity or the practicality of the goals of the African revolution in the form expounded by the strongest proponents of radicalism, e.g. Nkrumah, Nasser, Toure and Modibo Keita. The concern should rather be the effects that the commitments of these men to the revolution had on their foreign policies. The general goals of the revolution as they were enunciated in 1958 by Nkrumah was shared in large degree by the newly-independent states of Africa within the period under review. For Nkrumah, the goal of revolution in Africa was not simply a rapid modernization. He believed, with an almost missionary spirit, that the pattern of change which he advocated would bring about a profound social transformation that would ultimately restore dignity and equality to the former colonial subjects. The movement must encompass the continent; only through total and explicit acceptance of the revolution by all states would the African community finally gain an internationally-recognized status and dignity. Moreover, if the revolution was seen as a unified whole, its failure in one country would constitute a threat not only to African unity but, even more importantly to its success in every other country.

Direct Material Aid to Nationalists

The Ghanaian Government tried to speed up the liberation of the whole of Africa, including South Africa, by offering the nationalists direct material aid. Since Independence, according to Scott Thompson, Ghana had been providing small quantities of aid to some nationalist leaders.[16] Since the aid figures to the nationalists were not usually published, only very little could be said about them. In April, 1959, Dr. Banda's party received aid from Ghana to promote its nationalist campaign in Nyasaland (later Malawi).[17] Another form of aid offered to the colonial peoples in Africa by the Ghana Government was scholarships. Thus, during the 1963/4 academic session, the Ghana Government gave one hundred scholarships for secondary school and university education to students from various dependent territories in Africa.[18] In addition to this, Ghana was one of the fourteen members of the United Nations providing, by late 1963, special scholarships for Portuguese territories in Africa.[19] Thus, there were several of these students and refugees in exile in Ghana who were accused in their territories of origin of being propagandists for the Ghana Government.

Ghana's Foreign Policy in the Commonwealth

Ghana's foreign policy, as it is now, was from the period of her Independence to safeguard her position in the Pan-African movement and to maintain her relation with the Commonwealth of Nations of which the Queen of the United Kingdom is the Head. In other words, Ghana wanted to preserve the country's integrity as a Pan-African power, secure and strengthen her Commonwealth connections. While Pan-African unity may not in itself be sufficient to preserve an immediate peace, it is true that, without unity and co-operation, the individual states of Africa "out of a sense of insecurity, may be drawn into making defence pacts with foreign powers which may endanger the security"[20] of the present fragile African states. Equally in both defence and economic relations, such benefits as result from the close, informal relations within the Commonwealth are mutual.

In another respect, the relationship of the Commonwealth has provided particular advantages for Ghana and the newly-independent members of that union. These advantages arise out of Great Britain's facilities and position as a member of the Western Alliance and, more recently, the European Economic Community (EEC). Furthermore, Ghana as a member of the Commonwealth, has had the opportunity to make its points of view known through the Commonwealth media. During the 1960s, it was understandably-involved in its own problems; it was a matter of sheer survival for the Commonwealth as it weathered storms over such problems as Rhodesia. But that phase is now passed and the Commonwealth has been turning itself into a body of nations which increasingly works within the greater whole. The Commonwealth has been steadily realizing that its work can help and stretch into all the regional organizations like the EEC, the Association of South East Asian Nations (ASEAN), the Caribbean Community (CARICOM), and so forth, as well as into the Francophone associations and most importantly into the United Nations. More-over, more than a quarter of the membership of the Organization of African Unity (OAU) are Commonwealth countries. The South Pacific Forum (SPC) is almost all Commonwealth. Two of the five ASEAN countries are Commonwealth. Commonwealth countries such as Trinidad and Guyana are now members of the Organization of American States (OAS). A quarter of the membership of the UN are Commonwealth countries. Through its Secretariat, the Commonwealth is able to co-ordinate and increase its links with all these regional and international bodies. In several respects, Ghana benefited considerably from its Commonwealth membership.

At the Commonwealth Prime Minister's Conference in 1964 and 1965, Ghana was the most vocal in the defence of the Black African majority in Rhodesia and the most critical of the British Government's handling of the situation.[21]

Another factor which determined relations between Ghana and her Commonwealth partners on the problem of de-colonization was the role played by the British Press which virtually became an unofficial opposition to Dr. Nkrumah and his Government in the sense that, the press commented adversely on measures taken by the Ghana Government in the day-to-day running of affairs in Ghana. Even leading organs of the British press, *The Daily Telegraph* for example, had almost immediately after independence launched attacks on Ghana. Not only was Dr. Nkrumah accused of dictatorship but the British civil servants who had resisted the lure of £8,000 compensation were marked out for particular abuse. The *Daily Telegraph* had written as follows:

> If Dr. Nkrumah chooses to govern Ghana in an arbitrary and oppressive way, that is his affair and Ghana's. One thing he has no right to expect, however, and that is our assistance. There are still many British functionaries in Ghana. They are agents of the Ghana Government, compelled to do its bidding, to interpret its laws and to enforce them.
>
> The Judge who quashed an injunction preventing the Ghana Government from deporting two Moslem Leaders was British; the police officer who smuggled them out in a fast car to Accra was British. Both doubtless acted correctly in the context.[22]

Geoffrey Bing, who was then the Attorney General on the spot, has explained the circumstances which gave rise to this outburst of the *Daily Telegraph*. The Government had issued deportation orders against two Nigerians then living in Kumasi. One, Alhaji Amadu Baba, had claimed to be the Zerikin Zongo of the town, that is to say the Chief of its non-Ghanaian Moslem inhabitants. The other, Alhaji Othman Larden Lalemie, claimed to be the Chaplain to the Hausa community, or, in other words, asserted his right to the spiritual leadership of the Hausas whose homeland is in Northern Nigeria but who had settled in Ghana as Moslem traders. The Mosque maintained by Alhaji Othman Larden had been the centre of continual disturbance. It was suspected, whether rightly or not, that, itinerant Hausa had been employed in political crimes of violence and intimidation. Geoffrey Bing confirmed that upon his assumption of office he found a Report of a Committee of Enquiry into crimes of extortion and violence in Ashanti. It listed, with details supplied by the Police — still then of course under British Officers — 491 such incidents where prosecution had been impossible. In this dangerous situation, for anyone to try to establish himself as Zerikin Zongo was almost certainly liable to lead to rioting. On the last occasion, it had been attempted there was serious destruction of property and loss of life and the colonial authorities of the day had deported the previous claimant on that account. Bing gives it as his opinion that "it was not unreasonable therefore that the Ghana Government took the view that they ought to follow this precedent and deport the present one, together with his Chaplain."

It follows, therefore, that the *unjust Deportation Act of 1957* referred to by *The Daily Telegraph* was in fact a mere consolidation of two previous

British colonial laws on the subject and not a new enactment of the Ghana Government as The *Daily Telegraph* had urged its readers to believe. The two colonial laws were (1) the Aliens Ordinance and (2) the immigrant British Subjects (Deportation) Ordinance.

Another Commonwealth country's press which repeatedly sat in judgement over the activities of Nkrumah within Ghanaian territorial jurisdiction was Nigeria. When the bomb attempt was made on Nkrumah in August at Kulungugu, 1962, the *West African Pilot* of Nigeria left its readers in no doubt that it would have cheered had the assassination attempt succeeded. Referring to the arrest of Ako Adjei, Adamafio and others, the *West African Pilot* wrote as follows:

> ... bombing schemes are no longer hatched by a disgruntled opposition but, by those who built the glory of the CPP. Dr. Nkrumah can now hardly trust anybody in his party and to survive, he must constantly speak to the people over the head of the party. Rebels in the CPP will lie low for a while ... but they have to strike quickly and effectively soon ... It is dishonest not to acknowledge that events in Ghana are disturbing.
>
> Traces of Hitler are visible and the two official newspapers fit squarely into the shoes of Dr. Goebbels. They are calling for a public hanging of the "conspirators". Dr. Nkrumah's best hope ... is for him to slacken his pace ... Unless he sees wisdom in this course, he will realize too late that the circle has started and will reach an explosion point which will bury him in the rubble of his own folly ... [23]

The *Morning Post* of Nigeria, following the security measures taken immediately after the bomb attack on Nkrumah, in a leader titled "Fugitive from the ... Assassin's Bullet" deplored Nkrumah's actions as virtually turning Ghana into a "threepenny dictatorship".[24] The Daily Times ridiculed the bomb episode as being stage managed by Dr. Nkrumah to curb the activities and ambition of Tawia Adamafio who was considered by Nkrumah as being dangerously close to the presidency.[25] Later, the newspaper condemned Nkrumah's strong-arm measures against those suspected in the bomb attack, and warned that Nkrumah should realize he would "not achieve African socialism by liquidating his colleagues."[26] In 1964, the *Sunday Times* of Nigeria called for the expulsion of Ghana from the Commonwealth on the grounds that Nkrumah had become a dictator.

So scurrilous were the press criticisms of Ghana in Nigeria that, by mid-September, 1962, almost all Nigerian newspapers were banned in Ghana. Nonetheless, they continued to condemn the 'CPP dictatorship' at every available opportunity. Thus, when the special court set up to re-try Ako Adjei and Adamafio who had earlier been discharged on a charge of attempting to assassinate Nkrumah, now found them guilty and sentenced to death, the *West African Pilot* wrote one of the most scathing editorials ever written on

Dr. Nkrumah. This editorial is remarkable for the language used to describe a Head of State. Entitled "Judicial Murder", it described Nkrumah as a 'Frankenstein', 'Dracula' and 'Black Hitler'. It urged its readers as follows:

> ... Plainly the world must tell Nkrumah as we do today, that he impresses nobody with his Kangaroo court; that nobody is deceived when he decides to kill of his foes or former friends through the farce of his tame courts. Because the Redeemer is always talking of freedom and liberty when it concerns other parts of Africa he must be told the stark truth about himself — he is a one-man house of horror, a political bandit that has respect for nothing ... We say it today that this beast of Africa should be exposed for all his crimes ... Nkrumah can never get to heaven.[27]

Mr. Owusu-Ansah, Ghana's High Commissioner, protested against the language in the editorial of the *West African Pilot,* and questioned the right of the Nigeria press to set itself up as a judge, 'the only judge', over Ghana.[28]

The British press were relentless in their criticism of the internal developments in Ghana. The British were very unhappy about the series of measures taken by Nkrumah to establish a sort of one party administration. Thus, in May, 1960, some British MPs referred with disdain to what they called the quirks of the dictatorship in Ghana.[29] But the British press criticism of the trends towards what was alleged as dictatorship in Ghana was so severe as to provoke counter-attack by the Ghanaian press. By late 1961, one could talk of a sort of press war between Ghana and Britain. Although both Dr. Nkrumah and Mr. Sandys appealed in October 1961 to the news media in their respective countries for a truce[30] this was not heeded by either side.

The establishment by the Ghana Government of a Special Criminal Division of the High Court, from which there would be no appeal, in October 1961, was bitterly criticized by some sections of the British press,[31] especially the *London Times* which the Ghana Government accused of conducting a 'hostile campaign' against Ghana which it said 'can be compared to the similar campaign conducted by the *London Times* in 1938 against Czechoslovakia which had as its object the dismemberment of that country in the interest of Hitler'.[32]

Dr. Kwame Nkrumah's dismissal of Chief Justice, Sir Arku Korsah, on December 11, 1963 was condemned by almost all the British newspapers. The *London Times* criticized Dr. Nkrumah for being "so careless of his country's reputation".[33] Similarly, the turning of Ghana into one party democracy through the referendum of January, 1964 was widely criticized in the United Kingdom. The consequence of all this was a hostile reaction from the Ghanaian press and radio.

The Problem of the Republic of South Africa

Much of Ghana Government energy during the period under review (i.e. 1957–1966) was directed towards the eradication of colonialism, racism and neo-colonialism. For nearly two and a half years after her Independence, Ghana was virtually the spokesman for Africa on these matters. Nkrumah pursued this objective in a direct, aggressively militant and vigorous manner. There was no question of the Ghana Government mincing words about the evils of racism. At every available opportunity, Ghana's spokesman made violent verbal attacks on apartheid in Southern Africa. On the other hand, Nkrumah's anti-racist policy was informed by his belief in the co-existence of the races, majority rule, and sustenance of the human and legal rights of the minority.

In other words, Ghanaian policy was in general based on compromise and acceptance of the historical fact in South Africa. Whether or not, for instance, the European settlers were entitled to be in East Africa, Rhodesia and South Africa, they were there in fact and, in the Ghanaian view, the intolerable situation in South Africa had to be dealt with on its present merits irrespective of whether it arose out of some past wrong. Ghana, for example, never proposed that, in the course of African liberation, the European minorities should be expelled. On the contrary, the Ghana Government supported a reasonable safeguarding of their rights. It rejected divisions and supported multi-racial society. Ghana believed in majority rights and minority protection.

Put differently, Nkrumah and his Government supported the co-existence of the White and Black races in the Republic of South Africa. Abraham Lincoln was a liberal in a profound sense, and his views concerning the emancipation of slaves combined both the concept of the dignity of the individual and the worth of the collective community. In their struggle for Independence, the anti-colonial leadership in Africa was apparently influenced by the concept. They insisted on 'one man, one vote' as a basis of electing representatives to the colonial legislatures. The notion of 'one man, one vote' as advocated by Dr. Nkrumah was steeped in liberal assumptions of individualism, while his principle of undiluted democracy sought to realize the effective triumph of the numerically-preponderant and in the context of South Africa, the black Africans.

Unlike the picture painted of him by his critics, Dr. Nkrumah was not anti-white. He did not hate white people. On the contrary, he believed that there was some goodness in every racial group in this world. He assessed people on the basis of their merits. As he stated in 1960;

> We welcome men of goodwill everywhere to join us, irrespective of their race, religion or nationality. When I speak of Africa for Africans this should be interpreted in the light of my emphatic declaration, that I do not believe in racialism and colonialism. The

concept "Africa for Africans" does not mean that other races are excluded from it. No. It only means that Africans who are naturally in the majority in Africa, shall and must govern themselves in their own countries. The fight is for the future of humanity, and it is a most important fight.[34]

Thus, white, coloured and black liberal South Africans, including Leslie Rubin, a white South African lawyer and former Senator, found employment in Ghana during the administration of Dr. Nkrumah. In his view, these people were compelled to choose between either accepting a system which rejected the political and social ideas for which they stood or abandoning the country of their birth. He advocated the encouragement of these refugees. Those who had been so politically committed in South Africa, as to be incapable of living normal lives any longer there, tended to be drawn from the more able and more skilled of the professional classes and this was certainly so among potential white refugees. The skills which they had acquired in South Africa whether in the Foreign or Civil Service, mining or administration of industry generally, public health, teaching, journalism or law, were the skills most lacking in the newly-independent African states. Kwame Nkrumah remained unalterably opposed to apartheid until his death. He believed that, the solution to the problem of racial conflict in South Africa must depend upon the acceptance by all the races concerned of the principle of social, economic and above all, political equality.

In pursuance of his philosophy of racial co-existence, Dr. Nkrumah, for a brief period after Independence, attempted to maintain some contact with the South African Government to see whether he could thereby change their attitude about the ability of Africans to govern themselves and to co-exist harmoniously with white people. He invited the South African Government to participate in the First Conference of Independent African States of April 1958 at Accra, but the invitation was turned down by the Pretoria Government because, other colonial administering powers in Africa were not invited.

Early in 1960, there was a Ghanaian invitation to the South African Foreign Minister, then Sir Eric Louw, to visit Ghana, but this was turned down because, it was tied to the establishment of a diplomatic mission in Pretoria by Ghana which the South African Government, then led by Verwoerd, opposed because it would then become the headquarters for agitators in South Africa.[35] It became quite clear that, the South African Government was at that time most unwilling to accept diplomatic representation from any indigenous African state. In his 'sober analysis of the South African situation, looking at the position objectively and never allowing' his views to be influenced by sentiment or by racial prejudice of any sort, before the Ghana National Assembly on April 18, 1961, Dr Kwame Nkrumah said *inter alia* that in her foreign policy Ghana had experimented with 'two possible approaches to the South African Problem':

It has been argued that it might be possible to change the South African regime by persuasion and force of example. It was on that basis that it was argued that it was best to keep South Africa within the Commonwealth so that Commonwealth pressure might bring about a change.

I have always had the gravest doubts about the success of any such policy. However, we did attempt to apply it in the years which followed independence. We offered, for example, to exchange diplomatic representatives with South Africa and we continued negotiations with South Africa on the issue for over three years. It became quite clear, however, that the South African Government would never accept diplomatic representatives from any indigenous African states. We invited to Ghana individual South Africans so that they might see for themselves how Africans could run their own affairs and how racial harmony could prevail among white and black, but this policy was not reflected in the least change in South Africa's attitude to Africans or Asians in South Africa.[36]

Even at the Commonwealth Conference of 1961, where South African's withdrawal from the Commonwealth was discussed, Ghana took a soft line of approach as pointed out by Sir Alec Douglas-Home who observed that:

Gradually the place of South Africa in the Commonwealth, the members of which were pledged to the promotion of human rights, began to be questioned, and matters, came to a head at the Commonwealth Prime Ministers' Conference in London in 1961. On the whole, the mood of the Ministers attending was to give South Africa another chance. Even Dr. Nkrumah was on his best behaviour and did not want to see South Africa expelled.[37]

That Dr Nkrumah's policy was non-racial was proved by his general recruitment of men and women from all over the world to the re-organized modern administration of Ghana. S. Namasivayam from Ceylon, who was the author of two standard works on the Constitution of Ceylon (Sri Lanka) but who was unable to rise above the rank of Second Parliamentary Counsel. From Khartoum University, Patrick Atiyah (the son of Edward Atiyah the nationalist), who had a double first in Law from Oxford was the author of a Standard English work on the sale of goods, was recruited. He was just the type of expert which Ghana needed. Ulric Cross, originally a solicitor from Trinidad was pleased to practise his profession in Ghana. Cross had Distinguished Service records. He was a navigator in the RAF and Squadron Leader. He won the Distinguished Service Order (DSO). There was Professor L. C. B. Gower, a foremost expert on English Law — then Cassel Professor of Commercial Law at London University and who is now one of the law Commissioners, who came to Ghana to work on that type of progressive Corporation Legislation which he had been unable to do in England. At the same time as Professor Gower was engaged, Dr. Nkrumah also invited Professor John Lang (a practical commercial lawyer and a scholar) to be a

Professor of Law at the University and Head of the Ghanaian Law School. Professor John Lang had the support of London University, with which the University College of Ghana at that time was in special relationship. Indeed, his appointment had originally been suggested by Sir David Hughes Parry, a former Vice-Chancellor of London University well-known for his work on organizing Universities in Nigeria. Professor Lang's deputy was Leslie Rubin a South African lawyer and former Senator. There were several other foreign experts of various racial origins occupying prominent positions in the Government of Ghana including Geoffrey Bing, QC (a former Labour Member of the British Parliament for ten years) who was the Attorney General of Ghana. From October, 1961, until the coup d'etat of February 24, 1966, he was one of the officials attached to the President's office. Except in the case of Geoffrey Bing, QC, the foregoing analysis shows that, Dr. Nkrumah believed in a Ghanaian society where white and black races could harmoniously co-exist; a society advocated by his predecessor Dr. Aggrey 'of Africa'.

Returning to the problem of South Africa, the Ghana Government saw at an early stage the value of attracting to Ghana special skills of qualified South Africans. After the Sharpeville incident of 1960 an organized rescue of refugees of all colours was undertaken in Bechuanaland; the refugees were airlifted over the Federation of Rhodesia — where they would have been arrested if only in transit — to the Congo and from there to Ghana. Small as this operation was, its detailed planning, which involved illegal flights across South Africa, clandestine border crossings supervised by the wife of the Attorney General, Geoffrey Bing, etc., it deserved credit. It gave hope to those in South African jails and assured them that there was some country (Ghana) outside South Africa which, however meagre its resources, was prepared to help.

Ghana's efforts to persuade the Government of South Africa to end apartheid and the oppression of the black majority of South Africa were arrogantly ignored. The white minority regime, on the contrary, considered itself as being in a state of war against an avalanche of black domination in Africa. It thought, it was fair to oppose the freedom and development of black people in South Africa. South Africa's intransigence finally radicalized Ghana's anti-apartheid stance. Ghana, for example, played a dominant role in the anti-South African campaign at the 1961 Prime Minister's Conference which resulted in the withdrawal of South Africa from the Commonwealth. In the Prime Minister's Conference in 1960, the representative of South Africa had informed the Conference that, his Government intended to hold a referendum on the proposal that South Africa should become a republic. At that meeting, the Commonwealth Prime Ministers were asked to give their agreement in advance to the continued membership of a potential republican South Africa in the Commonwealth. But the Prime Ministers were unwilling at that time to agree. They were influenced by two considerations. First, such a decision might have been construed as an attempt to influence the referendum and, therefore, as an interference in a matter which was clearly one for the people of South Africa alone. Secondly, the precedents showed that although it was not necessary to withhold approval, it was not proper to give approval before the decision to make a constitutional change of this kind beyond all doubt. South Africa was accordingly invited to delay the application for renewed membership until after the referendum.

The referendum was held in October 1960. The result was in favour of a republic. Accordingly, the Prime Minister of South Africa put forward an application for South Africa to stay in the Commonwealth as a republic. But the Commonwealth Prime Ministers as a whole did not feel themselves able to treat the continued membership of South Africa as a purely formal or procedural question. In view of the strong feeling on the racial policies pursued by the Government of South Africa, the discussion could not be narrowed to the constitutional issue Dr. Verwoerd himself recognized this. It is an established convention that in their meetings the Commonwealth Prime Ministers do not discuss the domestic affairs of a member country without the consent of such a member country. The Prime Minister of South Africa agreed that on the occasion of the 1961 Conference the racial policy of the Union of South Africa deserved to be discussed for the general benefit; for the question had become more than a matter of domestic interest to South Africa. It had aroused widespread international interest and concern. It affected, in various ways, the relations between South Africa and other members of the Commonwealth. It even threatened to damage the concept of the Commonwealth itself as a multi-racial association.

There is no doubt that Presidents Nkrumah and Nyerere played a dominant role in the Commonwealth pressure on the Government of South Africa. While Dr. Nkrumah engaged apartheid on the conference platform, President Nyerere acted against the policy of apartheid in the British press. In an article published in the *Observer*,[38] President Nyerere vigorously denounced the South African policy of apartheid which makes a virtual mockery of inter-racial institution such as the Commonwealth. The article was entitled "Commonwealth Choice: South Africa or Us". President Nyerere said:

> ... we believe that South African membership under present conditions makes a mockery of the inter-racial composition of the Commonwealth ... the systematic attempt to degrade the non-European population of South Africa is not ... an internal affair and thus a concern of other Commonwealth members. Every country in Africa feels the effects of South African policies in its own life ... we believe that, the dignity of man is the idea that can defeat racialism; but we know that any action of ours which appears to compromise with the evil we fight must weaken the execution of our own policies. Thus, we cannot join any "association of friends" which includes a State

deliberately and ruthlessly pursuing a racialist policy... We believe that the principles of the Commonwealth would be betrayed by an affirmative answer to South Africa's application for readmission as a Republic.[39]

In his speech[40] before the Canadian Parliament on March 17, 1961, the Rt. Hon. J. C. Diefenbaker, Prime Minister of Canada echoed President Nkrumah and President Nyerere's sentiment as follows:

> All agreed that South Africa's constitutional change was not in itself an obstacle to continuing membership but the view was strongly held that the question of membership could not be divorced from the international implications of the union government's racial policies. Apartheid has become the world's symbol of discrimination; and in the eyes of the Prime Ministers present, ... to give unqualified consent to South Africa's application would be to condone the policies of apartheid.
>
> I took the position that if we were to accept South Africa's request unconditionally our action would be taken as approval or at least condonation of racial policies which are repugnant to and unequivocally abhorred and condemned by Canadians as a whole. Speaking for Canada.... I pointed out that we were opposed to racial discrimination, and made it clear that I could not approve any formula or solution which did not maintain beyond any doubt that non-discrimination in respect of race and colour is an essential principle of the Commonwealth association.[41]

Even the Prime Minister of Australia, the Rt. Hon. R. C. Menzies, who had given sentimental as well as historical reasons for advising caution on the problem of South Africa who was an original member of this 'multiracial association composed of representatives from all parts of the world' joined the other Commonwealth Prime Ministers in condemning apartheid as follows:

> I am against apartheid, against some of the modern manifestations and practices because they offend the conscience, against it as a basic policy because it seems to me to be doomed to a more terrible disaster.... The Union does not accredit or receive diplomatic missions to or from Commonwealth countries in Asia and Africa. This discrimination is, to me, offensive to the great countries concerned.... There is great value in such exchanges, and that to deny them is to suggest some notion of racial superiority, intolerable in form, and utterly unjustified in fact.[42]

He rejected the allegation of his critics that he equated apartheid and Australia's immigration policy. He explained that one policy, apartheid, related to a discriminatory policy in respect of people already permanently resident; the other, the Australian immigration policy, discriminated in the admission of persons for permanent residence. He believed that, the Australian immigration policy was both wise and just because it was based not upon any foolish notion of racial superiority, but upon a proper desire to preserve a homogeneous population and 'so avert the troubles that have bedevilled some other countries.

The transformation of the former British Empire into the present Commonwealth of Nations means that its special racial problem was carried over into the present Commonwealth, because the essence of the Commonwealth is that Great Britain did not terminate her relations with her former colonies but translated them into a continuing relationship between Asian, African and European nations. Consequently, for some time to come, a special tension in relationships between the various racial groups in these several communities of white and other coloured people would be an integral part of Commonwealth relations. That is why South Africa presented a special, unique problem for the Commonwealth, which shook the very roots of the nature of the Commonwealth.

Anti-racism was a supremely important component of the OAU's anti-colonial programme. At the OAU in Addis Ababa, the member states demanded the breaking off of diplomatic and consular relations between all the African states on the one hand and the Governments of Portugal and South Africa on the other. The call was to pave way for an effective boycott of foreign trade with the two countries because of their colonial and racialist policies. Dr. Nkrumah exhorted them as follows:

> It is for all the Independent African States to see that their total economic and political boycott is made complete without delay . . . if the great powers, or even a large enough body of the smaller ones, were to support us by joining the boycott, the moral effect would have tremendous repercussions throughout the African Continent, besides serving notice on the Verwoerd and Salazar regimes that they can no longer continue a policy of racial segregation, oppression and genocide.[43]

The Obstacle of South African Economic and Military Power

Be this as it may, the stark reality must be faced. The economic power of South Africa obviously posed problems for the Pan-African movement. South Africa was already heavily involved in the Cabora Bassa and Ruacana hydro electric schemes. The development of the huge integrated electric power grid which she was helping to set up would likely be the single most significant contribution to economic development of Southern and Central Africa.

There was a strong financial and ideological connection between South Africa and the Rhodesia which extended through Portuguese Angola to Mozambique. Besides, South Africa's powerful military machine presented a most threatening danger to the independence and African unity in Central, East and South Africa. It was unfortunate that the United Kingdom, even though South Africa had withdrawn from the Commonwealth following the heavy censure of her apartheid policy by the majority of the members, continued to give support to the Union's policy of military build-up. The accession to office of a Conservative Government in 1970 totally changed British policy of no-arms-sale to South Africa. Conservative oral pledges before the election to resume arms sales to South Africa (not, incidentally, set down in the Party's manifesto) were a potential Commonwealth problem. Within three weeks of the conservative victory, on July 7, 1970, the Foreign and Commonwealth Secretary, Sir Alec Douglas-Home, announced the Government's intention to sell arms to South Africa, a decision which could adversely affect the then impending Prime Minister's Conference. Now came something deeply disappointing so far as the development of the Commonwealth was concerned. The African leaders arrived in Singapore amid rumours that they would walk out of the Conference. From the outset, they gave assurances that they would not do so, and all were true to their words. They had come for serious discussions and they had brought with them as had everyone else, a desire to preserve the Commonwealth. It was this unanimous view that the Commonwealth was worthwhile and must be kept that saved the Singapore meeting from disaster.

The inevitable conclusion is that, South Africa's economic and military force had been a restrictive factor which held back to some extent the independent black African states. The black majority submit willingly to forcible control by the white minority although they resent coercion, and tend to resist it when they have the means, in every circumstance.

International Pressure through International Action

It is true that the best form of foreign pressure on a government is by a direct intervention to force the state concerned to be more tolerant or prevent it from being too brutal against a particular community. There is a general agreement that, by virtue of its territorial supremacy a state can treat its own nationals according to discretion. But there is a substantial body of opinion and of practice in support of the view that there are limits to that discretion and that when a state is guilty of cruelties against and persecution of its nationals in such a way as to deny them their fundamental human rights, intervention in the interest of humanity is legally permissible. Thus, Great Britain, France and Russia intervened in 1827, in the struggle between revolutionary Greece and Turkey when public opinion reacted with horror to the cruelties committed during the struggle. Intervention was often resorted to in order to put a stop to the persecution of Christians in Turkey. Undoubtedly, the practice of intervention had not been as frequent as occasion seems to have demanded.

The disinclination to take responsibility for an international conflagration likely to follow intervention or the consideration of the persecuted likely to suffer rather than benefit therefrom have been, to some extent, responsible for the relative infrequency of humanitarian intervention.[44] A most recent example of a direct intervention can be found in the Belgian intervention in the Congo soon after the independence of that state in 1960, when Belgian troops entered the country ostensibly to protect the lives and well-being of Belgian nationals. Then, there was the Stanleyville operation of November 1964 when American planes were used to enable Belgian paratroopers to descend on Stanleyville in order to rescue a group of European hostages. There are also direct cases of direct intervention to prevent what a state would regard as a danger to its own citizens in a foreign country, e.g. Israeli rescue of passengers of Jewish origin on a hijacked aeroplane in Uganda during the regime of Idi Amin.

Another type of international pressure is that of an economic blockade or some kind of strong economic sanctions on the defendant state. Some such sanctions were tried against Italy after the latter's invasion of Ethiopia, and more recently against Ian Smith's Government after Rhodesia's Unilateral Declaration of Independence (UDI) of Great Britain. In neither case was this international action simply an attempt to eliminate a racial situation; yet in both cases there were important racial principles compromised or endangered.

Internal Confrontation of Apartheid in South Africa

As we have shown, the revolutionary core of the Pan-African movement required a more militant position against apartheid in South Africa. They regarded the Organization of African Unity (OAU) as a purveyor of new and more co-ordinated revolutionary techniques for the liberation of colonial territories, indeed as an instrument for the liberation of African territories including those dominated by white settlers like South Africa and Rhodesia. It was at the initiative of the revolutionary core and to the great applause and relief of the independent states around South Africa that the Founding Conference of the Organization of African Unity created the African Liberation Committee. The same Conference also established a permanent organ to co-ordinate aid to liberation movements. The resolution which established the Liberation Committee, composed of nine nations with Headquarters in Dar es Salaam, tasked it with the responsibility of harmonizing the assistance from African states and for managing the Special Fund to be set up for that purpose. The resolution further established two guidelines for the action of independent states and one guideline for the strategy of liberation. Independent member states were enjoined 'to receive on (their) territories . . . nationalists from liberation movements in order to give them training in all sectors' and 'to promote in each state the transit of all material aid and the establishment of a body of volunteers in various fields with a view to providing the various African national liberation movements with the assistance they need in the various sectors'.

The mood of the first session of the Liberation Committee which was held in Dar es Salaam from June 25 to July 4, 1963, was moderately optimistic.

In British Africa, Kenya and Zanzibar had fixed dates for independence. Nyasaland (Malawi) had been permitted to withdraw from the Central African Federation and was certain to go forward to independence. That summer, Northern Rhodesia (Zambia) was placed in the same position by the decision to dissolve, on January 1, 1964, the Central African Federation.

In the opinion of Dr. Kwame Nkrumah, there were no precedents yet of white minorities in power in Africa giving it up without a major domestic upheaval. The precedents he knew of were more often than not convulsive, e.g. the liberation upheavals in Algeria and Kenya. Equally, Rhodesia and South Africa had to experience something similar before the white minority control could be broken. Nkrumah drew attention to some internal developments in South Africa which could eventually lead to the fall of the apartheid regime.

In the first place, he said, it must be noted that the South African regime exhibited similar contradictions which had preceded revolutions elsewhere but whose significance were often not appreciated until the revolution in question actually took place. There had occurred already in South Africa what was the prelude both to the French and to the Russian revolutions and, indeed, to the revolutions in many other countries. There was a significant repudiation of the regime by an influential section of the intelligentsia of the ruling class. The Dutch Reformed Church was the ideological pillar upon which apartheid rested, yet apartheid was denounced by Professor Keel, until recently the Head of the Theological Seminary of that Church at Stellenbeach University where Dr. Verwoerd himself was once a professor. The leaders of the Anglican, the Roman Catholic and the other churches in South Africa repudiated apartheid and indeed the whole system of racial segregation and racial domination. By itself, of course, this intellectual opposition was not significant. It was, however, one of the classic symptoms of an impending storm.

There came a division of the ruling class itself. The controversy which then divided the ruling class of South Africa was, in fact, of no importance in itself. The two main political parties in the country, the Nationalists and the United Party, were both dedicated to the maintenance of racial inequality. Where they differed, was how this inequality should be maintained. The two reactionary parties mistrusted each other on the question of how best racial superiority could be sustained. The then Government could not, therefore, claim undivided loyalty of the ruling class. Further showing division in the ranks of the existing ruling class, was the emergence of the Progressive Party, an organization of persons of good will allied to the shrewdest financiers of the country. The Progressives realized that, there was something radically wrong with South Africa and that if the social structure of the Union was to survive, radical changes must be made. Ultimately, however, they begged the only radical change which could solve the South African problem, namely, the establishment of the principle of one man one vote, irrespective of colour or racial origin. Like all reforming parties which spring up on the eve of a revolution, they saw an abyss opening up before them, but they were so conditioned by their membership of the ruling class to the existing situation that they were unable to formulate any acceptable alternative. The large vote cast in favour of Progressive candidates during by-elections and provincial elections showed that their fears were shared by a certain proportion of the ruling class but that the latter was nothing like sufficient to reform the existing regime.

Dr. Kwame Nkrumah was pragmatic enough to realize that, any action which was taken with regard to South Africa must be agreed upon beforehand by the largest number of states as possible. Consequently, he appealed to other countries interested in securing a solution to the South African problem to consider whether it would be helpful to hold a conference solely on South Africa. He admitted that, if such a conference were held, it would open the way to a 'positive action to deal with the South African situation.[45] Indeed, a combination of both internal revolution and external international pressures were necessary to liberate the suppressed black majority in South Africa. The earlier illusions about the image of South Africa as a stable country, largely invulnerable to external forces, appeared to have been finally dispelled in the latter half of the twentieth century — 'things ain't what they used to be'. In terms of political and economic power — as well as of military strength — South Africa might still be a force to be reckoned with; but in terms of its effective power over the black majority at home and in confrontation with black challenges abroad, its actual power was rapidly declining.

Southern Rhodesia

Rhodesia was a standard issue at African meetings for many years and the subject of resolutions of international organizations outside the Commonwealth. Such meetings included the extraordinary OAU session at Lagos in early 1964, at which the OAU Council of Ministers "again called upon the Government of the United Kingdom to meet its responsibilities and invited it ... to convene a new constitutional conference for the purpose of preparing a Constitution founded on universal suffrage of all inhabitants of the territory".[46] It is the 'again' that is most significant. At the meeting of Commonwealth Prime Ministers held in London from June 17 to June 25, 1965, the major issue of contention, apart from the abortive proposal of a peace mission to Vietnam, was Rhodesia. After much effort, the African leaders obtained the following promise from Britain:

> If the discussion (with the Government of Rhodesia) did not develop satisfactorily ... in a reasonably speedy time, the British Government, having regard to the principle

enunciated by the Commonwealth Secretary of unimpeded progress towards majority rule, would be ready to consider promoting such a constitutional conference in order to ensure Rhodesia's progress to independence on a basis acceptable to the people of Rhodesia as a whole.[47]

At that point, the issue was not pressed any further by the African members, except Tanzania, which dissociated herself from this section of the Commonwealth communique because she was unable to get 'assurances that the negotiations taking place between the British and Rhodesian governments are aimed at achieving independence on the basis of majority rule'. On the Rhodesia issue, Tanzania took over from Ghana as the leader of those pressurizing the British. Till the Unilateral Declaration of Independence[48] by the then Government of Rhodesia on November 11, 1965, along with attempts to enforce unity upon ZAPU and ZANU, the two major African nationalist movements in Rhodesia.

Great Britain's Rights and Duties

In international law and contrary to Ian Smith's Unilateral Declaration of Independence (UDI), Southern Rhodesia remained a colony of Great Britain and not an independent state. But, until genuine independence was achieved, the United Kingdom's responsibility for that colony, *vis-à-vis* other states and international organizations was retained. This legal position could not be obliterated by oft-repeated references on the part of Britain, to conventional privileges enjoyed by South Rhodesia over a period of years. In October, 1962, the General Assembly of the United Nations requested, by a majority of 81 to 2 (with 19 abstentions) that the United Kingdom secure for the people under its authority in Southern Rhodesia, the right to vote. This body made a similar request on October 14 and November 6, 1963. In May, 1963, the African Heads of State and Government, further requested in Addis Ababa that, Britain should not transfer to a foreign racial minority in the colony the 'attributes of sovereignty'.

However, critics maintain that far from making every effort to abort the growth of minority, racialist and unrepresentative Government in Rhodesia, the British government on the contrary made substantial concessions of such a nature as to make Rhodesia's power and policies all the more formidable and uncompromising. Due to lack of response to United Nations' demand that a fully-representative government be established in Rhodesia on a 'one man one vote' basis, critics never accepted the so-called 'internal settlement' supposedly based on adult suffrage. They rejected the British Government's argument that they were prevented by a parliamentary convention from exercising to the full, their legal authority over Southern Rhodesia. The convention, it was argued, derived from the fact that for 40 years successive

British Governments did not use their powers to safeguard the interests of the African inhabitants, and, in effect, these powers became obsolete. For the first 30 years of its colonial history, Southern Rhodesia was ruled by the British South Africa Company, a private trading concern. This company was nevertheless subject to the over-riding control of the British Government, which had granted the concern a Royal Charter setting out the broad lines of governmental policy. The Company was ostensibly established to prospect for gold etc., and as there proved little of it, proceeded to sell to European settlers, at profit, farmland which had been wrested from Africans. It was to satisfy these settlers that the Company set up a Legislative Council over which they, the settlers ultimately acquired control. Finally, during the First World War, the Company surrendered its 'rights' of administering the Protectorate in exchange for compensation paid by Britain and the settler government.

The small group of Europeans then living in Rhodesia were offered the choice either of affiliating the Colony with South Africa or of becoming self-governing. They opted for the latter by a vote of 8,774 to 5,989 in a referendum, which was held in 1923, without the participation of the numerically-vast African majority. Nevertheless, British representatives at the United Nations have argued that this referendum constituted the prime democratic event of Southern Rhodesian history, and legitimized future British non-interference and withdrawal. Despite the granting of self-government to the settlers, the British Government contemporaneously exercised by law the same control over their activities as it had over the activities of the Company. The motion that Southern Rhodesia had enjoyed control of its own internal affairs for forty years is thus false. The United Kingdom appointed the Governor whose official instructions by the British Government gave him express and lawful authority to refuse to accept the advice of his colonial ministers.

A convention, legally, is one only if it is recognized as such. If its recognition is essentially unilateral in a given case, that recognition maybe unilaterally withdrawn without prejudice to the law. The history of the recognition of the Southern Rhodesia convention went back to 1957. It is contained in a joint announcement by the United Kingdom Government and the Federation of Rhodesia and Nyasaland and does not actually refer to Southern Rhodesia as a separate political entity. The announcement reads:

> The United Kingdom recognizes the existence of a convention... whereby the United Kingdom in practice does not initiate any legislation to amend or to repeal any Federal Act or to deal with any matter included within the competence of the Federal Legislature except at the request of the Federal Government.

Subsequently, the Southern Rhodesian Government demanded from the United Kingdom similar recognition in its own regard; and this constituted a plea that the United Kingdom should undertake, unilaterally in respect of Southern Rhodesia, to follow a policy of domestic non-interference. The British Government at no time introduced legislation to this effect. But in June, 1961, a British White Paper, relating to constitutional proposals for Southern Rhodesia, declared that such a convention as spoken of above did exist.

It is impossible, however, to argue that in practice Rhodesia was independent. The Monkton Commission (including the Chief Justice of Southern Rhodesia and the Attorney General of the ten Central African Federation) which was appointed by the British Government in July, 1959, (Report published in October, 1960 — Cmnd.1148) was in unanimous agreement that the Federation, and consequently Southern Rhodesia, 'falls short of the status of a full international person'; that is 'is not an independent sovereign state', and that 'it is the United Kingdom who remain ultimately responsible in international law.' The Commissioners found, further, that 'the United Kingdom Parliament has inherent power to legislate for any part of Her Majesty's dominions except insofar as this has been qualified by the Statute of Westminster" and with regard to Southern Rhodesia, there was and there is no such qualification. As affecting the joint announcement of 1957, the Commissioners categorically stated that it referred 'only to powers conferred upon the Federal Legislature' without affecting 'the legislative authority of the United Kingdom Parliament to provide for the future constitutional development of the Federation, and, for this purpose, to make any necessary amendments to the Constitution itself.' The Monkton Commission, set up by the British Government to review the constitutional position in the Federation, clearly took the view that, British sovereignty remained even so far as to entail the right to amend the Southern Rhodesian Constitution, and, indeed, that it was and 'is essential that this right should be retained'.

The inevitable conclusion is that Britain's legal authority over Southern Rhodesia — in spite of UDI — remained intact. That authority imposed the need to accept certain responsibilities — as Britain accepted at the Commonwealth Prime Ministers' Conference 1979. Article 14(e) of the communique dated August, 1979, agreed that, the problem of Southern Rhodesia 'is the constitutional responsibility of the British Government.' One of the most basic of Britain's responsibilities is to establish secure conditions for representative government in Rhodesia and 'to grant legal independence to that country under the title of Zimbabwe on the basis of majority rule. And the government could not be truly representative if political expression and power were denied to the African majority on grounds of race. The European minority settlers had an undoubted stake in the future of the country. Article 14(f) provides that 'independence on the basis of majority rule requires the adoption of a democratic constitution including appropriate safeguards for minorities.'

Summary and Conclusion on Southern Africa

The case of Southern Africa has sometimes posed the question of whether any of the concerted international measures noted above could succeed in forcing modifications in the explicit apartheid policies of South Africa and similar ones in Rhodesia. It is true that, although, direct military intervention could correct the injustice of apartheid and uphold the international legal principle of racial equality, such a direct military intervention was scrupulously avoided by other states in general and black African states in particular. Some states felt that South Africa was too rich and too self-sufficient to be susceptible to external pressure whether from international organizations or from individual states. Through the help of the western industrialized nations South Africa had built up an arsenal of the latest weapons of destruction. The military strength of the independent African states south of the Sahara was not sufficient to defeat the military forces that had been built by the Republic of South Africa and Southern Rhodesia.

In a speech before the Malawi Parliament on the question of Southern Rhodesia, President Banda of Malawi said, 'if Mr. Ian Smith was pushed, the Rhodesian Air Force could reduce to ashes all the East and Central African capitals within 24 hours'. Dr. Banda was seeking MPs approval of his policy on Rhodesia. Stressing the point further, Dr. Banda said at the last OAU meeting in Accra in 1965 that 'within a week, ... the Rhodesian army could conquer the whole of East and Central Africa and the armies and air forces of Ghana and Nigeria could do nothing to prevent it.' Dr. Banda said that he had warned the Heads of African States not to push Mr. Smith into precipitate action which he did not want to take.

> The Organization for African Unity, with its talk of intervention could force Mr. Smith to declare unilateral independence "just to show who is boss". Talk of forcing Britain to send an army to Rhodesia to suspend the constitution and put the Africans in power by force was "childish prattle and unstatesmanlike" ... No matter how honest and democratic Mr. Wilson was, he could not countenance armed intervention. Sanctions would fail because if Britain refused to take Rhodesia's tobacco then some other country would. Sanctions unless applied by the major powers, were useless. South Africa had had ten years of sanctions and was now stronger economically than ever before.[49]

Dr. Banda went on to state that, the views he had expressed at the OAU meeting at Accra would make him unpopular but he refused point blank to be stampeded over on the Rhodesia issue. He maintained that the only way for Rhodesia to get majority rule was for the Rhodesian Africans to unite and fight for it constitutionally. They should not expect outsiders to put them into power by force of arms. He claimed to appreciate the Rhodesian problem better than other African Commonwealth leaders, and for that matter, other

African leaders of the Organization of African Unity because he had lived and worked in Rhodesia.

If what Dr. Banda said was true, then South Africa's vast military build up and activities would be considered by the newly independent African states as a serious threat to their independence and security. None of these black independent African states was capable of mounting an invasion of South Africa. The only states that could conceivably have any impact on South Africa — the western powers, especially the United Kingdom and the United States of America — felt somewhat vulnerable, economically, to the danger of South Africa's retaliatory measures. Consequently, they were reluctant to take any sort of direct military or economic action.

Ghana's Foreign Policy and the Institution of the British Monarchy

Ghana in 1961, adopted a republican form of government. The Governor-General (who represented the Queen as the Queen of Ghana) was replaced by an elected President. There was a wide variety of alternative constitutional systems which might have been applied in Ghana. But similar to countries such as the United Kingdom, New Zealand, South Africa, Ceylon and Indonesia, Ghana, in spite of strong internal regional differences, preferred unitary form of government in which ultimately complete authority was conferred on the central government. Unitary government may take several forms: centralized unitary government as in Ceylon, decentralized unitary government, in which some authority is devolved upon subordinate governments, as in South Africa, or unitary government with special minority safeguards, 'entrenched clauses', or a 'bill of rights' as in Ireland and some of the Scandinavian countries. Ghana adopted the centralized unitary government as in Ceylon.

Advantages claimed for a unitary concentration of authority in any of these forms, as opposed to a federal division of authority, are that, it provides a strong central focus for political integration and that it is more flexible and adaptable, particularly for economic planning. On the other hand, critics have argued that the concentration of power makes its conversion to autocracy easier, and that, therefore, it is unlikely to protect minority interests.

Why was the Britain's model of administration so consistently followed by the Government of Dr. Nkrumah? The simplest explanation is that Dr. Nkrumah and most Ghanaian politicians, educated in British political history, living in the milieu of British institutions, and with the precedent of progress to self-government and independence through the evolution of parliamentary government in the older Commonwealth countries before them, had simply been accustomed to expecting the British type of constitution with which they were familiar. To Dr. Nkrumah and his Convention People's Party, there was the further incentive that such a political form was more likely to inspire British confidence and, therefore, willingness to hand over power. Cabinet government was also justified because of its flexibility, enabling adaptation to varying circumstances, especially with regard to the representation of different elements in plural societies such as exist in Ghana.

The Monarchy

As a matter of pure political or juristic theory, the state remains the same whatever may be its form of government or constitutional jurisprudence. That jurisprudence with regard to monarchy may start with the premise that the original and continuing fountain of all legal authority is the Crown. Deductions from this premise are: that by the will of the ruling monarch all other organs of government have been created and continue to exist; that from that will such legal powers as they possess have been derived; and that by that will they may, at any time, be curtailed or wholly withdrawn; and that if a written constitution exists, its legal force is dependent upon that will. These are the constitutional doctrines upon which a system of pure monarch is founded.

Secondly, the constitutional jurisprudence of a state may take as its logical basis or starting point, the principle that certain organs of government other than the Crown, such as elected legislative chambers or an electorate having referendal legislative powers, shall divide with the Crown, upon a basis of full legal or constitutional equality, the various or certain powers of government, that is, in such a way that these several organs may act independently of each other as to the specific powers constitutionally vested in them, or that they may be legally obliged to co-operate with one another. In such a constitutional system it is obvious that all its provisions derive their legal force from some single source. If these provisions are to be found in a written constitution or fundamental instrument of government, the original and continuing fountain of all legality, corresponding to the legal autocracy of the absolute monarch, is the particular organ or complexus of organs of government, or electorate or determinate group of individuals acting *ad hoc* as an organ of government, which is recognized to have the legal right to change the terms of the written constitution, which constitution, therefore, however it may have been originally adopted, is to be regarded as continuing to have force of law only because the constitutional order or complexus of organs so wills it. This is the constitutional situation which now exists in practically all of the states of the world.

A third constitutional or government possibility is that exhibited by the United Kingdom which has a Queen, and does not possess a formal written constitution or instrument of government. It has built for itself a complicated and yet definite system of government and a body of constitutional principles which vests constitutional power in the Crown, and a Parliament, the members of one House which sit, for the most part, by hereditary right, and the members of the other House by selection by an electorate which has been broadened from time to time until now; it includes nearly all adult citizens. This institution of Monarchy as it exists in the tradition of Britain is not alien to the Ghanaian tradition of Chieftaincy.

Her Majesty is the great symbol of unity of the Commonwealth. This fact is given expression through her visits to overseas parts of the Commonwealth. When she visited Ghana in 1961, Her Majesty was underscoring her status as Head of the Commonwealth. In Ghana, the personal representative of the Queen in 1957 was the Governor-General. In the Commonwealth, the Governor-General holds the same constitutional relationship to the Prime Minister in the United Kingdom. Partly because of the working understanding between Dr. Nkrumah and Sir Charles Arden-Clarke, and later Lord Listowel, the then Governor-General, and partly because of the absence of any major issue which could drive a wedge between Accra and London, Ghana's attitude to Britain during the first period of Independence was very friendly. In addition to his respect for the Royal Family and Her Majesty the Queen, Dr. Nkrumah rarely took any position on major international issues between the period of independence and late 1960 without first consulting the British Government and the British officials in Ghana. In fact, the CPP Government was severely criticized by some of its own back benchers for relying too much on British officials in Accra for advice on foreign policy matters.[50] For example, Dr. Nkrumah forwarded a copy of the text of the Ghana-Guinea Union agreement of November 23, 1958 to Mr. Harold Macmillan, then the British Prime Minister, before its publication, with a note that the agreement would not affect Ghana's friendship with Britian.[51] The British Government in turn replied warmly to Ghana's friendly attitude.

The United Kingdom sent a parliamentary delegation headed by Mr. R. H. Turton to present to the Ghana National Assembly Speaker's chair which Dr. Nkrumah described as 'a symbol of the special relationship between the British people and the people of Ghana — the Commonwealth.[52] On his return to Accra from the Prime Ministers' Conference held in London in May 1960, Dr Nkrumah described the Commonwealth as 'a unique association of free, independent sovereign states, irrespective of their racial origins working for world peace.[53]

The foregoing facts are not to deny, however, that there were discordant note on which Nkrumah disagreed with Britain's colonial policy. In such circumstance, his critics condemned his attitude towards Britain as ambivalent in practice, whatever his innermost thoughts were. In spite of his affection for the Royal Family, he regarded partition of colonies, on a 'divide and rule' basis, as a normal British practice which he disapproved. Nkrumah regarded neo-colonialism as essentially an exploitative force.

British Commonwealth of Nations

Dr Kwame Nkrumah valued his Privy Counsellorship and the position of the Queen as Head of the Commonwealth. Equally, he maintained a formally-correct approach at all times to questions of Commonwealth connection, and defended Ghana's Commonwealth membership on the grounds that it did her (Ghana) no harm and it did not inhibit her freedom of action. He wrote as follows:

> States emerging from the tutelage of other colonial powers have not always understood Ghana's attachment to the Commonwealth. . . . That is because the loose, *ad hoc* nature of the structure is not correctly comprehended by those who have been or are members of a more formal association. It is difficult for those not accustomed to a free connection with Europe to appreciate that the Commonwealth is an association of sovereign states, each of which is free from interference from the others, including the United Kingdom (italics mine). Each decides for itself its own foreign and domestic policies and the pattern of its government. Members have the right to criticize each other, and they do. . . . There is no compulsion to remain within the Commonwealth, or even to become a member. . . . It (Commonwealth) grew out of the association of the white dominions within the British Empire and had adapted itself, with customary British flexibility, to the continuing evolvement of political independence among the non-European members.[54]

Ghana's British connection paved the way for continued use of British specialists, (including British Officers in the Military and Police Forces). The Ghana Government made the optimum use of the expertise it obtained from Great Britain in fields such as education and technical assistance.[55] Ambivalence in his actions and utterances with regard to Britain clearly indicated that he had more respect and affection for the British connection than he was prepared to admit.[56] However, in Ghana, and on the African stage at large, he was the most resolute of Pan-Africanists, the foremost opponent of European intervention in the Congo, and the target for attacks from other African leaders on the grounds of subversion which he allegedly introduced into their territories. He had a sharp disagreement with Great Britain over the Congo crisis in 1960 and the colonial and racial issues in Southern Rhodesia and South Africa.

Criticism of British neo-colonialist manoeuvres in Africa were incessant and widespread in the Ghanaian press and radio. The situation was so bad that in October, 1961, Mr Duncan Sandy's then the Commonwealth Secretary, had to say in the House of Commons that it appeared as if Ghana was becoming increasingly hostile to the United Kingdom and that she was supporting Soviet attacks against Britain.[57]

The Commonwealth Secretariat

That the Ghanaian leader's hostility to the British colonial policy, especially in Southern Africa, did not affect his attachment to the British Commonwealth of Nations is further proved by the fact that it was Dr. Nkrumah who put forward the suggestion of a Commonwealth Secretariat for the co-ordination of activities among the Commonwealth Prime Ministers in 1964. Derek Ingram observed that the formation of the Commonwealth Secretariat in 1965 as a result of an initiative by Ghana's President Dr. Kwame Nkrumah (the fruits of which he never saw in action since he was ousted from power in February, 1966) provided the necessary impetus and minimum infrastructure to mould the Commonwealth into its modern form.[58] I agree with him that without a Secretariat that took the administrative running of the Commonwealth affairs out of the British Government's hands, the Commonwealth would certainly have floundered. Dr. Nkrumah proposed the Secretariat at the Prime Ministers' Meeting of 1964. Support came from Eric Williams of Trinidad and Tobago, Milton Obote of Uganda and Jome Kenyatta of Kenya and the details were worked out by officials in January, 1965. The Commonwealth Conference of June that year set up the Secretariat and chose the Canadian Diplomat, Arnold Smith, as its first Secretary-General. Sir Alec Douglas-Home, then British Prime Minister, presided over the 1965 meeting and, whatever some British Administrative officials might have thought of the idea, he supported it. Canada was now wholeheartedly in favour, but Australia, represented by Sir Robert Menzies, had cooled. Publicly, Sir Robert welcomed the development, and was happy about the way in which the modern Commonwealth was developing. The appointment of a Canadian as Secretary-General was not very much welcome in Australia.

Much discussion at the 1965 Conference centred on the powers which the Secretariat were to be given. The older members of the Commonwealth were particularly anxious that it should not be able in any way to act independently. British officials really wanted it to remain purely a sorting house for information and communication between member countries — the 'clearing house for the Empire' concept of 1907. The agreed Memorandum of the Secretariat was restrictive and vague and reflected nervousness about the new body. It pointed out that 'The Commonwealth . . . does not encroach on the sovereignty of individual members' and, therefore, 'there would be disadvantages in establishing too formal procedures and institutions . . . its staff and functions should be left to expand pragmatically in the light of experience. . . .' It added that 'provided that it begins modestly and remains careful not to trespass on the independence and sovereignty of the member governments whose servant it will be, it will be possible for it to grow in the spirit of the Commonwealth association itself.' It was understood that 'the Secretariat should not arrogate to itself executive functions.' Thus, the independence of the members of the Commonwealth, and flexibility of the organization endeared Ghana to make Commonwealth amity one of the pillars of her foreign policy.

NOTES AND REFERENCES

1. CMD 1279 and 1433 of 1961.
2. *Ghana Press Release* No.397 of 1961, p.7.
3. Ghana Press Release No. 397 of 1961, p.8.
4. Kwame Nkrumah's Declaration at Polo Ground, Accra, 6, March 1957.
5. Nkrumah, Kwame, 1967. *Challenge of the Congo.* London: p.19.
6. Nkrumah Kwame, 1967. *Challenge of the Congo.* London: 21–22.
7. Text of a letter to the Secretary General, Dag Hammarskjold, September 12,.1960, reproduced in Nkrumah, Kwame 1967. *The Challenge of the Congo,* p.42.
8. Nkrumah, Kwame, 1967, *op. cit.:* 89
9. Nkrumah, Kwame, 1970. *Africa Must Unite,* (Panaf Edition). London: 145.
10. Nkrumah, Kwame, 1967, *op. cit.:* 119–133.
11. Du Bois, W. E. B. 1921. *African World Supplement* (London), p.16; A second journey to Pan Africa. *New Republic,* p.40.
12. Mazrui, Ali A. 1963. Consent, colonialism and sovereignty. *Political Studies,* xi, pp. 50–51.
13. Abrahams, Peter 1954. Last Word on Nkrumah. *West African Review* xxv, p.913.
14. Nkrumah, Kwame 1973. *Revolutionary Path.* London: 131.
15. Nkrumah, Kwame 1973. Tenth anniversary speech of the CPP. **In** Samuel Obeng 1972. *Selected Speeches of Dr. Nkrumah.* Accra, Ghana: 7.
16. Scott W.,Thompson 1969. *Ghana's Foreign Policy 1957–66.* Princeton: 65.
17. *Ibid.*
18. *African Diary,* September, 28–October, 4 1963, pp. 1364–1365.
19. *Ibid.*
20. Nkrumah, Kwame 1973, *op. cit.:* 226.
21. *West Africa,* March 19, 1966.
22. See Bing, G., 1968. *Reap the Whirlwind.* London: 217.
23. Editorial,'Shaping Up' *West African Pilot,* September 1, 1962.
24. *Morning Post,* Lagos, September 10, 1962.
25. *Daily Times,* Lagos, September 3, 1962.
26. *Daily Times,* Lagos, September 10, 1962.
27. Editorial, 'Judicial Murder' *West African Pilot,* February 10, 1965.
28. *Daily Times,* February 16, 1965.
29. *H. C. Deb.* Vol. 623, May 17, 1960, Col. 1133.
30. Joint Communique issued at the end of Mr. Sandys' visit to Accra in October 1961. *H. C. Deb.* Vol. 646, October 19, 1961, Col. 1–12, and Ghana Today, October 25, 1961.
31. Mr Sandys' expressed misgivings about this Ghanaian action, which was taken shortly after his return from Accra. See *H. C. Deb.* Vol. 646, October 19, 1961, Col. 477.
32. Statement by the Government on the Recent Conspiracy, December 11, 1961, Vol. **11**. No.7/61.
33. *The Times,* London, December 12, 1963.
34. Nkrumah, Kwame, 1960. Opening Speech to the Conference of Positive Action and Security (Accra) April 7, 1960, p.9.
35. Menzies, Sir Robert, 1967. *Afternoon Light: Some Memories of Men and Events.* London: 206–7.
36. *Ghana Press Release,* No. 397/61 of April 18, 1961, p.15.
37. Douglas-Home, Lord, 1978. *The Way the Wind Blows, an Autobiograph.* London: 133.

38. *Observer*, March 7, 1961. London.
39. Nyerere, Julius K., 1967. *Freedom and Unity*. London: 108–13.
40. *Canada House of Commons Debates, Session* 1960–61, Vol.3, pp. 3080–3083.
41. Mansergh, Nicholas, 1963. *Documents and Speeches on Commonwealth Affairs 1952–62*, pp. 367–368.
42. *Ibid.*, p.397.
43. Nkrumah, 1973. *op. cit.*: 265–267.
44. Article of Professor Jessup in *American Journal of International Law* Vol.32 (1938), pp. 116–19.
45. Address of Dr. Kwame Nkrumah to the Ghana National Assembly, April 18, 1961, U No.397/61, pp. 12–14.
46. Changes in the Constitution of Rhodesia are the concern primarily of Rhodesia herself and Great Britain', editorial *Daily Telegraph* (London) November 1, 1965.
47. Wallerstein, Immanuel, 1967. *Africa: The Politics of Unity*. London: .99.
48. *Financial Times* (London) November 11, 1965.
49. *National Assembly Debates*, Vol. 16, July 28, 1959, Col. 1087.
50. Mansergh 1963, p.605.
51. *National Assembly Debates*, Vol. 14, February 20, 1959, Col. 24.
52. See *Ghana Today*, June 22, 1960.
53. Nkrumah, 1970, pp. 185–186.
54. Bing, 1968, Chapters 9 and 10.
55. Speeches during the Royal visit of H.M Queen Elizabeth II and H.R.H the Prince Phillip, Duke of Edinburgh, published by Ministry of Information, November 1961. Accra.
56. *H. C. Deb.* Vol. 646, October 19, 1961, Col. 646.
57. Ingram, Derek, 1977. *The Imperfect Commonwealth*. London: 4.

Chapter 4

AFRICAN UNITY — THE ASPIRATION

The Ghanaian Approach

In the movement toward African Unity, there has been much talk, not always reflecting real and considered commitment. Since the independence of Ghana in 1957, for example, there has been the Conference of Independent African States (CIAS), the Afro-Asian People's Solidarity Conference (AAPSC) and the All-African People's Conference (AAPC). The roles of AAPC and CIAS have been discussed in Chapter 3. Certain sovereign states have, at specific points, taken the lead, some more consistently than others. The contribution of significant student organizations has also been relevant, particularly of those Africans studying in Europe.[1] However, although the nature of the colonial system in Africa and the economic interests of the petty-bourgeois sections of the nationalist leadership inevitably dictated a comparatively conservative political style and none too broad an interpretation of Pan-African unity, the basic ingredients of Pan-African ideology — i.e. racial autonomy, unity and economic independence — were never unravelled and properly presented until the arrival on the scene of Kwame Nkrumah who was the foremost advocate of continental unity in Africa. In his New Year Message to the Ghanaian people in 1963, Dr. Kwame Nkrumah declared as follows:

> I, my Party and Government are completely devoted to the achievement of the political and economic unification of Africa. This is not an idle dream. It is not impossible. I see it; I feel it; it is real; indeed I am living in it already.[2]

In their response to the theme of African Unity, African political leaders had been paying tribute to the ideological force of unity as a movement, very often even when some of them were not themselves supporters of the movement. One of the marks of a movement effective only on the social level is that it can often induce others within its social milieu to share its rhetoric, pay lip service to its ideals, and even applaud its 'victories'. Compelling ideas can incarnate too many hopes and aspirations and assuage too many frustrations for them to be scorned publicly.

During the period under review the Pan-African movement, indeed, found its locus in Ghana, which was a key centre of the movement, but it was by no means its only *locus*. Ghana provided some of the organizational basis and some of the money, and it contributed significantly to the beginnings of the ideology of African Unity, although it was not the only active participant. The movement toward African unity enjoyed freedom to organize and propagate ideas both among its followers and its opponents between 1957 and 1965. The end of that period, however, was to witness some decline and the fall of President Nkrumah in February, 1966, may be said to have marked its effective end — or at least interruption.

The contemplation of ultimate African unity was emphasized in the Republican Constitution. In the Preamble, the people of Ghana declared that they enacted their Constitution "in the hope that by their actions this day might help to further the development of a Union of African State". Article 2 provided that "In the confident expectation of an early surrender of sovereignty to a union of African states and territories, the people now confer on Parliament the power to provide for the surrender of the whole or any part of the sovereignty of Ghana". Article 13 includes the following two fundamental principles: "that the union of Africa should be striven for by every lawful means, and when attained, should be faithfully preserved, that the independence of Ghana should not be surrendered or diminished on any grounds other than the furtherance of African unity."

A further step in the direction of African unity was taken on November 23, 1958, when Kwame Nkrumah and Sekou Toure, President of the Republic of Guinea, issued a joint statement, which was duly ratified by the Ghana National Assembly during the following month. The joint statement declared:

> ... we have agreed to constitute our two states as a nucleus of a Union of West African States.... We appeal to the Government of independent African States and peoples of territories still under foreign rule to support us in our action. In the same spirit, we would welcome the adherence to this union of other West African States.

In November, 1960 it was announced that Ghana and Mali had agreed to have a common parliament. On December 23–24, 1960, President Nkrumah of Ghana, Modibo Keita of Mali, and Sekou Toure of Guinea held talks in Conakry. A joint communique issued at the conclusion of their discussion announced that they had decided to establish a union of the three states, with common diplomatic representation and a common economic and monetary policy. Two special committees were set up to examine practical methods of achieving the objectives of the union. It was agreed that the three Presidents should meet four times a year — twice in Accra, the capital of Ghana, once in Conakry, the capital of Guinea and once in Bamako, the capital of Mali. On April, 1961, the three Heads of State, after several days of secret talks in Accra, announced that they had signed a Charter which would be submitted to their Parliaments for ratification. The Charter provided for the establishment of the Union of African states. It also provided for the subsequent entry of other African States and Federation into the Union.[3]

From what has been said, it is clear that Kwame Nkrumah and the Convention People's Party were totally dedicated to the principles of African

Unity. In effect, the surrender of sovereignty was a condition which Ghanaians were to accept as necessary in order to promote the cause of unity in Africa. In the view of the Ghana Government, a united Africa should seek three objectives.

1. Overall economic planning on a united continental basis (which would increase the industrial and economic power of Africa) must be achieved. So long as Africa remained disunited; so long as it remained balkanized regionally or territorially, it would be at the mercy of colonialism.

2. A Joint Military Command should be created. There was no wisdom in the then current separate efforts to build up or maintain vast military forces for self-defence which, in any case, might well prove ineffective in any major conflict. If the problem was examined realistically, Africans would be able to ask themselves this pertinent question: which single African state could protect itself against an imperialist aggressor? It was feared that if African states did not unite and combine their military forces for common defence, the individual states, out of a sense of insecurity, might be drawn into making defence pacts with non-African powers which would endanger the security of the continent. There was also the financial aspect of the problem. The maintenance of military forces would impose a heavy financial burden on even the most wealthy African states. In any case, newly independent African states needed every penny they could get for development. It would be ridiculous — indeed, suicidal — for each State, individually, to assume such a heavy burden of military expenditure alone when the weight of the burden could be shared among them all.

3. The third objective of African Unity derives from the first two just discussed above. If the African states were to set up a common economic planning organization and a joint military command, they would be compelled to adopt a common foreign policy in order to give political direction to their continental economic and industrial development planning. The burden of separate diplomatic representation by each state on the continent of Africa would alone be crushing — not to mention representation outside Africa. The desirability of a common foreign policy which would enable the proposed union of African states to speak with one voice in the councils of the world, was considered so obvious, vital and imperative that it needed hardly to be emphasized.

The 'Regional Arrangements'

However, on closer examination, the union government of Africa proposed by several countries proved rather amorphous — complex and without centralized direction. In Africa, much of the sentiment for unity has, in the past, focused more on small regions than on the whole of Africa. North Africa, West and East Africa, have all been suggested as the areas which might unite, or unite first. An example is the joint statement of November 23, 1958, by the Presidents of Guinea and Ghana 'agreeing to constitute our two states as nucleus of a Union of West African States. . . .'[4] And such regional concepts have often been spoken of as African unity — a terminological confusion that is a true reflection of the fluidity of the overall concept in the minds of its advocates.

In discussing the whole question of African emancipation and unity at Sanniquellie in Liberia, the Presidents of Liberia, Guinea and Ghana in July 1959, described the proposed African Unity as a 'Community of Independent African States'. Members of such a Community would maintain their own national identity and constitutional structure; and each member of the Community would agree not to interfere in the internal affairs of any other member. The general policy of the community would be to build up a free and prosperous African Community for the benefit of its peoples, and the peoples of the world. The policy would be founded on the maintenance of diplomatic, economic and cultural relations on the basis of equality and reciprocity, with all the states of the world which adopted positions compatible with African interests. One of its main objectives would be to help African territories not yet independent. The motto adopted for the proposed Community was 'Independence and Unity'.

There came into being, again more ambitious in intent than implementation, the Ghana-Guinea-Mali Union described as 'the Union of African States'. That union envisaged a common currency which never materialized. There was a proposal that each country should have a resident minister serving in each other's capital, but this was never fully worked out. There was a proposal to co-ordinate internal economic and social policies, but no concrete implementation was achieved. In fact, nothing was achieved except periodic consultations on African and international affairs by the three Presidents — Kwame Nkrumah, Sekou Toure and Modibo Keita.

There was also the proposed union of Upper Volta (Burkina Faso) and Ghana. In June, 1961 there was even a ceremony of 'knocking down the wall' when President Kwame Nkrumah and the Voltaic President, Maurice Yameogo, declared their determination 'by concrete measures quickly to achieve the total independence and effective unity of Africa' — and as a first step, they agreed to knock down a symbolic wall (specially erected for the purpose). This was to symbolize the agreement that 'freedom of movement for persons and groups shall be the rule'. More concretely, there was an agreement for the equitable refund of customs dues collected on re-exports from Ghana to be paid into the Upper Volta Treasury. Ghana's economic agreement with

Upper Volta cost Ghana approximately three and half million pounds. Kwame Nkrumah looked upon it as a stage towards the imminent inclusion of Upper Volta in the Ghana-Guinea-Mali Union, but his Co-Presidents in the Union, Sekou Toure and Modibo Keita were less optimistic about Voltaic participation. Indeed, the Presidents of Guinea and Mali pointedly stayed away from the ceremony of 'knocking down the wall'.[5] On the whole, Presidents Sekou Toure and Modibo Keita have been proved right in their pessimism about the seriousness of Upper Volta's intention. Kwame Nkrumah's optimism was misplaced.

The Mali Federation, which united the states of Senegal and Sudan, not of course to be confused with the Republic of Sudan, another Sahelian state, was the end product of a train of events arising out of the splitting up of the eight territories formerly known as French West Africa, namely, the Ivory Coast, Dahomey, Guinea, Upper Volta, Mauritania, Niger, Senegal and Sudan. The disintegration of the Federation was in part the deliberate work of the Ivory Coast, whose leader, President Houphouet-Boigny, made the liberation of his territory from the tutelage of the West African Federation his principal objective in the constitutional reform of 1956. He was partly successful. Senegal and Dahomey took the opposite position, and during the initial period, this conflict resulted in a split between the Rassemblement Democratique Africain (RDA) and the other political parties in French West Africa. The RDA itself, during the 1958 crisis, was divided on the issue, with the dominant group in Niger following the Ivory Coast view, and Guinea and Sudan, with minority support elsewhere, the opposite. Guinea even conditioned her adherence to the new French Constitution upon the continued existence of the West African Federation. But this attitude, so contradictory to that of the Ivory Coast, in fact worked to the same end and proved to be a decisive element in breaking up the Federation.

After the independence of Guinea, four of the seven states that had been members of the French Community — Dahomey, Upper Volta, Senegal and Sudan, agreed in conferences at Bamako (December 29–30, 1958) and Dakar (January 17, 1959) to establish a union. However, the Dakar agreement was finally approved only by Senegal and Sudan. Thus, the Mali Federation was born on April 4, 1959. But by July 1–2 of the same year, during a convention of the Parti de la Federation Africain (PFA) in Dakar, indications appeared to the discord that was to bring about the rupture of Mali; disagreement as to the respective roles of the central government and the constituent states, and opposition for the sake of opposition, without regard to principle.

In French North Africa, nationalist movements initially thought of unity in terms of the anti-colonial struggle. That is to say, in their struggle for independence from France, the relevant unity movements were those fighting the same immediate battle. In March, 1956, both Morocco and Tunisia gained full independence from France. Shortly, thereafter, a meeting between President Bouguiba of Tunisia, King Mohammed V of Morocco, and the leaders of Algerian FLN was planned. It was to be held in Tunis on October 22, 1956, but this was made impossible by the kidnapping by the French of Ben Bella and other Algerian leaders *en route* to the meeting. Despite this, talk of unity grew until it reached a climax at a meeting on April 27–30, 1958 at Tangiers, of representatives of the three nationalist parties — Front de Liberation Nationale (FLN) (Algeria), Istiqlal (Morocco) and Neo-Destour (Tunisia). The Conference insisted that North African Unity pre-supposed the independence of Algeria. It was decided at the Conference that, as a major next move, the FLN should create a provisional government. This was the crux of the meeting — the total commitment of Morocco and Tunisia, as independent states, to the fight for Algeria's independence.

The six-man permanent secretariat which was established, did in fact meet three times that same year, and on 19th September, 1958, the Government Provisoire de la Republique Algerienne (GPRA) was officially announced. But the proposed inter-state Consultative Assembly was never convened. From then on, the momentum seemed broken. Thus, once the movement for Maghreb unity, as symbolized by the Tangier meeting, achieved its major immediate goal, namely to aid the liberation of Algeria, its zeal for regional unity waned. In December, 1958, the All-African Peoples' Conference met in Accra and the Algerians, in particular, decided to place greater stress on African Unity, hoping thereby to solicit united African support for their struggle with France. Insofar as North African revolutionaries wanted to transform world society, they needed a larger arena in which to operate than the Maghreb alone. In 1958, they met in Mwanza in Tanganyika, subsequently part of Tanzania, to participate in a meeting of East and Central African leaders. This was the meeting that, in effect, launched the Pan-African Freedom Movement of East, Central (and later Southern) Africa. (PAFMEC (S) A). The credit for this Conference must go to President Julius Nyerere of Tanganyika and his powerful movement, The Tanganyika African National Union (TANU) and to the Secretary, Mbiu Koinange, then still in exile from Kenya. Both the Afro-Shirazi Party and the National Party of Zanzibar were represented. TANU and the Tanganyika Federation of labour attended, while from Kenya some African members of the Legislative Council as well as two leading politicians were present. Uganda and Nyasaland had one representative each. The members present knew their task was to undertake all the ground work necessary for ridding their territories of colonialism as quickly as possible and for establishing an East African Union or Federation.

The agenda included such topics as 'Co-ordination of Policy and Tactics of the Nationalist Movements in East and Central Africa', 'Eradication of Tribalism,' 'Harnessing the Forces of Traditionalism for Political Struggles',

'Problems of Non-Africans' etc. It is interesting to note that, while the idea of an eventual unity of East Africa was enthusiastically supported, the time of its implementation was not addressed. It was resolved that the first priority was that 'Colonialism must go'. In addition, the Conference felt that common political principles and economic patterns should be established in all the territories concerned — and to that end, even the democratization of independent African states was urged. The Freedom Charter adopted at the Conference spelt out the political ideology and the general economic approach the freedom movements were to follow. The charter stressed the need for the people of East Africa and Central Africa to commit their lives, their wealth and all their endeavour to the 'setting up of the Pan-African Freedom Movement to establish in each territory, in East and Central Africa, a government of Africa by Africans for Africans on Pan-African lines.'

Thus, all the movements for sub-regional unity were similar in several respects. They all represented militant demands in the immediate political context. They all led to the rise of close co-ordination not only between political parties but between other popular organizations in their respective regions, whether in the North, East, Central or West Africa. Most of them reached their climax just before total independence and served as effective rallying points of pressure on the colonial power, for example, the pressure of the FLN in Algeria before independence. Several of them collapsed as movements quite quickly thereafter, e.g. East African federal unity movements. In August ,1964, President Kenyatta of Kenya said in a speech that the independence of his country had been obtained by his 'ingenuity' in talking about federation. The speech was in Swahili. The first translation used the word 'trick', but the Kenya Government then corrected the translation to read 'ingenuity'.[6]

The Continental Union of Africa

As the political struggle for unity proceeded, the sub-regional unity idea increasingly gave way to that of continental unity. A major debate nevertheless developed among the advocates of African Unity. There were some who thought that African Unity should be a loose alliance and those who saw African Unity in the context of United States of Africa. As indicated earlier, in 1958, a joint declaration was made by Kwame Nkrumah and Sekou Toure that they were setting up a 'Ghana-Guinea Union as a nucleus of the United States of West Africa'.[7] In 1959, both Presidents issued another declaration setting out the basic principles of a 'Union of Independent African States'.[8] The Conakry Declaration alarmed President Tubman of Liberia because its emphasis on 'union' (although the basic principles set out in the declaration showed that neither Sekou Toure nor Kwame Nkrumah meant a supranational state) was believed to mark a radical departure from the 1958 Conference of

Independent African states where the emphasis was on 'co-operation' and 'exchange of views'. Such was the power of the word 'union' in the language of Pan-Africanism that once it was used, people and governments concluded that whoever used the word meant a supranational state. Tubman, therefore, called for a meeting with Nkrumah and Sekou Toure which was held at Sanniquellie on July 19, 1959. There, they agreed to present a 'Declaration of Principles' to a special conference of all independent African states 'as well as non-independent states which had fixed dates on which they expected to achieve independence.[9] This declaration contained ten principles. Two of these principles, the third and fourth, were believed at that time to represent a major victory for Tubman's views on Pan-Africanism, which were what the writer would call 'factionalism' rather than political union. The third principle stated as follows:

> Each State and Federation, which is a member of the Community shall maintain its own national identity and constitutional structure. The community is being formed with a view to achieving unity among independent African states. It is not designed to prejudice the present or future international policies, relations and obligations of the states involved.

The fourth principle stated:

> Each member of the Community accepts the principles that it shall not interfere in the internal affairs of any other country.

The fourth principle of the Sanniquellie Declaration appears almost diametrically opposed to the type of African Unity proposed by Presidents Nkrumah and Sekou Toure, namely, continental unity. The establishment of such a United Africa required the political and economic unification of the whole of the continent of Africa including an overall economic plan on a continental basis, the establishment of a unified military and defence strategy, and the adoption of a unified foreign policy and diplomacy which would give political direction to the joint efforts for the protection and economic development of Africa. Nkrumah said, 'the survival of free Africa, the extending independence of this continent, and the development towards that bright future on which our hopes and endeavours are pinned, depends upon political unity.[10] He believed that, through a major political union of Africa, a United Africa could emerge, great and powerful, in which territorial boundaries, as mere relics of colonialism would become obsolete and superfluous, thus working for complete and total mobilization and economic planning under a unified political direction. Thus, in his speech before the OAU in Addis Ababa, 1964, he analyzed the framework of the proposed union government as follows:

> This union government shall consist of an assembly of Heads of State and government headed by a President elected from among the Heads of State and governments of the independent African States. The executive of the union government will be a cabinet or council of ministers with a chancellor or Prime Minister as its head, and a House consisting of two chambers — the Senate and a House of Representatives. If you agree, even in principle, we can appoint our Foreign Ministers, assisted by experts, to work out a constitution for a union government of Africa.[11]

But this position adopted by Ghana in Cairo, 1964, was later modified; for the OAU Conference held in Accra, October, 1965, Ghana only proposed the setting up of an Executive Body consisting of a cabinet or council of ministers. The difference between the stand adopted by Ghana in Cairo and in Accra, was that in the case of the Cairo OAU Conference, acceptance of Ghana's proposal for setting up an 'Assembly of Heads of State and Government' headed by a President would have given sufficient power to such a President to direct the affairs of the OAU or the continent. The President, once elected, could give political direction with or without the concurrence of his colleagues. On the other hand, the Accra proposal was a Prime Ministerial type of administration, in the sense that the cabinet or the council of ministers would comprise the respective Foreign Ministers of the OAU and the current Chairman of the Organization. The latter would then, as Chairman, act as a 'Chancellor' or 'Prime Minister', who could not, in fact, take decisions on his own without discussions and agreement arrived at within the cabinet or council of ministers.

The advantage of the Accra proposal was that the Cabinet or Council of Ministers was already established by Article XII of the OAU Charter. It would have been easier for the cabinet to meet, and unlike the previous proposal the chancellorship or premiership would rotate among the Heads of State or Governments of the OAU. The only change was that instead of the Foreign Minister of the country hosting the meeting directing affairs, this responsibility would have been passed on to his Head of State or Government. Such an arrangement would facilitate contact with the Heads of State or Governments and make it easier for decisions to be taken. Consequently, the Assembly of Heads of State and Governments at their second ordinary session on October 25, 1965, passed a resolution which took note that there was a need for an 'Establishment of an Executive Body' and requested the governments of the member states of the OAU to examine the problem in order to express their opinions on the matter.[12]

The historical importance of the Sanniquellie meeting was that, firstly, while many other African leaders had spoken out against Kwame Nkrumah's ideas of political unity, only President Tubman came out with a concrete suggestion aimed at slowing down what was believed to be a rush by Nkrumah and Toure towards political unity. Indeed, to most outside observers and well-wishers, Kwame Nkrumah was right in seeing the political significance of Ghana in continental terms, but they were equally agreed that a functional approach was more profitable and realistic than the immediate establishment of a political union of independent African states. For example, the Ghanaian call to member states at the 1960 Tunisian Conference of Independent African States to provide the framework within which 'any plans for economic, social and cultural co-operation can, in fact, operate . . .', was rebuffed by the leader of the Nigerian delegation. M. Maitama Sule — a Cabinet Minister, as follows:

> No one in Africa doubts the need to promote Pan-Africanism but we must not be sentimental, we must be realistic. It is for this reason that we would like to point out that at this moment, the idea of forming a Union of African States is premature . . . too radical — perhaps too ambitious — to be of any lasting benefit.[13]

When the Ghanaian delegate, Ako Adjei, said that as a result of faith in African unity, the Ghanaian electorate had 'recently voted in a plebiscite on the new Republican Constitution of Ghana to . . . surrender her sovereignty in whole or in part, in the interest of a Union of African States . . .' Maitama Sule replied that 'At the moment we in Nigeria cannot afford to form union by government with any African state by surrendering our sovereignty . . . We believe that many of the African states would very much prefer to rule themselves, and that they would like to taste the atmosphere of freedom after having been under foreign domination.'

It is necessary to describe, briefly, the nature of the African political scene in which the conflicts on African unity were taking place. The French-speaking African states, except Guinea, became independent in 1960. At this time, the primary issues which faced the African states were the Algerian war of independence, the Belgian invasion of the newly-independent Congo and the Moroccan claim to the whole of Mauritania. Because of the different and conflicting positions adopted by the African states on these issues, it was inevitable that these differences would spill over into the area of African unity. How these differences led to the emergence of political groups will be briefly discussed.

The Approach of the Brazzaville Group 1960

In view of the impending admission of the newly-independent French-speaking African states to the United Nations, Houphouet-Boigny of the Ivory Coast convened a meeting in Abidjan in October 1960 to formulate a common position on the African issues before the United Nations. Though all black French-speaking states were invited, Guinea refused to go and Togo declined because Morocco and Tunisia had not been invited. Olympio objected to Algeria being on the agenda and the Malagasy Republic also declined because it regarded Algeria as a French internal problem. Both Mali and Congo (Kinshasa) sent observers after Lumumba was dismissed as Prime Minister.

Another meeting of this group, referred to as the Brazzaville Group, was held in Brazzaville in December, 1960, where it was decided to form a permanent association. This was called the Union Africaine et Malgache (UAM) since Madagascar (later the Malagasy Republic) also attended the meeting. The members of UAM were Congo (Brazzaville), Ivory Coast, Senegal, Mauritania, Upper Volta, Niger, Dahomey, Chad, Gabon, the Central African Republic, Cameroon and Madagascar. At the conference, the member states called for the admission of Mauritania to the United Nations and reaffirmed their recognition of her as 'an independent and sovereign state.' They called for bilateral negotiations between France and Algeria to allow 'the Algerians freely to choose their destiny', but opposed any United Nations action on the issue. On the Congo, they declared their support for Kasavubu.[14]

For the first time in the conflict over African Unity, a bloc of independent African states was created on an ideological basis, with membership that excluded other African states. It was clearly inevitable that the formation of this Brazzaville Group would elicit reactions from those who disagreed with the policies of the member states. The first to react were those states whose views and those of the Brazzaville bloc diverged on the specific issue considered by that group. Morocco disagreed with the group's recognition of Mauritania. Ghana, Guinea, Mali, Morocco and the United Arab Republic (UAR) disagreed with the group's support for Kasavubu of the Congo in his dispute with Patrice Lumumba. Indeed, when the Kasavubu delegation was finally seated in the UN General Assembly, Guinea, Mali, Morocco and the UAR agreed to withdraw their troops from the United Nations command in the Congo. These states preferred United Nations intervention in Algeria to the bilateral talks being urged by the Brazzaville Group. Under such circumstances, Morocco took the initiative in calling for a Casablanca Conference.

The Approach of the Casablanca Group

The Casablanca Conference, held on January 3–7, 1961, was attended by Morocco, Ghana, Guinea, Mali, the UAR, the provisional Government of Algeria, Libya and Ceylon. Morocco, Ghana, Mali the UAR and the provisional Government of Algeria were represented by their respective Heads of State or Government, while Libya was represented by its Minister of Foreign Affairs and Ceylon by an Ambassador. Participants discussed Palestine, Mauritania, Rwanda-Burundi, South Africa, Algeria, the French nuclear tests in the Sahara and the Congo. On Mauritania, they supported Morocco's claim and pledged their approval of 'any action taken by Morocco on Mauritania for the restitution of her legitimate rights'. They condemned France, over Algeria, called for the breaking off of diplomatic relations with France, the enlistment of African volunteers in the 'Army of National Liberation' and recognition of the provisional Government as the only government in Algeria. 'On the Congo, they confirmed 'the intention and determination of the respective Governments represented to withdraw their troops and other military personnel placed under the United Nations Operational Command . . .' and affirmed their support for Lumumba.

On African Unity, the difference between the Brazzaville and the Casablanca groups were clearly evident. Whereas the Brazzaville bloc rejected the idea of any political inter-state economic institutions, the Casablanca Group decided to set up: (1) an African Consultative Assembly composed of representatives of every African State, (2) an African Political Committee of Heads of State, (3) an African Economic Committee, (4) an African Cultural Committee, and (5) a Joint African High Command of Chiefs of Staff.

The Approach of the Monrovia Group 1961

The creation of both the Brazzaville and Casablanca Groups still left a substantial number of African states uncommitted to either group. The origins of the Monrovia group cannot be traced to any particular Head of State. Early in 1961, Houphouet-Boigny of the Ivory Coast canvassed the Heads of African states not identified with Brazzaville Group over the need for a general conference to discuss the Congo and Algeria, and where the participants could subscribe to a principle of non-interference in one another's domestic affairs.[15] At the time, Balewa of Nigeria and Senghor of Senegal were canvassing for the same type of conference. Senghor himself did not play a leading role but persuaded Olympio of Togo to take the initiative. After further consultations, it was agreed that Cameroon, Guinea, Ivory Coast, Liberia, Mali, Nigeria, and Togo should sponsor a conference of Heads of State in Monrovia on May 8, 1961.[16]

The choice of the sponsors was a deliberate attempt to arrest the formation of Groups in African politics. Cameroon and Ivory Coast were chosen to ensure the attendance of the Brazzaville Group; Guinea and Mali were selected from the Casablanca Group; Togo, Nigeria and Liberia were among the uncommitted African states. Whether the absence of any Arab states among the sponsors has any significance is not known, but the sponsors were chosen to ensure that the Monrovia Conference would be attended by the Heads of all African states. This conference was then the largest convocation of representatives of African states ever held. At the conference, the delegates of twenty countries adopted a set of broad principles governing relations between their states and outlining procedures to assist in the pacific settlement of disputes arising amongst them. A second conference was held in January 1962, in Lagos, to which were invited the leaders of all independent African states (except South Africa). Although eight of those invited did not attend because the Algerian Provisional Government had not been invited, the Lagos Conference achieved marked success in institutionalizing African co-operation. The charter which was proposed and later ratified called for the establishment of a permanent secretariat, an assembly of Heads of State and Government, a council of ministers and organs for co-ordinating economic policy and mediating in disputes.

The Monrovia Group stressed the importance of the sovereignty of individual members, rejected the interference of any outside power, African or non-African, in the affairs of African states and agreed to preserve full political sovereignty while gradually developing mechanisms for economic co-operation. In Lagos, the group stressed the legal equality of all African states regardless of their size.

When the Monrovia Conference was convened in Monrovia on May 8, 1961, members of the Casablanca Group, except, Libya stayed away. Morocco, a member of the Group, also stayed away because Mauritania was invited; Sudan withdrew its acceptance of the invitation because she supported Morocco's claim to Mauritania; the Congo (Kinshasa) was not invited because of the controversy over which was the 'legal' government there. All the other states (i.e. Cameroon, Central African Republic, Chad, Republic of Congo, Dahomey, Ethiopia, Gabon, Ivory Coast, Liberia, Libya, Malagasy Republic, Mauritania, Niger, Nigeria, Senegal, Sierra Leone, Somalia, Togo, Tunisia, Upper Volta) were represented either by their Heads of State or Government, or high level delegations. Of the members of the Casablanca Group, only Morocco had a substantial reason for staying away. The rest of the Casablanca Group stayed away in all probability, because they knew that their views on Pan-African union were simply not acceptable to the majority of the states gathered in Monrovia.

The emphasis at the Monrovia Conference on non-interference in one another's internal affairs should be understood in the context of accusations of subversion African states were levelling against one another. For example, Nigeria accused Ghana in May 1961 of subversion in Nigeria, Morocco laid claim to the whole of Mauritania and Togo accused Ghana of planning her annexation. Dr. Nnamdi Azikiwe, in an opening address to the second Conference of the Monrovia Group, emphasized what he said was the basic difference between the Casablanca Group and Monrovia Group:

> But there is one basic difference... It is the conspicuous absence of a specific declaration on the part of the Casablanca states of their inflexible belief in the fundamental principles enunciated at Monrovia regarding the inalienable rights of African states, as at present

constituted, to legal equality ... To self-determination ... and to safety from interference in their internal affairs through subversive activities engineered by supposedly friendly states.[17]

This issue of subversion remained for a long time the main point of friction in African inter-state relations.

In terms of the positions adopted by the Monrovia and Casablanca Groups on various issues, how far apart were the respective members? On South Africa, the difference was in degree rather than in kind. The Casablanca Group condemned South Africa for its policy, and the imperialist powers who supported it. The Group then called on the United Nations to impose economic and diplomatic sanctions on South Africa. The Casablanca Conference resolution actually cited Articles 40 and 41 of the United Nations Charter as those under which the United Nations should act. This would have made the implementation of the sanctions mandatory on all United Nations members. However, they did not advocate the use of force. The Monrovia Group, using more temperate language, called for political and economic sanctions by African states.

On Angola and colonialism in general, the Casablanca bloc pledged 'aid and assistance' to the nationalist forces while the Monrovia Group pledged 'material and moral support'. However, while the Casablanca Group proclaimed its determination'.... To liquidate neo-colonialism in all their forms' the Monrovia Group pledged 'non-interference in the internal affairs' of states.

It was over the Congo, that positions differed considerably. For example, while the Brazzaville Group supported Tshombe, the Casablanca Group threw its weight behind Gizenga-led Lumumba force. However, till the assassination of Lumumba, it would be correct to say that the Casablanca Group members and some members of the Monrovia Group were working for a reconciliation of Lumumba and Kasavubu. After Lumumba's death, the more radical members of the Casablanca Group withdrew recognition from Kasavubu's government and recognized the Stanleyville regime. The Monrovia Group, on the other hand, continued to recognize the Kasavubu Government while working for reconciliation between the Leopoldville and Stanleyville regimes.[18]

There were further differences on the role of the United Nations in the Congo. While both groups expressed general dissatisfaction with the United Nations, the Monrovia Group expressed its faith in it. The Casablanca Group, on the other hand, presented the UN with an ultimatum.

On Algeria, the Monrovia Group did not want to antagonize France and hence limited itself to appealing to both sides in the conflict to negotiate. This fear of antagonizing France did not, however, stop it from calling for independence for Algeria. The Casablanca Group not only condemned France but also called for United Nations intervention rather than bilateral negotiation.

On disarmament, the Monrovia Group, obviously reflecting the wishes of the French-speaking states, took a conciliatory line on French nuclear tests. While appealing to all nuclear powers to desist from the manufacture and testing of nuclear weapons, it simply noted the 'assurances' given by the French Government not to carry out any more tests in Africa. The Casablanca Group, on the other hand, singled out France for condemnation and called on African states to 'reconsider their relations' with France.

Opposite stands were taken on Mauritania. The Monrovia Group supported Mauritania's claim to statehood and sovereignty and the Casablanca Group opposed it. Morocco's membership of the Casablanca Group and Mauritania's membership of the Monrovia Group deepened this difference.

On the issue of African Unity, there was the myth that the Casablanca Conference participants embarked on a programme of political unity while the Monrovia Group did not. A careful study of the resolutions and post conference activities of each Group, in fact, reveals little difference. The members of the Casablanca Conference affirmed their will to intensify efforts for the creation of 'an effective form of co-operation among the African states in the economic, social and cultural domains (and aimed) at the consolidation of liberty in Africa and building up its unity and security.[19] The Monrovia Group agreed on 'the need for pooling resources and co-ordinating efforts in order to overcome the barriers of growth which confront all African countries on their way to development,[20] but stressed that unity must be a 'unity of aspirations'. Colin Legum draws attention to public misconception about the Casablanca Group's stated position on African Unity. The concept of immediate political unity was never endorsed by any of the conferences of independent African states; however, it usually found a place in resolutions of conferences of non-governmental organizations such as the All-African People's Organization.[21]

In conclusion, it is correct to say that differences over conceptions of 'unity', 'union' and their applicability engendered long debates. The Casablanca Group, for which the major spokesman was Ghana's Kwame Nkrumah, emphasized immediate political unification with the subsequent growth of economic co-operation. It is this notion that is most directly identified with 'Pan'Africanism', although Pan-Africanism has been used loosely in connection with both stands on African Unity. The Monrovia Group's more conservative leaders particularly Houphouet-Boigny of the Ivory Coast and Tubman of Liberia advocated gradual economic co-operation out of which might evolve, at some later and unspecified date, a loose political confederation whose structure would correspond to the needs of the time at which it would come into being. The two positions were finally brought together in May 1963, at the Addis Ababa Conference from which emerged the Organization for (and later of) African Unity, designed to be the formal base upon which a unification of the continent would henceforth be built.

The Legal Nature of the Union

The foregoing analysis demonstrates that without exception, the leaders of the newly-independent states placed African unity in the forefront of the foreign policy goals for their countries. However, not all proved prepared to accept the submergence of their new-found sovereignty within a union government structure of the type that was advocated by Kwame Nkrumah and the Casablanca Group of states. But at the same time, African Unity was accepted as an ideal to be pursued and all were prepared to make at least some sacrifice of autonomy in order to gain a greater measure of unity and co-operation. Their commitment to some form of unification stemmed essentially from the feeling that only in this way could the ultimate objectives of the African revolution be accomplished. Only when Africa speaks with a united voice, it is argued, can the final stage of liberation of Africa from colonial bondage and full political equality for Africa in the eyes of the outside world be brought about.[22]

By 1959, at least the problem of African Unity had not assumed major proportions, for Nkrumah's approach to Pan-Africanism up to 1962 was regional.[23] The Pan-Africanist political movement, espoused and developed by Kwame Nkrumah, was a form of macro-nationalism which has been described variously as racial, cultural, and political. In fact, the three components have been emphasized and regarded as indispensable in building African unity. The passionate commitment to Pan-Africanism can best be appreciated in the light of his early contacts in London with George Padmore, the West Indian theorist of Pan-Africanism, and with Jomo Kenyatta, the late President of Kenya, in the Pan Africanist Conference in Manchester in 1945 and even earlier at Lincoln University in the United States of America. Almost since the day of Ghana's independence, Nkrumah had stressed over and over again in public, the necessity of building a United States of Africa designed to bind together the independent states of the continent into a single political federation which would, in some aspects at least, resemble the constitutional structure of the United States of America.

The arguments for greater unity in Africa, then were generally accepted, but the method by which this unification was to be brought about posed perhaps the greatest single problem faced by the African community. However, persuasive the doctrine of African unity might have been, the emphasis by Nkrumah on the submergence of individual African sovereignties into a single union government of Africa, created suspicion as regards the motives of those who most loudly advocated the ideals of unity and Pan-Africanism. Many leaders saw, in the man who might eventually become the leader of a union government of Africa, a threat to their own position. This has been one of the major reasons for the reiteration at all conferences of the necessity of respect for national sovereignty.

Moreover, as the members of the African community travelled further and further from the moment of independence, diverse national interests inevitably became more deeply entrenched. Consequently, the advantage of political unity became increasingly less apparent. All African leaders had long realized, of course, that there were formidable hurdles in the way of true African unification. Differences of language and cultural background and the rivalries of ancient nations and tribes remained natural barriers to African solidarity. Despite the desire of the nationalist leaders to overcome the colonial heritage, the most natural groupings of the African states appeared to be those whose colonial and especially linguistic background were similar. As the abortive Ghana-Guinea union clearly proved, the task of devising common institutions for countries that were the product of different colonial systems could be a difficult and arduous one. The struggle for independence was carried on by nationalist parties within the confines of existing colonial territories and the emphasis since independence had heavily been on the creation of nations within these boundaries. A common African bond, forged in the anti-colonial struggle, gave way, at least in part, to the desire of new governments to create first and foremost an awareness on the part of their people of belonging to a common nation.

It was clear in discussions in Addis Ababa, which preceded the establishment of the OAU, that the Heads of State were not yet ready to accept Nkrumah's ideas of a political union of Africa. The foundations of unity were to be built on sovereign states which would determine the form and degree of their co-operation entirely on the basis of their own individual policy decisions. The framework of organized and voluntary co-operation and co-ordination was designed to leave room for sub-regional organizations that would represent the special interests of groups of members. In the circumstances, CPP stalwarts prevailed upon Nkrumah to adopt a flexible approach to the problem of African Unity. Consequently, in something of a Volte-face, in a speech in Accra on May 24, 1964, he conceded that "A Union Government for Africa does not mean loss of sovereignty of independent African states. A Union Government will rather strengthen the sovereignty of the individual states within the Union."[24]

The Committee of African Organizations (CAO) also played an invaluable role in respect of African Unity. Its policy of unity for Africa and freedom for all African countries enabled it to bring African leaders together. Perhaps quite apart from the OAU itself, no platform enjoyed greater attraction for the African leaders than that of CAO. The organization acted as a common platfom for the leaders of the Casablanca, Monrovia and the Brazzaville groups. The African unity included Nnamdi Azikiwe (Zik), Jomo Kenyatta,

Julius Nyerere, William Tubman, Houphouet-Boigny, Modibo Keita, Milton Obote, Sekou Toure, Kenneth Kaunda and Kwame Nkrumah. Zik's speech was rather significant, he said *inter alia*, "As I see it, there is bound to arise an African Leviathan in the form of a political organization or association or union or concert of states."[25]

CAO, by getting Zik to speak, bridged the gap which threatened to divide the Pan-African movement on the continent. The fact that CAO officers and committee members are today to be found in distinguished offices of the continent, helped to create understanding with the OAU.[26] And CAO conferences held in the following cities — Belgrade in August, 1962, London in April, 1963 and Moscow in September, 1964 — and attended by the All-African students union from Europe and America, and their message of flexible approach to the ideal of unity, greatly influenced the African states.

It is difficult to subsume the theme, Union Government, under a specific juristic category. It is neither a Union of States nor a federation in the classical sense of the word. A **Union of States** is in existence when two or more sovereign and independent states are, by a treaty, recognized by third states and linked together under the same government or Monarch, so that they make one and the same subject of international law. They form a compound power and are by their treaty of union prevented from making war against each other or one another. On the other hand, they cannot make war separately against a foreign power nor can war be made against one or other of them separately. Each state can enter into separate treaties of commerce, extradition and the like, but is always the Union which concludes such treaties for the separate states.

Viewed as a quality or faculty of statehood, and as connoting legal omnipotence rather than physical power, sovereign independence is, by its very nature, a unity. It is the name ascribed to the will of a legally-supreme political power. It is the plenary faculty which that entity is assumed to posses or to express its will in the form of commands legally binding upon all persons over whom it sees fit to claim jurisdiction and with respect to any matters which it may select. Thus, conceived, it is clear that sovereignty is not regarded as a bundle or aggregate of jurisdictional powers.

A **Federal State,** on the other hand, is a perpetual union of several states which has organs of its own and is invested with power not only over the member-states, but also over their citizens. The union is based first, on an international treaty of the member-states, and secondly, on a subsequently-accepted constitution of the federal state. A federal state is said to be a real state in international law, standing side by side with its member-states, because its organs have a direct power over the citizens of those member states.

If there is any analogy to the proposed Union Government of Africa or the suggested Pan-African Union of States it is that of a **Confederacy**. In a confederacy, the individual states retain their character and their relations to each other or one another are of international or treaty character. Consequently, no central state is created and sovereignty lies wholly within such individual political units. What union there is in the Confederacy is the creation of the wills of the individual states. In a Federal State, on the other hand, its foundation rests in itself. It is created by the people as a whole and the individual states are creations of its will. In the case of a Federal State, historically founded upon a union of previously-existing sovereign states, the citizens of the Federal State are regarded as having first divested themselves of their old state sovereignties and then, as a people, established a national Federal State.[27]

The concept of a union government of the African continent appears to allow for the formation of a loose supranational administrative union of independent African sovereign states, which union would leave untouched the international legal personalities of the respective member states. For example, it can be readily seen from the Saniquellie declaration of July 19, 1959, how matters as extensive as political economy and defence (which are matters capable of causing the greatest loss of autonomy among the member states of a composite union state) have been discussed with calculated concern to avoid the creation of a rigid centralized supra-national organism.

Even so, in conclusion, one is bound to agree with Professor Gray-Cowan[28] that in spite of the obstacles to African Unity, Pan-Africanist political unity is more than an emotional slogan, the appeal of its symbols is a strong one. The dream of a continent united under one government which would speak for the people of Africa with a powerful voice in international circles continues to have great attractions, especially in the light of the often discordant voices within the African community in recent times. The conception of how this unity is to be obtained, however, has been undergoing a quiet change over the years. No longer is it possible to expect the immediate political unity that was the theme of Kwame Nkrumah and the Casablanca Group of political leaders. Instead, a much more gradual approach, based on a clearer realization of the pre-requisites of genuine unity has taken the place of the emotional aura that surrounded the Pan-Africanism of an earlier period. Yet, if, as Professor Gray Cowan propounds, it is more fully realized by African leaders that the road to unity will be long, it will involve many compromises of national interests. The relatively minor successes of Pan-Africanism up to this point have by no means dimmed the lustre of African Unity as the far-off goal of African leaders. And in this at least, the original Ghanaian approach remains fundamental.

NOTES AND REFERENCES

1. Kwesi Armah, 1965. *Africa's Golden Road*. London: Heineman: 6–16.
2. *Axioms of Kwame Nkrumah – Freedom Fighters' Edition* 1967, Panaf Books, p.11.
3. New York Times, April 30, 1961. For the full text of the Charter see, Legum, Colin, 1962. *Pan-Africanism* Appendix 14 (Revised 1965).
4. Legum, 1962, p.139.
5. For the declaration of the Ghana-Guinea Union, as worked out by May 1, 1959, See Colin Legum's *Pan Africanism: A Short Political Guide* (Pall Mall Press, London, 1965). On the agreement between Ghana and Upper Volta and the ceremony which accompanied it, see *Ghana Today* (London) July 5, 1961. See also State Opening of Parliament, July 4, 1961 (Speech of the President), p.5.
6. Wallerstein, Immanuel, 1968. *Africa: The Politics of Unity*. London: 118–119.
7. *Ibid.*
8. *Ibid.*
9. Legum 1962, p.162.
10. Nkrumah, Kwame, 1970. *Africa Must Unite*, (Panaf Edition), London: 221.
11. *Africa Research Bulletin*, Vol.1, 1964. London: 123B.
12. Assembly of Heads of State and Government Resolution, 28, October 25, 1965. Accra
13. Legum 1962. Appendices 10 and 11, for the extracts of the speeches of both Ako Adjei and Maitama to the Conference.
14. Legum 1962. Appendix 13, pp. 176–182. *See* also Wallerstein 1967, pp. 45–46.
15. Wallerstein 1967, p.54.
16. Wallerstin 1967, p.54 and Legum 1962, p.52.
17. *West African Pilot*, January 26, 1962.
18. Wallerstein 1967, 1967, pp. 42–54.
19. Legum 1962, *op. cit.*, 187–192.
20. Legum 1962, *op. cit.*, 198–201.
21. Legum 1962, *op. cit.*, 42–43.
22. Nkrumah, Kwame 1963. *African Must Unite,* passim.
23. Nkrumah, Kwame 1962. *Towards Colonial Freedom*. London: x–xi.
24. *Axioms of Kwame Nkrumah: The Freedom Fighters' Edition*. London: 13. *See* also Programme of the Convention Peoples Party for Work and Happiness (Accra) 1962, p.46.
25. Armah, Kwesi 1965, p.12.
26. *Ibid.*
27. The distinction between federal state and confederacies in Austin 1961. *The Province of Jurisprudence Determined*, pp.223–224.
28. Cowan, Gray L., 1968. *The Dilemmas of African Independence* (revised edition), pp. 74–75.

Chapter 5

THE ECONOMIC ASPECTS OF FOREIGN POLICY

The Colonial Economy

At the time of independence, Ghana's comparatively slow rate of economic growth could be attributed to the general characteristics of an underdeveloped country. There were impediments too, which were the direct results of the colonial legacy. Under colonial rule, the country had very restricted economic links with the international community. Its natural resources were developed only insofar as they served the interests of the colonial power. The modern sector of the economy was organized around the production of raw material, employing very few skilled persons. This had not been the traditional historical pattern. The trans-saharan trade had reached many nations — but it had declined in favour of contact with Europe via the coast. In the twentieth century, at least up to the end of the Second World War, the colonial administrators of Ghana were not concerned with the foreign economic policy of the country. Their major objective was the maintenance of law and order and the balancing of a budget which was designed, as far as possible, to serve British economic well-being.

The economy of the country developed only slowly in the period of colonial rule punctuated by two world wars and a series of economic depression. The colonial government expressly acknowledged their obligations not only to govern but to develop the country economically and politically. At the same time, however, they asserted that what was best for foreign traders was also best for Ghana (then the Gold Coast), so providing ample occasion for generations of Ghanaian nationalists to complain that the Ghanaian economy was being developed merely to serve foreign interests. The colonial administration in a way limited the export of raw material to its metropolitan market. Ghana's colonial position was, of course, little different from that of other African colonies. Immense profits were made and repatriated out of the country. Significant mineral deposits attracted foreign capital, but this served mainly to enrich alien investors. There was no partnership in development, simply because there was no partnership at all.

The British and French metropolitan powers (and the German until 1914) ran their colonies on shoe-string budgets. The British, indeed, insisted from the beginning that each territory should be self-supporting.[1] Thus, the cost of administration and public services was met from the Ghanaian budget out of taxes and revenues, the first charge upon the revenue was the salaries of officials of the administration. The transportation network, for example, was designed primarily by the colonial administration and the roads and railways were built from the sea coast particularly the capital of the period to the hinterland. Links with the roads of the neighbouring French colonial territories were not favoured. All the metropolitan powers of colonies in Africa created patterns of transport of this type. Commenting on this situation in the then 'Gold Coast', Geoffrey Bing referred to a 'lopsided' effect of colonial development which 'the railway from Ouagadougou (the capital of the Voltaic Republic) did not follow the direct route to the coast which would have been through Ghana but was diverted to meander endlessly through French territory. The external cable service was similarly based on these colonial principles. To telegraph to Accra it was necessary to route one's message via Paris and London and even letters to Ghana had to follow this route.'[2] Nevertheless, as long as the colonial economies were functioning 'adequately', i.e. to the satisfaction of the Colonial Office, colonial officials were happy to go about their daily task of administration. The economies were fairly static. This factor made work easier since innovation and development are invariably administratively taxing. The operations of the expatriate companies, together with systems of protective tariff, ensured that the trade of African colonies should remain largely with their metropolitan countries. Thus, France in the mid 1930s took over three-quarters of her colonies' exports, while Britain's share of the exports from her colonies in West Africa ranged between nearly two-thirds for Sierra Leone and a little over one-third for Ghana.[3]

Post-independence Economic Policy Objectives

Ghana continued its open economy after independence, and maintained the traditional outlook of the pre-independence period until 1961. Substantial emphasis was, however, placed on changing the structure of the economy from a lop-sided primary goods-producing economy to, at least, a balanced agricultural and light industrial economy. The main objective behind this was to attain a certain measure of economic independence by reducing the country's economic vulnerability.

The Government believed that to attain the envisaged economic independence not only did it have to lessen the dependence on mono-crop farming but also had to initiate and encourage the type of industrial production that would free the level and composition of consumption from depending on foreign exchange. In addition, while industries in the cities would help employ and train the youth who migrated to the cities, the establishment of rural industries would curb future migration.

The economy in the period under review, was geared towards the creation of the necessary institutional structures that would mobilize and direct domestic and foreign savings for industrialization and provide the basic infrastructure necessary for such action. The budget of 1958 set out to create conditions which would attract foreign capital and encourage the re-investment in Ghana of a substantial portion of profits from such investments. The conditions created included the granting of special concessions to new industries, low taxation and generous depreciation allowances. In 1959, under the Pioneer Industries and Companies Act, duty paid on raw and semi-processed materials used in Ghanaian industries became refundable. The Government guaranteed as little interference as possible with the production and distribution processes and with the market structures as a whole. In return for these concessions foreign enterprises were required to (1) recognize the Trade Unions, (2) train Ghanaians for superior posts, and (3) develop local sources of raw materials.

The Government was also to be given the first option to buy the shares of foreign enterprises when they themselves decided to sell them and sixty per cent of net profits were to be re-invested in the country. The Government's plan envisaged a mixed economy in which 'a vigorous public and co-operative sector operated along with the private sector.[4] The Government encouraged Ghanaian businessmen to form British-type co-operative organization. The co-operative sector was used in broadening the vitality of the economy; it was also used in harnessing indigenous private capital formation both in agriculture and industry. Economically, this appeared to be a solution to the chronic financial needs of the small Ghanaian businessman.

The economic policies during the period under review were meant, among other things, to attract foreign capital. By virtue of the Capital Investment Act 1963, a Capital Investment Board was established for the purposes of initiating measures to encourage foreign investment in the country. Moreover, by this Act, the Government undertook to refrain from any expropriation of foreign enterprise in Ghana. In exceptional cases where the Government took over a project in the public interest, fair compensation for the take-over was paid in the currency in which the investment had been originally made. As a result of the country's economic backwardness, the Government was determined to expedite economic development. But the infrastructure was terribly underdeveloped. It, therefore, became necessary for the Government to indulge in a massive expenditure required for the resuscitation of the economy. The bulk of the materials needed for such massive industrialization and infrastructural programme, particularly machinery and construction materials, needed to be imported. The country, therefore, faced large import bills for the period and, despite rising export revenue (up to 1961), had to fall on its foreign exchange reserves to finance these imports. As a result, the net foreign exchange assets of the banks depleted considerably by 1966.[5] Given limited resources, deteriorating terms of trade and its reluctance to curtail the industrialization and development programmes, the government introduced import licencing at the end of 1961. More emphasis was placed on the importation of capital equipment and raw materials at the expense of consumer goods.[6] Exchange control regulations also checked repatriation of profits by foreign firms. These controls, however, served to make foreign capital wary and despite the rather favourable terms offered under the Capital Investment Act of 1963, the inflow of foreign capital abated considerably. Despite all these controls, Ghana's medium-term debt burden did not show a healthy picture.[7]

As the import bills rose with the development programme and export earnings continued to fluctuate with the unstable world prices of commodities exported, particularly cocoa, the Government adopted a new policy involving increased trade with the centrally-planned economies of Eastern Europe and Ghana. Under agreements, these countries offered generally-stable prices which on the average led to higher export earnings. Furthermore, following the rapid development of infrastructure and rundown of Ghana's reserves, the country's request for aid to continue with its development programmes received a favourable response from the Eastern European countries, particularly USSR. Aid led to more trade and vice versa. Ghana signed its first bilateral trade agreement with USSR in 1960 and trade increased rapidly between them from then on, reaching its peak in 1965.[8] Despite this trend, Ghana's percentage of trade with the Eastern European countries including China was very small in comparison with that of her traditional trading partners of the Western countries. Like the Western Powers and other third world countries, Ghana adopted a policy of diversification of trade as a means of making her foreign policy meaningful.

Ghana's objectives with respect to trade were: (1) to boost its existing exports so as to increase its earnings, (2) to develop the export of non-traditional but promising items to lessen dependence on the traditionals, particularly cocoa, and (3) to diversify its trade and create competition for fair prices. To boost exports, the best thing for Ghana to do was to find new trading partners. In diversifying its trade links, Ghana primarily wanted to trade with third world countries particularly in African and Eastern Europe. Unfortunately, the African countries exported very much the same items as Ghana, and had the same import needs.

This led to very slow development of trade between them. Trade with East European countries and China was on a large scale but turned out to be mainly on cocoa and other traditionals. A policy of diversification in trade links was responsible for the increase in the number of countries buying Ghana's cocoa from 15 in 1957 to 22 in 1961, rising to 25 by 1965; it also accounted for about 20 per cent of sales in 1965.

Ghana's expansion of trade to embrace China and Eastern Europe was crucial in the period under discussion. The first phase of the country's industrial and infrastructural development had so taxed its resources that Ghana was in need of credit for its imports and the bilateral trade agreements contracted with the East European countries under which imports were paid for with commodities exported in return suited Ghana. As Stevens points out[9], for primary goods producers, fluctuation in the size of harvests is a major problem and given the general inelasticity of demand in the traditional markets for these goods and the attendant unfavourable prices, any new outlets for siphoning off excesses during periods of heavy harvest help to maintain prices and benefit from the increase in production. The development of the Eastern European markets would, it was hoped, fulfil such a need. China and the countries of Eastern Europe constituted the largest potential market for counter balancing the price glut resulting from good harvests.

Domestic Factors which Influenced Foreign Economic Policy

The domestic factors which influenced Ghana's foreign economic policy were both political and economic. The considerably undeveloped economy inherited at independence, the Government's determination to embark on an accelerated developed programme and the obvious lack of the requisite expertise and capital to implement the envisaged programme called for a liberal investment policy which aimed at enticing foreign capital. The open-market policy adopted in the early post independence years was also greatly influenced by the 1953 report by Professor Arthur Lewis on Industrialization in Ghana. The fact that both the 1951 and 1957 manifestos of the CPP promised to rapidly develop and industrialize the economy put pressure on the Government to pen up to foreign investors. At the same time, Ghana's fears of possible total domination of the economy by multi-national enterprises gave rise to the country's attitude towards foreign capital.

There were two phases of Ghana's foreign economic policy. While during the first phase (i.e. 1957–1960), the open-market policy ruled, controls were in force throughout the second phase (i.e. 1961–1966). This was because of the following factors: first, the massive government spending on development coupled with the free trade greatly deplenished the coffers of the country. Secondly, the pursuit of the policies of African Unity and de-colonization, although beneficial to Ghana and Africa, were a drain on Ghana's resources. Thirdly, a lot of Ghana's industries were not related to available local primary products and so additional resources had to be imported to feed them. Fourthly, indigenous private entrepreneurship was beset with problems which frustrated Ghana's industrialization programme, despite measures taken to assist and promote Ghanaian enterprises.[10] Fifthly, Ghana had a youthful population, with 45 per cent of the people under the age of fifteen. Sixthly, Ghana, just like other under-developed countries, was a victim of unfavourable terms of trade. She imported mainly manufactured items (from the West) the prices of which had rarely fallen, but rose during the previous decade, whereas her exports, mainly of primary products, had a long-term tendency to decline.[11]

In April, 1970, this situation compelled Mr. J. H. Mensah, Minister of Finance and Economic Planning in the Government of Dr. K. A. Busia, to reveal in a lecture at the University of Ghana, to the National Union of Students, as follows:

> There has been a tendency to play down or even completely to ignore the impact of international price fluctuation on Ghana's exports, and hence to overlook the contribution of the primitive organization of the world cocoa market on our balance of payments problems. Ghana's terms of trade deteriorated gravely over the period 1960 to 1968. In money terms, this deterioration has accounted for 86 per cent of the total deficits on the Current Account, which the Ghana economy accumulated during the nineteen-sixties. In other words, the external deficit which has been financed by running down reserves, and by getting so heavily into debt overseas, would have been only 14 per cent of what it actually was in the terms of international exchange. The rate at which Ghana can exchange cocoa and timber, for machinery, vehicles and other imports, had deteriorated so sharply against Ghana and in favour of her trading partners.[12]

The view expressed by Mr. Mensah had a profound effect on the economic policies of Dr. Busia's Government. Consequently, in the same period, the Progress Party Administration of Dr. Busia, forwarded to all Western Creditor Countries, a memorandum in which the Government stated *inter alia:*

> The most important single factor affecting the balance of payments in the nineteen-sixties was the adverse movement of the country's commodity terms of trade . . . Had price movements been less adverse to Ghana, the balance of payments deficits would, other things being equal, have been much smaller and the large external debt would not have arisen.[13]

Ghana's long pre-independence economic ties with the West, particularly Britain, were responsible for the country's immediate post-independence large volume of trade with that zone.[14] Long-established commercial contacts with Britain yielded positive dividends. A lot of commercial houses then operating in the country were incorporated in the West with Western suppliers. The long association with the West helped Ghana in terms of technical expertise and finance for the capitalization of her industrial programme. However, the Government's anti-neo-colonialism posture was quite at variance with the spirit of some of the agreements that it was out of necessity signing with some Western multinationals. The personal embarrassments to Nkrumah over some of these agreements increased his aversion for government state-owned company dealings, particularly with multinationals. The West's reluctance to engage at state level in business transactions made the CPP Government to extend its trade with the East, where the converse was the case. Economic transactions with the East were always at governmental level. Further, it was argued by the proponents of trade with all countries that, unlike the West, the East were prepared to enter into bilateral trade agreements that did not involve cash payments for imports, and at a time when Ghana's foreign exchange reserves were running desperately low, this was most welcome.

Impediments to Industrialization

During the colonial period, advanced processing of raw materials and industrial development in the territory were seldom. Manufacture of consumer goods or even the processing of raw materials was virtually absent. Private capital came entirely from abroad. By implication, a substantial part of the profits accruing from production were remitted there i.e. to the metropolitan source of the capital. The Government's share of these profits augmented public capital, and this helped in the development of the infrastructure. Few industrial skills were imparted to Africans, especially those employed in the public services, with the workshops of Public Works Departments, the railways and the electricity corporations. Even in the case of cocoa, which was encouraged as an export crop, a new and particularly dangerous situation developed which tended to render the cocoa industry even more vulnerable to fluctuation in the world prices of cocoa and over which the Ghanaian cocoa producer had no control. Attempts were made to minimize this risk by the use of a marketing device which, by paying the producer somewhat less than the world price for his product when the market price was high, sought to cushion the price paid in the country by drawing on previously accumulated reserves in the years when world prices dipped seriously below previous levels. Indeed, when the cocoa price in the world market soared, the Government still paid the farmer a predetermined fixed price which did not vary with the world market. The use to which the surplus, thus accumulated, was put, was it came to be argued, a mater on which the colonial government could legitimately be attacked. It was invested abroad, but so as not to affront the colonial authorities directly the opposition did not raise this aspect in Parliament. Instead, what the opposition demanded was a higher price for the farmer — which was politically attractive, although going too far, in the then condition of the country, could produce disastrous internal inflation.

In addition, during the period of internal self-government, 1951–1956, and after independence, 1957–1960, the opposition attacked the Government's and the Marketing Board's policies generally. The Nkrumah Government had used the resources of the Board to give low interest loans to farmers. The larger farmers and many of the chiefs had long made profitable business by lending to the poorer farmers. The Government's policy thus split the previously united farmers front. The poorer farmers and those looking to Government development support in order to open up more land for farms aided with the CPP. Wealthy farmers lined up with the chiefs and perhaps to give the 'Committee for Higher Prices' a more ethical look, it was transformed into the 'National Liberation Movement'. The chiefs, however, would not allow this new organization to be called a 'Party'. Party politics were contrary to the tenets of traditional rule. As a price for their support, they proposed the re-division of the country into old provinces which had existed as almost separate entities in the heyday of indirect rule. On 14th September, 1956, amid the firing of muskets and the singing of Asante war songs in Kumasi, Bafour Osei Akoto, Senior Linguist to the Asantehene, ritually slaughtered a sheep in order to inaugurate 'the Movement'.

One fact remained, however, and that was that despite the measures adopted by the colonial officials, the Ghanaian cocoa producer remained in a precarious position. His production remained based entirely upon the European export market. During and immediately after the war, when Britain was in dire need of hard currency, the idea was even mooted to purchase cocoa for sterling at a low controlled price and sell the same for dollars at as high a price as possible. This was done through the Gold Coast Government Board, controlled of course by the colonial authorities, who banked the profits in Britain with an obligation to repay at least part of these at some future date. In fact, in the long run, Ghana benefited immensely from this exercise, but that is another matter.

After the war, there was a plan by which cocoa was both bought and sold at fixed prices below its real market value. While the prices at which the principal export product was bought was strictly controlled, no similar restrictions were put on the price of imports. A piece of cotton print which had sold before the war for twelve shillings, cost ninety shillings by 1945. In addition, an absolute shortage of imports led to black marketing. In terms of purchasing power, the West African pound was well below its pre-war value. Meantime, the colonial government, assured by the chiefs that all was well, did nothing.

The inevitable conclusion to draw from all this is that overseas capital in the then country, even when provided, was still used principally for the development of primary products for export to overseas markets. Investments in the primary producing export sectors and in other necessary services such as in the railways from the supply sources to the seaports was favoured, almost to the exclusion of any conscious development of domestic markets in the country. Commercial and industrial enterprises received scarcely any foreign investment if they were locally based in the territory.

Investment in public utilities was not an exception in a pattern which was dominated by export considerations, since the existence of public utilities was generally necessary before exports could be expanded. Directly in the agriculturally-rich and the mineral-producing regions, and indirectly in public utilities, foreign capital almost invariably facilitated the production of primary products for exports. There was, of course, an increasing demand for imports from overseas; but another factor combined to create a congenial environment for foreign investment in the country; a general atmosphere of optimism — a hangover from the Victorian era — characterized many of the people of the country. There was a confidence in the general imperial aspects of British foreign economic policy — albeit ill-informed. Had not the Colonial Stock Act of 1900 placed the securities of the country and other British colonial governments on the list of 'trustee securities', thereby enabling trust funds to be invested in them?

Independence — and the struggle which preceded it — changed all this. It was, however, the Government of the First Republic which immediately set about removing these impediments by a direct appeal to significant number of international and national agencies who could make available the necessary corp of expertise for rectifying this problem.

The structure that was developed by Kwame Nkrumah's Government to bring about the modern development of Ghana was based on mixed economy. It had a strong egalitarian emphasis on 'full employment, good housing and equal opportunity for education and cultural advancement for all the people up to the highest level possible. Thus, prices of goods were not to be out of step with wages; house rentals were to be within the means of all groups; social welfare services were to be open to all, and educational and cultural amenities were to be available to everyone.[15] Nonetheless, the Government was faced with the fundamental problem of creating a modern economy out of a system essentially based on subsistence farming. Although the economy was increasingly diversified, the basic characteristic remained that of agriculture. The bulk of the primary products were for home consumption to raise nutritional standards, and of introducing commercial crops for the export market. The comparatively small sector of agricultural production which was designed for the export market was based upon the needs of the European markets for raw materials, in return for which Ghana was apparently still expected to import the manufactured goods of the United Kingdom.

The Quest for Economic Independence and Foreign Policy

One major advantage of Ghana's independence was the liberty to dispel the inherited colonial market forces, a prerequisite for Ghana's direct participation in the world trade. Nkrumah phrased this as the liberty "to arrange our national life according to the interests of our people, and along with it, the freedom, in conjunction with other countries, to interfere with the play of forces in the world commodity markets."[16] The Government was aware that fluctuations in primary product prices were some of the insecure variables that made planning difficult for less developed countries like Ghana. This did not, however, invalidate planning which was considered the prime medium by which development was to be undertaken. The Government was determined to emulate the adventurous pioneers who had created the capital basis of industrialization in the advanced countries. The aim in the industrial sphere was to encourage the establishment of plants which could exploit the natural advantages of local resources and cheaper labour and produce essential commodities required either for development or for domestic consumption. During 1961, over sixty new factories were opened, including a distillery, a coconut oil factory, a brewery, a milk-processing plant and a lorry and bicycle assembly plants. In addition, agreements were signed for the establishment of a large modern oil refinery, an iron and steel work, a flour mill, sugar, textile and cement factories.[17] Nkrumah and his Government refused to accept the argument according to which the newly-independent states of Africa were criticized for indulging in 'wasteful' expenditure in duplication industries and ventures which were already 'perfected' by the older industrialized nations of the world, whose products were available at lower cost than those produced by the new nations emerging from colonialism. Nkrumah argues:

> It may be true in some instance that our local products cost more, though by no means all of them, and then only in the initial period. But even if it were substantially the fact, it is not an argument that we can accept. It is precisely because we were, under colonialism, made the dumping ground of other countries' manufactures, and the provider merely of primary materials, that we remained backward, and if we were to refrain from building, for example, a soap factory simply because we might have to raise the price of soap to the community, we should be doing a disservice to the country. . . . Every time we import goods that we could manufacture if all the conditions were available, we are continuing our economic dependence and delaying our industrial growth. It is just these conditions that we are planning to provide, so as to make ourselves independent of the importation of goods and foodstuffs that we can produce ourselves. These are the conditions which will assist to build up our body of knowledge, techniques and skills, to make us more self-confident and self-sufficient, to push towards our economic independence.[18]

On the communication networks in Africa, the Government was aware that one of the factors making contact between African states difficult was the absence of proper and adequate means of communication. There were few, if any, intra-African communication networks. As we have noted, transport networks connected African states with countries overseas rather than with neighbouring African countries during the colonial period. Shipping was not planned to go along the coast of Africa from port to port. At the time of independence, connecting roads across the African continent were non-existent, and even the existing international air route were planned to serve travellers from Europe rather than Africans wishing to go from one part of the

African continent to another. The routings of the European airlines frequently made it necessary for Africans to go, for instance, from North or East to West Africa by way of Europe. The absurdity of this situation, observed by Nkrumah, was too obvious to need emphasis. He, therefore, ignored advice or suggestions that the newly independent nations of Africa should refrain from entering the field of communications. The Government of Ghana knew well that Africa was a considerably larger continent than Europe, and there was more than enough reason for African nations to develop communications between themselves as a means of bringing them closer together and making their common intercourse easier and more fruitful. He announced that difficulties of getting the new Ghanaian Black Star Shipping Line launched had been overcome, and that the Government had even decided to enlarge it with a number of vessels whose keels had been laid in Germany, England, Holland and other European countries. He was convinced that an efficient and adequate Ghanaian shipping fleet was capable of establishing a powerful instrument to break the hold which monopolistic interests had upon Ghanaian trade. The revenue that went into several countries abroad each year in the shipment of Ghanaian cocoa alone, was very high.

> Without shipping of our own, we are placed at the mercy of the foreign shipping lines, who could hold us to ransom, as they have in the past, at any time they wished. With our own shipping we shall become independent of external maritime agencies. We shall bring revenue to our own coffers, and once more make a fine addition to our skills and experience.[19]

Attitude to International Aid

Before independence, the main source of technical assistance for the economy of Ghana (then the Gold Coast) was the Colonial Development and Welfare Fund of Great Britain. From 1945, those funds, as well as private investments, continued to be extended to Ghana in increasing amounts. But after independence, the sources of outside aid available to Ghana multiplied. New European sources opened up, and countries like Germany (West), Holland, Denmark, Scandinavia and some East European countries, became important donors of aid to Ghana. Israel also extended technical assistance to Ghana and to several African countries.

A wide variety of international bodies, such as the World Bank (WB), the United Nations Technical Assistance Fund (UNTAF), the United Nations Development Fund (UNDF), the International Monetary Fund (IMF), etc., made available loans, grants and technical personnel. The Government of Ghana was well aware that aid frequently carried with it invisible political strings. But given its special economic needs, the Government had to accept the aid proffered. Skilful statesmanship was, however, required to steer a course that retained the greatest possible independence and freedom of action. Nkrumah made sure that the Government of Ghana was, in the final analysis, the one to decide whether or not to accept the foreign aid, and how far it should go in co-operating with the donor nation as to its use.

Foreign Investment

In a speech on the Seven-Year Development Plan, Dr. Kwame Nkrumah said,

> We welcome foreign investors in a spirit of partnership. They can earn their profits here, provided they leave us an agreed portion for promoting the welfare and happiness of our people as a whole as against the greedy ambition of the few. From what we get out of this partnership, we hope to be able to expand the health services for our people, to feed and house them well, to give them more and better educational institutions and to see to it that they have a rising standard of living . . . Ghana's economy, particularly at the present stage has room for all the investment capital which is likely to be provided by foreign investors, by the central and local governments and by individual Ghanaians'.[20]

The inflow of foreign capital was necessary in several respects. It provided Ghana with the means of acquiring local resources for domestic investment; it generated foreign exchange for importing necessary materials and equipment directly needed for development programmes and it also allowed the importation of other commodities which were indirectly required as development proceeded. Private capital came entirely from abroad, and its profits were remitted there, while public capital was used to develop the non-productive infrastructure needed by the country including expatriate commercial firms. Without the use of external resources, the pace of development under the First Republic of Ghana would undoubtedly have been slower, a situation which would no doubt adversely affect the standard of living.

The Ghana Government left no one in doubt that it welcomed 'foreign investors in a spirit of partnership', i.e., it required local ownership participation in some industries or investment project. In other words, Ghana was not prepared to allow a hundred per cent foreign ownership where investment was open to foreign investors. In effect, the bulk of Ghanaian industry still remained closed to a hundred per cent foreign ownership. Ghanaian basic policy was to foster joint ventures in which Ghanaian participation was raised to a percentage of equity. The Government always insisted that the operation of all economic enterprises in Ghana conform to the national economic objectives and be subject to the rules and regulations which were made in pursuance of the Government's policies. The Government's experience was that foreign investors were willing to invest in the country so long as the limits within which they worked were fair and clearly defined. It was the Government's intention, therefore, to regularly consult them in order to ensure that co-operation was as full as possible.

Although, in West Africa, Ghana was unique among the newly independent states in terms of joint ventures, many developing countries had adopted that policy earlier; Mexico, for example, required at least fifty-one per cent Mexican ownership in a broad range of new industries. For many years, Mexico pursued a policy of progressive 'Mexicanization' of foreign-owned companies by converting them into joint ventures with local business interests. In 1971, Anaconda, a major United States copper producer, sold fifty-one per cent of its Mexican mining affiliate to Mexicans. In 1965, American Smelting and Refining Company (another United State copper producer) did the same with its Mexican affiliate.[21] The Government of India insisted that the 'majority interest ownership, and effective control of an undertaking should be in Indian hands.' In developing countries where there is no legal requirement for local ownership participation, the host government nonetheless, may 'persuade' foreign investors, in one way or another, to enter into joint ventures with local entrepreneurs.

In fact, Ghana limited the activities of foreign investment to the contribution of 'personal initiative, managerial ability and technical skills towards the development of the country. They will also further the growth of similar initiative, ability, technical skills and habits of saving among Ghanaians.'[22] Investors were essentially expected to assist in the expansion of the economy of the country in line with the general objectives of the Government.

Thus, the Ghana Government continued to look to the outside world for a contribution to development of the country. They expected that more advanced and industrialized states would facilitate Ghanaian trade in primary commodities and manufactured goods so that the bulk of the development plan could be financed out of the country's own resources and earnings. The Government hoped that, where necessary, they would be able to borrow on reasonable terms for essential and productive projects,

> Let me say again that we welcome foreign investors to come and invest in Ghana's progress. We offer them every assistance, substantial material benefits, and the advantages of a coherent long term economic strategy which will give them plenty of scope for planning and development. At the same time, we expect them to re-invest an adequate share of their profits in the further progress, both of Ghana and of themselves.[23]

Capital Accumulation and Exchange Control

A major requirement for Ghana's development was internal accumulation of real capital. The requirement of capital accumulation could not be met simply by creating financial institutions and by monetary expansion as advised by many commentators. A strong financial structure was important in influencing the mobility and allocation of capital and in channelling savings into productive investment. The country's economy after independence had more than enough room for all the investment capital that was available from foreign investors, central and local governments as well as individual citizens. But there were a considerable number of individual Ghanaians who invested their profits abroad and outside the country. Although it was argued that an investor who laid out his money wisely in Ghana was likely to make a larger profit than if he had invested it in a more developed country, a considerable number of Ghanaians still maintained their savings — even after independence — in foreign investments and in properties outside of Ghana.

Exchange control was one of the means adopted by Nkrumah's administration to retain and employ revenue for the economic development of the country. The colonial administration had considerable difficulty in collecting revenue, income and other direct taxes for development. The personnel and the skills required to administer direct taxes in Ghana, were not available. Moreover, it was politically impossible to impose taxes on wealthy individuals who maintained their savings in foreign investments and in properties outside the country. While the Government maintained a liberal trade policy, it was convinced that a system of exchange control offered a ready-made apparatus for the collection of revenue with only slight additional administrative experience. Moreover, exchange control regulations made it difficult to avoid tax whether in the form of a penalty exchange rate or an exchange tax. An exchange tax is a charge levied on transaction in foreign exchange. The Government was determined to make certain that all foreign exchange received by residents of Ghana was actually surrendered to it. It was feared that foreign exchange outside the control of the Government might have been used for illegal purposes. It would then be unavailable for financing imports that the CPP Government considered desirable.

The surrender of foreign exchange to a control authority or a government is usually accomplished in one of two ways. Under one method, all exports may be licensed by a trade control authority or government, and, before the merchandise is allowed to pass through customs, the export licence must be validated by an authorized bank. To obtain a validation of his licence, the exporter is required to inform the bank of the destination of his export shipment as well as the amount of the payment and the currency in which it is to be made. The exporter also agrees to surrender to the bank his receipts of foreign exchange. When the exporter arranges for payment by drawing a bill of exchange against the foreign importer or against a bank, he must either discount the bill with the authorized bank or send it through that bank for collection. Thus, the authorized bank is certain to acquire the foreign exchange when payment is made on the bill.

In the second method, the surrender of foreign exchange receipts is insured by requiring the exporter to secure a sworn declaration from an authorized bank before his exports are allowed to pass customs. In obtaining the declaration, the exporter must inform the bank of the destination of his exports and the amount and kind of payment he expects to receive for them. He also agrees to surrender to the bank his receipts of foreign exchange within a stipulated period. The two methods of effecting the surrender of foreign exchange receipts apply to merchandise exports only. It is more difficult for the control authority or government to capture foreign exchange receipts arising out of exports of services, gifts, and capital movements.

Thus, where there is a strict exchange control, a close watch must be kept over all foreign-owned bank balances in the exchange control country; foreign securities owned by domestic residents must be registered with the control authority or government and sometimes held by an authorized bank, and the international mails must be screened for domestic and foreign bank notes. Failure to surrender foreign exchange in accordance with the regulations of the control authority is made a criminal act. The guilty party could be punished by the imposition of a fine, or, in the case of an exporter, the denial of permission to export in the future. Violations of the exchange control laws of Nazi Germany, for example, carried the death penalty. Nevertheless, evasions of exchange control was widespread and surrender procedures are never one hundred per cent effective.

Under the 1963 Exchange Control Law of Ghana, it was, of course, illegal for Ghanaians to have property abroad without having declared it to the appropriate authorities. However, this aspect of the laws of Ghana was not always understood by the people of Ghana and, therefore, the Government leaned backwards to accommodate this ignorance and take a lenient view of the violations of the law in this respect.

Nkrumah informed Parliament that his Government understood that this aspect of the country's laws was not understood by the population which had just emerged from colonial law. His Government was, therefore, tolerant in their enforcement of it. He assured the people of Ghana that his government had decided 'not to penalize any Ghanaian firm or individual who, within the next three months, repatriates foreign holdings of money to Ghana, or who declares ownership of foreign property.[24] He assured Parliament that a thorough investigation was afoot to discover the extent of holdings of foreign exchange and properties by Ghanaians, and those who 'do not take advantage of this offer but continue to conceal their foreign assets', must expect, after the three months period of grace, to be subjected to the full rigours of the law.

European Common Market and Africa

Although not directly related to foreign aid, an aspect of African economic development may be examined with regard to Ghanaian reaction. The continuing relationship of Africa with the countries of Europe took on a new dimension with the association of the former French territories with the European Economic Community (Common Market). Under the original terms of association of the Treaty of Rome in 1957, the African states became the beneficiaries of the Development Fund for Overseas Countries and Territories (DFOCT). This fund was designed to supplement the aid normally given by the European powers. The two largest contributors were France and Germany (West). The bulk of this aid went to the French territories before 1960.[25]

In fact, the eighteen associates were former colonies of France, Belgium and Italy in Africa. With the coming of independence and the increase in the number of sovereign African states after 1960, the Rome Treaty was replaced by the Convention of Association signed by six European states and the said African states in 1963. Under the Convention, the African states continued to receive favoured treatment by the European signatories while the African signatories were expected to reduce their tariffs against European commodities by a fixed percentage annually, although provision was made for protection of African infant industries. Some African Heads of State objected to such an association of African states with European states because it constituted a form of neo-colonialism and stood in the way of Pan-African Unity. Until the end of his regime, Dr. Kwame Nkrumah set his face firmly against any type of formal link with the European Economic Community. He campaigned against it with a view to dissuading other African no-associates from joining the Community and the associated African countries from continuing their association. Thus, in his address to the All-African Conference on Positive Action and Security in Africa, in April 1960, he declared that he hoped the Congo (Leopoldville) and the other African territories associated with the Community would sever their former links with it on the attainment of their independence.[26] The African signatories maintained, however, that the advantage to be gained from association with the European Community far outweighed any possible threat to African political independence that might be associated with it.

When after independence these countries continued to maintain their links with the Community, Dr. Nkrumah intensified his denunciation of the Community. In July 1961, he warned the Africans associated that the financial gains they were getting through their association with the EEC would be very small when compared with the 'losses they would suffer from perpetuating their colonial status — losses in terms of retarded economic and cultural development, and harm to African unity.[27] He states:

> Our trade, however, is not between ourselves. It is turned towards Europe and embraces us as providers of low-priced primary materials in exchange for the more expensive

finished goods we import. Except where we have associated and formed a common selling policy, we come into a competition that acts to force down the prices we receive to the profit of the overseas buyers. It is because of the effects of this colonial relationship in limiting their economies, that some of the African states have joined the European Common Market.

They have the hope that by this means they will inject new life into their economies. But this is an illusion, because the benefits received by way of aid will do nothing to change the fundamental nature of these economies, and they can, therefore, never thrive in the way that most advanced countries do.[28]

At meetings of African nationalists, Ghana attacked the EEC and the African countries associated with it. There were other reasons for Ghana's opposition to the EEC. To Ghana, the EEC was not merely an attempt to effect the political, military and economic union of Western Europe, but was also an economic means of impeding progress and development of African states. The general implication of the Commonwealth Finance Ministers Conference in Accra in September 1961, was that the Community had 'political, social, economic and even emotional features' which made it unsuitable for African countries. From the Ghanaian point of view, to associate with the EEC under Part IV, Article 131 of the Rome Treaty would be contrary to the Ghanaian foreign policy of non-alignment. This view was reinforced by the attempt of West Germany during the early sixties to use association with the EEC as a weapon against the recognition of East Germany.[29]

The Ghana Government believed that the association with the EEC under Article 131 of the Rome Treaty would hamper the industrialization programme of Ghana. The tariff arrangements of the Community deepened the divisions between the overseas members and the non-members on the African continent. Quota restrictions and depressed prices could be the only outcome. Even united African arrangements for the maintenance of a common selling policy for certain raw materials such as cocoa, could be upheld if one or more of the parties to the arrangements adhered to the European organization. The prices which would be fixed by the European members would apply to all the overseas members supplying the EEC, and the EEC states within the African alliance would have to conform to the fixed prices if they were to enjoy the aid for which they joined it. African loyalty would be split between the European attachment and the African association, and the obligation to the former would nullify fidelity to the African interest.

The fear of losing the warm and informal atmosphere of the Commonwealth, with its historical and familiar links, in an enlarged European Community was an important factor as regards Ghana's opposition to Britain's application for EEC membership between 1961 and January 1963. To prevent this, Mr. Goka, then the Ghanaian Finance Minister, appealed to Britain during the Commonwealth Prime Minister's Conference in London in September 1962, not to sacrifice 'Commonwealth values' to 'new loyalties'.[30] On another occasion, Ghana used stronger words and made powerful arguments in a further attempt to prevent the United Kingdom from joining the Community. Nkrumah argued that if the United Kingdom joined the EEC in a way which might prove disadvantageous to Ghana, then Ghana might have to consider withdrawing from the sterling area 'to safeguard' its trading position. He argued that the United Kingdom, as a senior member of the Commonwealth, should not join the EEC unless she could give assurances that her own treatment of her colonies and ex-colonies would be no less favourable than those which existed at the time; and thirdly, unless she could assure that whatever financial assistance was offered by the European Powers was given unconditionally.[31]

The Government believed that any association with the Community would be detrimental to African Unity. Its view was that any formal link between African countries and the Common Market would at once involve commercial, financial and other discriminatory actions between those associated and those not associated; and that the effect of this would be to preserve the artificial boundaries and other barriers of the colonial era which Ghanaians had committed themselves to eliminating. Furthermore, they believed the link would make it almost impossible to establish an African Common Market, which was very dear to Ghana. However, President Nkrumah's hostility to the EEC was severely criticized. The proponents of Ghanaian connection with the European Common Market based their criticisms against Nkrumah on the grounds that the Associate membership offered to Africa and other Third World countries, would be brought about by means of a unique treaty, and that this treaty would place economic, trade, financial and industrial co-operation between developed countries on contracted basis. And for the first time, the volume of aid to African countries which would have association with the EEC would be set out in a treaty.

The critics argued further that if Ghana refused association with the Common Market by March 1980, she would lose about 80 million cedis worth of food aid from the EEC. Food items were received free under this programme. Under the Lome One Convention proper, about 300 million cedis worth of projects were under construction in Ghana. These included the Weija Irrigation Project, Twifo Oil-Palm Project and the Axim-Mpataba-Elubo Road which would link Accra with Abidjan. Moreover, the EEC money was being used for the study of the Ayensu Irrigation Project.[32]

Nevertheless, Nkrumah called on All African states to unite to build an African Common Market, rather than serve as appendages to the European Common Market.[33]

> An African Common Market, devoted uniquely to African interests, would more efficaciously promote the true requirements of the African states. Such an African

> market pre-supposes a common policy for overseas trade as well as for inter-African trade; and must preserve our right to trade freely anywhere. If it is a good thing for the European buyers to regulate their affairs with their overseas suppliers by combination, then it must be equally good for Africans to do likewise in offering their wares.[34]

The importance of African Common Market presupposing common policy for overseas trade as well as inter-African trade is that Africa as a continent handling billions of dollars of trade cannot indefinitely rely on foreign-owned financial institutions for the handling of its trade. It would not be easy for African countries to establish individual financial institutions in the developed financial countries of the world because it would be difficult to raise the initial large sums of money required to float financial institutions of that nature. Moreover, it would not be easy to command immediately the confidence required of such financial institutions. But as countries or as groups of countries in Africa constituting a common market, and acting in concert with other countries of the world, viable and respectable institutions for financing their own trade could be established. This kind of combination would yield a financial and economic benefit which would provide the greatest stimulus for development.

It is, therefore, clear that despite the fact that the structure of the economy of the African states did not make an African Common Market a very attractive proposition, Ghana believed that such a market would be of immense benefit to the continent of Africa. To Ghana, an African Common Market using a common currency and operating a common external trade policy — as we have noted above — would be in the best interests of the whole of the African people. First, it would eliminate competition among the African states in the bid to sell their primary products in the world market. Under an African common market system, the African would obtain better prices for his products. Furthermore, it would eliminate the difficulties of exchange, and what Nkrumah called 'illegitimate trade dealings' in Africa.[35] An African Common Market would also attract into the continent more foreign investment, and would also promote the growth of great industrial complexes in Africa. Finally, Nkrumah believed that it would turn Africa into an economic giant as powerful as any of the existing economic giants such as the United States, the Soviet Union, West Germany or Britain.

The Ghana Government believed that the African Common Market had to be considered along with the formation of a Union African Government. Indeed, the position of the Government was that the latter could genuinely establish the former. Thus, in May 1963 at the OAU Inaugural Conference at Addis Ababa, where the Government strongly advocated the formation of a Union Government of Africa, it was also proposed that a commission of such a Union Government should work out a continent-wide plan for a unified, or common, economic and industrial programme for Africa.[36] The plan was to contain proposals for the establishment of a common market for Africa, African currency, an African monetary zone, an African Central Bank, and a continental communication system. In accordance with this stand, the Government reiterated its call several times for the establishment of the African Common Market on a Pan-African basis; this could only come about, as stated above, with the establishment of a Continental Union Government. In the opinion of the Ghana Government, half-hearted attempts at economic co-operation would not go much further without a political machinery.[37] The Government's position was supported by Professor Willie Abraham who held that:

> Pan-Africa would be a sort of mutual insurance, economically speaking, for the different regions of Africa. They would practically be guaranteed against total collapse, and that insurance would enable them also to rationalize their agriculture ... Pan African can diversify and plan its agricultural efforts, thus regulating the amount of produce in world markets in order at once to prevent surfeits, and obtain the maximum reward for its export effort.[38]

Nevertheless, the obstacles to the creation of an African Common Market were many. These obstacles included a variety of trade and payments systems in Africa, political and economic ties with other countries, lack of transport facilities and legislative practices. Africa also faced the problem of lacking political will, and non-availability of qualified personnel.[39]

However, if these difficulties to the creation of an African Common Market could be overcome, then the major short-term disadvantage of losing or renouncing the certainty of favourable tariff arrangements and generous inflow of capital as Associate Common Market member, would be virtually inconsequential. A continental African Common Market, with a population approaching 500 million by the end of the century and associated with a potential industrial revolution would be something which could not be dismissed as an insignificant alternative to the Common Market.[40] These factors influenced the policy of the Ghana Government to work for the creation of an African Common Market as opposed to the Associate Status offered by the European Community.

Intra-African Trade and Foreign Policy

Ghana was in favour of an African Common Market because she believed it would boost inner-African trade and enable the continent of Africa to stand on its own economically as other parts of the world. Thus, Ghana took some bilateral steps to improve trade with other African countries, such as the customs abolition agreement with Bukina Faso (then Upper Volta) in June 1961, and the trade and payment agreement with Benin (then Dahomey) in principle on June 25, 1961.[41]

On March 8, 1965, Ghana and Mali entered into a trade agreement according to which Ghana was to export locally manufactured goods such as aluminium, household utensils, pineapple juice and cocoa products to Mali. The latter agree to export to Ghana various food items, including live cattle, fresh meat and dried fish. This trade agreement was followed by subsequent agreements including that of 9th June, 1965, according to which the two countries agreed to exchange various manufactured products and certain raw materials for meat and livestock.[42]

The United Arab Republic and Ghana signed a trade protocol which came into effect in April, 1965 and provided for a trade exchange between the two countries amounting to £3 million sterling to be increased to £4 million by the end of the year. The UAR was to export to Ghana cotton textiles, short-staple cotton and pharmaceuticals in exchange for cocoa, tobacco and other commodities.[43] At the increase to £4 million of this trade agreement, Egyptian experts were despatched to Ghana for helping on farming projects.[44]

By the foregoing example of trade with independent African states on the African continent, the Government of Ghana was gradually laying the foundation to a common political basis for the integration of the Pan-African policies in economic planning. Such a process was to enable the independent African States to move away from the directions which exposed them to the dangers of trade restrictions. Such inner — African trade would also make possible an overall economic planning on a continental basis, and increase the industrial and economic power of Africa. This approach by the Ghana Government was in accordance with the objectives of the economic and social commission of the organization of African Unity,[45] namely, co-operation and co-ordination of economic and social activities of Africa.

NOTES AND REFERENCES

1. For example, Southern Nigeria relied initially on its income from customs and excise; and since Northern Nigeria shared little of this revenue, Lugard was obliged to develop for his own needs the Fulani system of direct taxation. The French colonies, on the other hand, were integrated with their metropolitan country to a high degree. French officials were frequently paid from Paris. France paid higher prices than those ruling on the world market for many exports from her empire; and budget deficits in the colonies were erased with grants from the metropolitan treasury.
2. Bing, Geoffrey 1968. *Reap the Whilwind.* London: 242.
3. Bauer, P. T. 1954. *West African Trade passim.* London (is now a classic on the subject).
4. Nkrumah, Kwame 1964. Speech to Parliament on Launching the Seven-Year Development Plan on Wednesday March 11, 1964.
5. *See* Appendix 3 of this book.
6. *See* Appendix 2 of this book.

7. *See* Appendix 4 of this book.
8. *See* Appendix 5 of this book.
9. Stevens, Chris 1974. In search of the economic kingdom: The development of economic relations between Ghana and the USSR. *The Journal of Development Areas,* October 1974, p.5.
10. Killick, Tony 1978. *Development Economics in Action: A Study of Economic Policies in Ghana.* London:37.
11. Birmingham, W. and Ford, A. G. 1966. *Planning and Growth in Rich and Poor Countries.* London: 179.
12. Memorandum: Radical Economic Research Bureau (Accra) July 24, 1979, p.8.
13. *Ibid.,* p.8.
14. *See* Appendix 4 of this book.
15. Nkrumah, Kwame 1970. *Africa Must Unite.* London: 119.
16. *Ibid.,* p.109.
17. *Ibid.,* p.111.
18. *Ibid.,* p.112.
19. *ibid.,* p.114.
20. Speech by Nkrumah in launching the Seven-Year Development Plan on Wednesday, March 10, 1964, p.6.
21. Anaconda to sell Mexico 51 per cent of its Cananea Mine' New York Times August 28, 1971, p.31.
22. Speech by Nkrumah in Launching the Seven-Year Development Plan, on Wednesday, March 10, 1964, p.6.
23. *Ibid.,* p.9.
24. *Ibid.,* p.7.
25. Article 131 of Part IV of the Rome Treaty, March 25, 1957.
26. *Ghana Today,* April 27, 1960.
27. *National Assembly Debates,* Vol.24, July 4, 1961, Col. 8.
28. Nkrumah 1970, *op. cit.,* p.161.
29. Mazrui, Ali 1963. African attitudes to the European Economic Community. *International Affairs* (London), January, 1963, p.34.
30. Minutes of the Commonwealth Prime Minister's Conference (1962).
31. Kwame Nkrumah, Speech at State Opening of Parliament (Accra) July 4, 1961, p.7.
32. *The Ghanaian Times,* 'Ghana and the EEC', June 27, 1980, p.4.
33. *National Assembly Debate,* Vol.24, July 4, 1961, Col. 9.
34. Nkrumah 1970, *op. cit.,* p.162.
35. *Ibid.,* p.163.
36. Supplement, *Ghana Today,* June 5, 1963.
37. OAU —Verbatim Report of the Assembly of Heads of State and Government Accra, October 21–26, 1965, p.8.
38. Abraham, W. E. 1967. *The Mind of Africa,* pp. 196–197.
39. *Africa Research Bulletin,* 1964. Vol. 1, p.27.
40. Birmingham, W. 1966. The economic development of Ghana. In *Planning and Growth in Rich and Poor Countries* (ed. W. Birmingham and A. C. Ford), pp. 193. London.
41. *National Assembly Debate,* Vol.24, July 4, 1961, Col. 7.
42. *Le Moniteur Africaine du Commerce et de l'industrie,* Bamako, June 26, 1965 (The African Monitor of Commerce and Industry).
43. *Africa Research Bulletin,* Vol. 3, No. April 3, 1965, p.265.
44. *Ghanaian Times,* January 11, 1966.
45. Article 20(1) OAU Charter, 1963.

Chapter 6

GHANA AND WORLD PEACE

From its first day of independence, Ghana was concerned with world peace as a priority for its own development and for humanity's survival of the nuclear age. The balance of nuclear forces between the Soviet Union and the Warsaw Powers, on the one hand, and the United States of America and the NATO Powers, on the other hand, reached such a stage that the only avenue open to mankind was peaceful co-existence. The alternative to this would be chaos, destruction and annihilation.

Thus, the basic aims of Ghanaian foreign policy under the First Republic were: (1) African independence, and (2) the maintenance of world peace through positive neutrality and non-alignment.

Ghana and the United Nations

That, it was the cardinal foreign policy to co-operate with the third world in general and independent African states in particular after an era of foreign domination, and in the light of their immediate task of nation-building, is hardly surprising. Living in constant fear of neo-colonialism and the possible loss of their independence to super powers, and involved in economic development that often necessitated the adoption of rigid internal and external policies, the Government and people of Ghana naturally treasured their new international status and independence. Thus, Ministers and Envoys of the First Republic of Ghana lost no opportunity to make their voices heard clearly and unequivocally on issues of war and peace. An important forum where Ghana could forcefully articulate her peace mission was the United Nations Organization and its specialized agencies which can be "counted on effectively to promote international peace".

> At the moment there exists only the United Nations Organization which offers, with all its defects, the possibility of working towards a peaceful world.[1]

In order to obtain appropriate representation in these international organizations, Ghana and other members of the Third World insisted upon the principle of equality. It is true that the United Nations has always recognized the principle of equitable geographical distribution and of geographical representation on its non plenary organization. However, the emergence of so many new Afro-Asian independent states within a short time caused practical problems with regard to the implementation of this principle.

In state practice the idea of equality among states has given rise to a plethora of generalities including the United Nations Charter's "sovereign equality" as periodically expressed in the General Assembly Resolutions. For example, the appendix to Assembly Resolution 375 (IV) in 1949 admitted that "every state has the right to equality in law with every other state". Equally, Article 6 of the Charter of the Organization of American States (OAS) stipulated that "states are jurisdically equal, enjoy equal rights and equal capacity to exercise these rights, and have equal duties. The rights of each state depend not upon its power to ensure the exercise thereof, but upon the mere fact of its existence as a person under international law". International courts are inclined to accept the other version of legal equality; namely, that states are equally protected in the rights they possess and are committed to equal fulfilment of their obligations. They hold this view in the full and often regretful awareness that there may be great differences between equality in law and in fact, and they do so by referring to the principle of equality rather than by interpreting it. Their reluctance to commit themselves to any precise meaning may be due to the fact that nobody doubts the validity of the principle of legal equality, and that its content changes with the needs and spirit of the times. It changes, in particular, with the role power is played at any given moment in the development of the international system, which, in turn, depends largely upon the changing instruments of power. Smaller, weaker states are not any more willing than large powerful ones to abandon these principles. For occasionally, it provides them with a measure of protection and even some political influence, for instance, when votes become relevant. Much of the time, however, the principles of legal equality is little more than a fig leaf to cover naked power between states.

Equality, before the law, means little when the law itself results from an unequal distribution of power and, therefore, tends to confirm rather than ameliorate inequalities in the international community.

Nkrumah believed that, in emphasizing that formal equality before the law without substantive equality is not justice. That all men are created equal needs social implementation to ensure that they do not become unequal after creation. In referring to the general trend toward greater discrepancies between states especially in terms of political and economic unevenness of development, Nkrumah declared that the international community had an obligation to rectify these unfavourable trends and create conditions under which nations, in general, and the newly-independent states of Africa, in particular, could enjoy political freedom as well as economic and social well-being. As long as the governments of the new nations remained in the hands of colonial administrators, their economies would be set to a pattern determined by interests, not of the indigenous inhabitants but of the national beneficiaries of the metropolitan powers.[2] This theme became the leitmotif of Ghanaian diplomats at international conferences and organizations.

Their strategy, in this regard was to offset the effects of past inequalities and forestall future instances of disparity. At the United Nations, they identified themselves with projects and discussions which aimed at protecting the right of states to sovereign equality and to full and equal participation in the life of the community of nations. They participated in the creation and modification of rules of the international community; and protected jealously the entitlement of the newly-independent states to every assistance by the international community especially in the economic field. Ghana's spokesmen maintained that the economic aspects of the principle of sate sovereignty could not be separated from its political and legal aspects, for economic independence was one of the main guarantees of the effective and complete exercises of state sovereignty. The Government interpreted state sovereignty, among other things, as entitling all states to participate in multilateral conferences and international organizations, or in the solution of international problems.

Criticism of Ghana's tactics to exploit the well established international principle of legal equality for results normally obtainable by political means were at once dismissed by the fact that the political methods used previously to make occasional exceptions to the principle of equality (e.g. in the Security Council or the International Monetary Fund) had not been encouraging for the under-developed states of the Third World. Most of the important exceptions were not made to make weaker, poorer, or under-developed states more equal. They were made to legitimize the inequality bred and sustained by the superior position of the more powerful states. There are extremely few instances (of which perhaps the General Assembly of the United Nations may be one) in which more powerful states have sacrificed something to bring the principle of legal equality more in line with factual equality. A Soviet international writer has gone on record[3] in his rationalization of the special privileges of the big powers in the Security Council as a protection of the smaller powers against the "imperialist powers", in which, of course, he does not include the Soviet Union. The principles of socialist internationalism mean, according to him, that the principles of equality and non-interference "include, for example, not only the mutual obligations not to violate each other's respective rights. . . ." Professor Tunkin's observation appears inadequate in the sense that the power of veto, which is exercised by the five Permanent Powers of the Security Council including the Soviet Union, is an instrument of inequality. The veto undermines the whole concept of equality as accepted by the United Nations completely theoretical. Consequently, far from being an instrument of protection and stability for the smaller states, as suggested by Professor Tunkin, the privilege of the veto possessed by the five Permanent Members of the Security Council is suspect among the smaller states in the United Nations. To redress the situation, it might be appropriate to substitute the principles of two-thirds majority for the veto. This will give the Security Council real authority and dignity in the discharge of its responsibilities.

The Government of Ghana was concerned that the stock-piling of atomic weapons for mass destruction, and the failure of the Super Powers to agree on the cessation of nuclear testing on the globe were the greatest source of danger to mankind. Ghana was convinced that, the conduct of the Super Powers was dictated by political expediency of the moment and it was in no way related to the welfare of mankind as a whole. People in Africa had a vested interest in peace and the salvation of the world from a nuclear destruction. Nkrumah observed:

> there must be an enduring peace to enable us to consolidate our hard-won freedom and to reconstruct socially and economically, the possessions of our heritage devastated by colonialism.[4]

The Ghana Government was conscious of Africa's vulnerability to potential nuclear warfare. No present or future African leader should, therefore, ever gamble on the assumption that the continent of Africa would remain neutral throughout a major nuclear conflict.

> We do not threaten anyone and we renounce the foul weapons that threaten the very existence of life on this planet. Rather we put our trust in the awakening conscience of mankind which rejects this primitive barbarism, and believe firmly in positive action.[5]

The Government found this awakening conscience of mankind in the activities of the United Nations Organization. Ghana believed that the UN was capable of contributing greatly to the maintenance of peace. The world Organization offered the opportunity for the statesmen of competing nations to work out compromises, or for statesmen of neutral countries to act as moderators and conciliators. International agreements as well as the decisions or suggestions of the Security Council, may provide face-saving devices to enable would-be nuclear aggressors to yield gracefully. As time went by the working out of international compromises could become habitual, as in fact it has become in the dealings between Super Powers.

The UN has been particularly important in casting a shadow of global disapproval on two phenomena which had been regarded as legitimate for hundreds of years — war and colonial subjugation. On colonialism itself, the Organization's record could be pronounced as successful. It became the main forum of censure against colonial policies. The colonial powers first resisted these challenges from the world body. Ghana's foreign policy was strictly opposed to colonialism and neo-colonialism wherever it raised its head. Ghanaian anti-colonial activities in the UN were well known. Sometimes the UN was implicated directly, as could be discerned in the case of the argument between Indonesia and the Dutch over the control of West Irian.

The World without the Bomb — Peace Plan of Ghana

It was the policy of the First Republic of Ghana to secure the preservation of Africa as a non-nuclear zone. In the circumstances, Ghana went all out to obtain the co-operation of other independent African States towards the achievement of that objective. African and other non-aligned countries demonstrated that, on the issue of nuclear pollution of the planet, they were concerned regardless of who was exploding the device. On 1st September, 1961, the Soviet Union resumed nuclear tests at a time which coincided with the Belgrade Conference of the twenty-five non-aligned states. Russia's fifty megaton explosion was described by Kwame Nkrumah at Belgrade as "A shock to me". Nehru asserted, "I regret it deeply". And Nasser of Egypt called the Russian tests "another cause for deep regret".[6] The existence of the nuclear stalemate reduced the credibility of nuclear diplomacy. This type of diplomacy involves the traditional diplomatic instrument of persuasion using some elements of force as basis of negotiation with other nations. By the summer of 1962, the Third World remained obstinately a third world. Nationalism had proved stronger than Marxism; and communism had encountered one frustration after another in Lagos, in the Congo, in Latin America. The changes of this period placed Nkrumah's desire for a breathing-spell in a new frame. Ghana, therefore, organized an eight day ban-the-bomb conference in Accra, rallying international opinion behind a commitment to control this particular way of polluting the world's atmosphere.

This Conference, which symbolized Ghana's non-alignment, increased Ghana's prestige.[7] The Conference was attended by more than 130 people from about 40 countries; the participants included atomic experts, journalists, eminent scholars, politicians and university professors. The Conference called for a positive campaign by all peoples of the world to awaken the conscience of the world and to secure the banning of atomic tests. It also advocated the destruction of all weapons of mass slaughter and the reduction of conventional armament. The menace of nuclear warfare could be removed if every individual was convinced that he had a personal duty to prevent the destruction of mankind in an atomic holocaust. What the world lacked was a code of international morality which could measure up to its technological progress — a new public morality which would teach that what was wrong in private life was equally wrong in international relations. The advocates of disarmament, of the abolition of nuclear weapons and the ending of the cold war, should not only stir the conscience of the world, but should also teach a new doctrine of hope.

In his address to the Conference, President Nkrumah reminded all persons and organizations engaged in the struggle for the abolition of nuclear weapons that their task would be just as difficult and arduous as those who struggled against slavery. The latter had to overcome ingrained habits of mind; by courage and perseverance, the abolitionists of slavery won their day. He believed an almost exact parallel existed with the issue of war and peace in our own time. He cautioned the Conference that, in the struggle to rid the world from the threat of nuclear warfare, vehement protest was an essential ingredient in arousing man's conscience. In discussing the Government's four classes of tension above, he continued that "the very fact that peace is today threatened by tensions created by the Second World War underlines the point that world war cannot solve our difficulties. The victors in a world war, by their very victory, create problems which contain the seeds of a new world war. Lessons of the last two great wars teach, above all else, the uselessness of world war in the conditions of the present world. Indeed, the consequences of these last two wars have been the very opposite of what either victor or vanquished anticipated when they entered the conflict." The Conference accepted the recommendations of its commissions, endorsed the concept of a nuclear-free Africa and welcomed the initiative taken by the people of Africa. It proposed the creation of nuclear-free zones in other areas, such as South-East Asia, Middle East and Latin America, along with a number of other recommendations. The Ghana Government offered facilities for the establishment of a secretariat in Accra to implement the recommendations of the Conference and plan future conferences.

These were, indeed, the days of high Ghanaian sensitivity to issues concerned with nuclear ecological abuse. Nkrumah and de Gaulle clashed on the issue of nuclear pollution of the world atmosphere. For de Gaulle, the leader of a big power, the acquisition of nuclear status was inseparable from a resurgence of France as a world power. He ordered the entire technocratic and scientific manpower of the French Community to address themselves to the great ambition of France to enter the nuclear age. He looked forward to Europe, self reliant in defence. But for the time being, he wanted to ensure that France was not a mere puppet in American nuclear strategy. He refused to allow American nuclear weapons to be stockpiled in France except on condition that they should be under French control. Concurrently, he pursued the policy of developing a separate nuclear capability for France. By contrast, Ghana's vision of the world included a commitment to the elimination of nuclear weaponry. Ghana was consistent in this policy as expressed in the positions taken on the eve of independence with regard to the Bandung Conference of Afro-Asian countries in 1955. Ghana was capable of censuring both the West and the East on matters connected with nuclear power. She capitalized on the considerable world-wide unease about the implications of nuclear tests, particularly in view of the dangers of the fall-out and spread of radiation. The most direct clash between Nkrumah's vision and de Gaulle's came over the issue of French nuclear tests in the Sahara. De Gaulle had steadily pushed on with his ambition to create a French nuclear capability, and 1960 was the year when France's entry into the nuclear age could at last be tested by the explosion of a nuclear device in the Sahara. Ghana became the platform from where international protests could be launched against the French experiment. In December, 1959, and January, 1960, an international team of representatives from Africa, Britain, the United States of America, and even from France, attempted to enter the testing site at Reggan in the Sahara. Their starting point was Ghana, under the leadership of the Reverend Michael Scott. However, the team was prevented from proceeding beyond the borders of Burkina Faso (then Upper Volta). They were confronted by armed guards under the direction and control of the French authorities. The guards not only ensured that the team could not get past them, but also prevented them from reaching the testing site from any other direction. They confiscated the vehicles and equipment of the group. Nkrumah was indignant about this event. Just as he maintained that Ghana's freedom was incomplete as long as any part of Africa was still under foreign rule, so he held that Ghana's safety was not secure as long as any part of Africa was used for nuclear purposes. Nuclear fall-out was no respector of boundaries. Neither was Ghana's plan for Pan-Africanism. These two tenets caused an outcry of protest as de Gaulle pursued his plan to take France into the nuclear age. Ghana called for positive action against French nuclear tests — a mass non-violent protest movement crowding into the testing area. Nkrumah viewed the situation as follows:

> It would not matter if not a single person ever reached the site, for the effect of hundreds of people from every corner of Africa and from outside it crossing the artificial barriers that divide Africa, risking imprisonment and arrest would be a protest that the people of France, with the exception of the de Gaulle government ... could not ignore. Let us remember that the poisonous fall-out need not and never will respect the arbitrary and artificial divisions forged by colonialism across our beloved continent.*

As soon as the French tests took place, the Ghana Government froze French economic assets within Ghana 'until the extent of the damage to the life and health of her people become known'. And when France exploded a second bomb, Nkrumah recalled the Ghanaian Ambassador to France. In April, 1960, he called a special conference in Accra to discuss "positive action and security in Africa". He called the conference in consultation with other African states. Many of the French-speaking states in Africa were lukewarm if not hostile. But for once, Nigeria and Ghana were eye to eye on the gravity of de Gaulle's nuclear experiments in the Sahara. Ghana saw the utilization of the Sahara for nuclear tests as a violation of the sanctity of Africa's soil, and as a manifestation of the arrogance of a big power.

Positive Neutrality or Non-Violent Positive Action

Why the Ghana Government opted for positive neutralism in foreign policy will now receive our attention. The term neutrality is derived from the Latin word, *neuter*. It may be defined, in political context, as the attitude of impartiality adopted in international affairs by third states towards belligerents and recognized by belligerents, which attitude creates rights and duties between the third or impartial states and the belligerents. Persuaded by the nature of the cold war which existed between the Soviet Union and the United States by the time of the First Republic of Ghana, third states including Ghana considered the two Super Powers as belligerents. Whether or not Ghana adopted an attitude of impartiality in that cold war was entirely a question of international politics. It was not possible for a state, in the modern world, to secure its safety by withdrawing from international affairs and refusing to take a stand on issues which affected peace and war. This would lead to a policy of negative neutralism which is tantamount to the fatal notion that war between the Super Powers would bring destruction only to the Super Powers. In other words, whether remaining neutral or not, in the absence of a treaty stipulating otherwise, is entirely a question of policy. However, all states which did not expressly declare the contrary by word or action were supposed to be neutral, and bound by the rights and duties arising from neutrality. Since neutrality was an attitude of impartiality, it excluded such assistance and succour to one of the cold war parties as it was detrimental to the other, and further, such injuries to the one as benefit to the other. The independent African states that accepted the status of neutrality in the cold war were expected to prevent either of the parties in the conflict from making use of their neutral territories, and of their resources, for military and naval purposes as long as the cold war existed and menaced mankind. Further, neutrals must, by all means, falling short of becoming involved in the conflict or of abandoning their attitude of impartiality, prevent each party to the conflict from interfering with their legitimate intercourse with the other party to the conflict through commerce and the like, because a party to the conflict could be expected passively to suffer vital damage resulting to themselves from the violation by their enemy of a rule, which, while it operated directly in favour of neutrals, indirectly operated in their favour as well.

Under the impact of the cold war, the most important basis of non-alignment was abstention from permanent alignment with either bloc. Such abstention was primarily defined in pure military terms, as is seen from the criteria for membership of the movement spelt out at the first conference of the "non-aligned" countries in Belgrade in 1961. Burton summarized the criteria as follows:

> That a state belonged to neither the Communist nor the Western military bloc, that it had no bilateral military arrangement with a bloc country, that it either had no foreign military base on its soil or was opposed to those which were there; that it supported liberation and independence movements; and that it pursued an independent policy based on peaceful co-existence.⁹

Thus, non-alignment does not and did not require politico-ideological or social structural differentiation from the two blocs. Internally "non-aligned countries" were free to pursue the kind of policies they wished. They had a right to claim non-intervention in their own affairs from countries inside as well as outside the movement. To what extent non-alignment is practical or applicable when there is strong similarity or congruence with aspects of the political and social systems of any one bloc member is another matter.

However, the development of areas of tacit agreement between the two big powers, including a degree of agreement on "spheres of influence", to a considerable extent changed the environment in which the "non-aligned" found themselves. Whereas earlier under the impact of bloc expansion drives from both camps, they were openly courted by the two camps, later they found themselves less "attractive" in the old way. Courting still went on, but it took other and more subtle forms, considerably blurring the borderline between what was alignment and what was not. The complexities created by the development of the international system in the 1960s went even further. As President Nyerere pointed out in his important speech in to the Dar es Salaam preparatory meeting, the blocs were no longer monolithic as they had been; military relationships alone were no longer a sufficient indicator of alignment; and there was much more interaction across the "curtains". Moreover, the system had changed from a predominantly bipolar to an increasingly tripolar structure, with China emerging as the third Super Power. But Nyerere's interpretation of the concept of non-alignment is not so different from the one which emerged from the 1961 Belgrade Conference and also from the 1964 Cairo Conference.

> It is a statement by a particular country that it will determine its policies for itself according to its own judgement about its needs and the merits of the case. It is thus a refusal to be party to any permanent diplomatic or military identification with the Great Powers; it is a refusal to take part in any alliances or to allow any military bases by the Great Powers of the world.¹⁰

The newly independent African states in general and Ghana, in particular, felt at the time under review that their independence of big power politics placed them in a position to exert pressure on the big powers to ease international tension, to settle their disputes peacefully, and to bring about an atmosphere of international justice. Of course, it was not a case of non-alignment making international peace and justice possible — it was more a case of the fear of war making non-alignment possible. But Ali A. Mazrui pointed out that, "although indulgence toward the weak may be the child of a mutual fear between the strong, that indulgence may already be changing into genuine respect. This respect would in turn make non-alignment more effective as a moderating influence on the big powers".[11]

The complexities created by the development of the international system sooner than expected compelled the non-aligned movement, at least in theory, to develop certain more or less specific roles which member states were expected to play. In order to avoid being manipulated by the powerful blocs, the non-aligned had to unite to defend their position. This is "positive non-alignment" or "positive neutrality". Already at the time of the Belgrade Conference in 1961, Nehru, Sukarno, Nassar and Nkrumah had made it clear that they reserved to themselves the right of positive involvement in any dispute. They would even go to the extent of taking sides in the dispute, but, as a matter of principle, they declared themselves against any permanent or long-term involvement on the side of one or the other of the parties to the cold war. Thus, Nkrumah's principle of positive neutrality or positive non-alignment was pragmatic. It was essentially a foreign policy of pragmatic non-committal. By eschewing commitment to super power bloc alliances in the early post-independence period, and by rejecting the notion of automatic alignment in the cold war, Ghana gave herself time to think. Non-alignment as a foreign policy was well suited to that period of experimentation. It enabled Ghana to try out relations with countries in both the Western and the Eastern blocs, and to find out for Ghana what the rest of the world was like. The opening of embassies is expensive, and if the policy of non-alignment had not required contact with both sides it might have seemed wasteful for Ghana to establish so many embassies.

Many Ghanaians did not feel that relationship with the East was necessarily inimical to their interests. They were aware that, the Soviet Union was a consistent champion of African nationalism in the United Nations and other international bodies in the early part of their independence. The Eastern bloc had also been giving substantial assistance to development programmes in most newly-independent African states. But as the conflict within the socialist camp became more pronounced, more and more Africans began to suspect that the motivation for Eastern interest in their welfare was a desire on the part of one or another group of the socialist bloc to use African nationalism as a tool for its own political interests. The consequence was a reaffirmation of non-alignment in the fullest sense of the term.

Non-alignment then, for Ghana and most African states after independence, did not mean lack of commitment or interest in events taking place in the world arena as suggested above by Nehru. Rather its real significance lay in the reservation by Ghana and the newly-independent African states of the right to make a policy choice on any particular international issue on the basis of the merits of the issue without ideological commitment to one side or the other. As it was aptly explained by Nkrumah:

> Positive neutralism and non-alignment" does not mean keeping aloof of burning international issues. On the contrary, it means a positive stand based on our own convictions completely uninfluenced by any of the power blocs. We believe that we could help to bridge the unfortunate and undesirable gap between the East and West blocs by not aligning ourselves to either side. We hold the view that as to the issues between them, neither bloc can claim to be permanently right or permanently wrong. As such, it will not be in the interest of international understanding and unity for us and the other independent states of Africa to involve ourselves in the disputes of the power blocs by taking sides. We should be free to take our stand without previously committing ourselves to any bloc on any matters which affect the peace, progress, and, indeed, the destiny of Africa. We believe that it would be suicidal to involve ourselves in the disputes of the great powers by taking sides. We will continue to cultivate and maintain friendly relations with all countries, and to be enemy to none.[12]

The crucial question then, of course, was whether non-alignment was feasible or desirable in the cold war situation that existed. In view of the economic and political pressures from both East and West to which Ghana and the newly-independent states of Africa were subjected because of their physical and economic weakness, there was considerable difficulty in making non-alignment work. Thus, the foreign minister of one African state, Doudou Thiam of Senegal, argued that such criteria as were required to make non-alignment work in the difficult circumstances were unrealistic and indeed, in the long-range interests of the African states entirely untenable.[13] This is not to deny the right of the non-aligned states to preserve their independence against outside forces and reject foreign interference in their internal affairs. The criteria for a policy of non-alignment laid down at the Cairo Conference of Independent States in 1960, provided that non-aligned states should have an independent policy, should not be committed by military agreement to any of the major power blocs and should be prepared to support any liberation movement especially in Africa. Indeed, the pattern formulated by Nehru set the stage for a period of diplomatic maturation. It allowed the developing states a period of trial and error in a variety of relationships. Of course, there was always the risk of having one's fingers burnt. It has been suggested that India's faith in Chinese good intentions, stemming in part from the policy of non-alignment, resulted in India's unreadiness to meet the Chinese invasion in 1962. If this interpretation were true, it could still be argued that burning one's fingers as a result of direct trial and error was part of the process of growing up in a world of diplomacy.

However, as the foreign minister of Senegal argued, the criteria of non-alignment are unrealistic. According to him, it may well be that it would be in the interest of an African state such as Senegal or Ivory Coast, to belong to a particular military bloc; the simple avoidance of such commitment in order to remain "non-aligned" would not, in the opinion of Doudou Thiam,[14] necessarily constitute an independent foreign policy. Instead, he asserted that the operative question to be asked in the formation of foreign policy is "Are foreign policy decisions arrived at freely without external coercion?" If the government is satisfied that a decision which results in the alignment of an African state with one or another bloc was freely taken in the national interest and provided the commitment is made in such a way that if these interests change, the commitment may be ended, then the state may be said to be pursuing a policy of non-alignment. The major criterion of non-alignment should be freedom of choice of commitment and not avoidance of commitments. In this connection, Doudou Thiam raises the question "Are the United States or Great Britain or France any less independent because they have committed themselves to the NATO alliance?".[15]

What emerges strongly from these analyses is that, in the 1960s, the non-aligned movement increasingly shifted its emphasis from cold war issues to issues of economic confrontation between the developing and developed world. The Non-aligned Movement in the days when it was dominated by Nehru of India, Nassar of Egypt, Nkrumah of Ghana, and Tito of Yugoslavia, was a Movement eager to avoid entanglement in the ideological and military issues which divided the West from the Communist world. Non-alignment was, at the least, a refusal to be tied to a military alliance with one of the major powers. But gradually non-alignment developed into a broader concept of autonomy and the right to experiment, a reaffirmation by newly-independent states that they were entitled to an independent say in world affairs. Issues of trade and the use of world resources were still substantially outside the preserve of the Non-aligned Movement as such. The first major economic factor to concern the Movement was the issue of foreign aid. A doctrine of balanced benefaction emerged, by which it was assumed that relative independence for poor countries lay in diversifying their benefactors. A country which was heavily dependent on the United States was less autonomous than a country which managed to get foreign aid both from the United States and the Soviet Union. Non-alignment became an exercise in balanced dependency — an assumption that a client with more than one patron was freer than a uni-patronized dependent. However, by the time the non-aligned countries were assembling in Algiers in the summer of 1963, a major shift had taken place. Non-alignment was now concerned with more than just keeping out of military alliances or getting the most in foreign aid from Western and Communist countries. The concerns of the Non-aligned Movement now embraced not only issues which were previously handled only by the United Nations Conference on Trade and

Development (UNCTD) but also the need to use the natural resources of the poor countries as political and economic weapons against the affluent sectors of the world.

The conclusion is that, the policy of non-alignment in the period under review operated to the advantage of Ghana in the sense that, the country for the most part was able to avoid clear identification with either camp (East or West), although the tendency was to have more extensive relations with the West through the United Kingdom because of established former colonial trade and cultural channels and because more aid was forthcoming from the Commonwealth. Notwithstanding, it is doubtful, whether the present success of non-alignment as a policy among developing states has been a result of decisions taken by the non-aligned themselves. In reality, non-alignment has been possible not only for the non-aligned African states but for the other states of the developing world in large part because the two major opposing super and great power military blocs, NATO and Warsaw Pact had reached balance of military power and had to seek support of the smaller nations, all of which possess votes in the United Nations in their quest for political advantages. Despite denials to the contrary, the foreign aid policies of the major powers have inevitably been used in some degree to win the support of the smaller states. Their decision on which power to support on a particular issue before the United Nations has become a matter of interest to the Great Powers. Had the Great Powers not cancelled out each other's force by nuclear balance, it would, in fact, have been largely irrelevant whether the African states, or, indeed, any of the states of the Non-aligned Movement, had decided to adopt a policy of non-alignment.

It is equally true that, were the United States of America and the Soviet Union to arrive at an overall agreement reducing mutual antagonisms, the policy of non-alignment would have been much less meaningful under the circumstances, although Communist China (People of Republic China) had become a third centre of power. With the Chinese condemnation of the Soviet position as being a deviation from true socialism (hegemony), the non-aligned African countries that were publicly committed to pursuing a socialist pattern were placed in the position of having to choose between the two socialist groups. Ideological commitment became, in effect, an obstacle to non-alignment, and many African non-aligned states subsequently took refuge in African socialism regarded by both sides of the socialist group as a deviation from the correct theoretical position as interpreted either by the Chinese or by the Soviets. In the beginning, non-alignment was real, though limited, when the distinction between the two big power blocs was made reasonably simple. Although the usefulness of non-alignment declined in the face of tripolar world power centres, non-alignment proved to be of genuine assistance to the African states since under its umbrella it was possible for the latter to insist on an all-

African solution to African problems, and from time to time prevent either the East or West from exploiting to their own advantage what was essentially an intra-African dispute.

Cuban Missile Crisis

Major crises during the period 1957–1966 ranged from Hungary and Suez in 1956 to the US incident in May, 1960 through to the Cuban Crisis in 1962. The Cuban missile crisis, started when Nikita Kruschev, the Soviet Prime Minister, and President John Kennedy of the United States of America confronted each other in 1962 on Cuba and the world hovered on the brink of nuclear war. With astute statesmanship, Krsuchev capitulated to John F. Kennedy's challenge, promised to remove the missiles from Cuba, moved towards establishing a hot line between Washington and Moscow, and began at least to respect the canon of international diplomacy. On his part, Dr. Fidel Castro, Prime Minister of Cuba, agreed to halt the construction of the missile bases which the Soviet Union had planned to establish.

In his message to the Soviet Prime Minister, President Nkrumah said;

> I congratulate you most sincerely on your bold decision to dismantle equipment in Cuba regarded by the United States of America as offensive. This I consider to be a most welcome first step towards the progressive elimination of ground-to-ground missile bases in the territories of non-nuclear powers and vital contribution to world peace. I believe that the urgent and essential cause of general and complete disarmament could be most powerfully assisted by a planned and co-ordinated dismantlement of ground-to-ground missile sites established outside the territories of the powers providing and controlling such weapons . . . the whole world has been gravely disturbed by the course of events leading to the United States blockade of Cuba. This action has brought the world to the brink of disaster. A world war involving the use of nuclear weapons cannot be contemplated. I, therefore, appeal to you to exercise the greatest restraint in this most critical situation. Mankind would, indeed, be grateful to you if you can turn this moment of distress to the path of peace."[16]

In reply to President Kennedy's communication on the matter, Dr. Nkrumah stated as follows:

> I have received your urgent message from your Charge d'Affaires on the Cuban situation and would like to thank you for informing me of the action you have taken in the matter. I also have been gravely concerned at the turn which events have taken and have instructed my representative at the United Nations to support all the efforts being made to secure a peaceful solution. Mankind may not survive another world war. I, therefore, appeal to you personally in the name of humanity to see to it that this calamity is averted. The world will be greatly beholden to you if you can save it at this critical moment. . . . The world welcomes your timely and important reassurance that the United States will not invade Cuba. This action of yours is, in my view, a definite step towards world peace".[17]

He also congratulated Dr. Fidel Castro, Prime Minister of Cuba, on his readiness to agree to halt the construction of missiles in Cuba in the light of the statements made by President Kennedy and Mr. Kruschev.

In his capacity as a Head of member state of the Commonwealth, Dr. Nkrumah addressed similar message to Mr. Harold Macmillan, Prime Minister of the United Kingdom as follows:

> I thank you for your personal message concerning the United States-Cuba situation. The risk of another world war is so great that I consider it extremely urgent for us to exert ourselves to secure that the parties concerned seek a peaceful solution without delay. To this end, I have instructed my representative at the United Nations to support all the efforts now being made to secure a peaceful solution. I, therefore, ask you, Mr. Prime Minister, to appeal to Mr. Kennedy to see to it that no precipitous action is taken by the United States Government that might involve the world in another war. Can't you use your good offices to get Mr. Kennedy and Mr. Kruschev to meet on this critical issue? I have addressed messages to Mr. Kennedy and Kruschev on the situation.[18]

In the Security Council of the United Nations Organization, Ghana and the United Arab Republic tabled a joint resolution calling on America, Russia and Cuba to refrain from any action which might aggravate the crisis. The Ghana Government proposed that the United States should give a written guarantee that it had no intention of interfering in Cuba's internal affairs or taking offensive military action against her, directly or indirectly. It was suggested that Cuba should give a similar undertaking not to interfere in the internal affairs of any other country or taking military action against any other country in the western hemisphere.

In some respects, the Cuban missile crisis was the beginning of the *embougeoisement* of the Soviet Union. The successors of Kruschev, though in some cases descended from origins as humble as Kruschev's, were by now bureaucrats rather than rural folk in style and temperament. In the first thoroughgoing revision of Marxist doctrine and practice since Lenin's time, Nikita Kruschev reflected a dynamic capacity for surprising initiatives which he had brought into the role of the socialist super power. In the course of a dramatic speech before the United Nations General Assembly on 23rd September, 1960, he launched what Christian Herter, then United States Secretary of State, described as "an all-out attack, a real declaration of war" against the office of Secretary General and, by implication, against the United Nations itself. He proposed a de facto abolition of the Office of Secretary General and its replacement by a "collective" executive; that is, one official each from the Western, the Communist, and the non-aligned camps. Each of these officials would possess a veto over the actions of the collective executive. In practice, the Office of the Secretary General would be rendered as ineffectual as the Security Council in dealing vigorously and promptly with threats to international peace and security. Kruschev's *troika* scheme thus indicated a deep ambivalence in the official Communist mind about the consequences of a non-aligned-controlled United Nations. On the one hand, an important prong of Kruschev's strategy of peaceful co-existence was aimed at winning and holding the friendship of non-aligned countries, regarded by the Kremlin ideologists as "fraternal partners" and as members of the "peace zone". Moscow's increasingly bitter dispute with China put a greater premium than ever upon maintaining cordial relations with nations throughout the Afro-Asian-Arab world. On the other hand, communist policy makers may have been even more surprised than Western officials to discover that their non-aligned "proteges" were unwilling to serve as diplomatic sycophants. In the Congo and elsewhere, the diplomatic independence espoused by the non-aligned world applied to Communist as much as to Western efforts to control and direct the destiny of newly-independent nations and to reduce them to unwilling participants in disputes were of secondary concern to them; the troika idea seemed an ingenious way both of flattering the non-aligned countries (by offering them more formal participation in the United Nations decision-making) and of negating their influence (by subjecting their role to a Communist veto) in the Organization which they had come to rely upon heavily for achieving their diplomatic objectives.

But the Soviet Union under the administration of the successors of Kruschev relinquished some of the dynamic capacity for surprising initiatives which Kruschev had brought into the role of that country. The Soviet Union became internationally more predictable, more stable, more congenial to the science of forecasting the country's own moves. The *caste factor* had once again intruded to influence issues of predictability. Kennedy was killed in 1963. Kruschev was replaced in 1964. In many ways, the brief period of congruence between Kennedy and Kruschev in their interpretation of the Third World constituted the heyday of Africa's centrality in world politics.

By contrast, under Nixon and Brezhnev, the total ideological tension that had been rampant in the days of Kennedy and Kruschev receded. The clarion called from both the White House and the Kremlin was the call of détente. But although the Super Powers agreed, it was not an agreement that augured well for Africa in general and Ghana in particular. Compared with their predecessors, both invested Africa with less importance than it had enjoyed in the early 1960s. On balance, however, it could still be said that the Soviet Union was a decade ahead of the United States in understanding some of the forces at work on the continent of Africa. The Soviet Union spent far less money on Africa than the United States did, and there was less Soviet commitment to the alleviation of African problems of poverty and underdevelopment. Yet in spite of this, Russia displayed in the developing world as a whole more awareness of future trends. Detente between the

Soviet Union and the United States reduced even the competitive motive behind the favours bestowed by the Super Powers on the smaller countries of the world.

Financing the United Nations Emergency Force

One of the most important events in the General Assembly of the United Nations was the nineteenth session debate of that Assembly with respect to the expense on the Organization's peace keeping operations. This debate was chaired by the Representative of Ghana, Alex Quaison-Sackey, as President of the Assembly in this period.[19] For the first time in history, a force of this type was necessary to work toward the peaceful settlement of dangerous international disputes. Efforts to achieve this goal had been made many times in the past: always they had failed.

The total expense incurred by the UNEF is not inconsequential. Subject to certain reimbursement procedures, salaries and equipment of individual soldiers are paid and supplied by their national governments, but UNEF itself is responsible for providing a substantial amount of gear, transport, fuel, currency, and food. A daily overseas allowance for all members of the Force is financed by the United Nations. But a number of contributing states made known to the Secretary General their desire for reimbursement of the "extra costs" which they were obliged to incur in making troops available for service with the Force. Some governments considered that resolutions 1089 of the Assembly had altered the earlier rule that a nation providing a unit would be responsible for all costs of equipment and salaries; they believed that these costs should now be shouldered by the Organization. The issue became increasingly complicated with regard to the United Nations activities in the Congo.[20]

Expenses for the Congo Force, like those for the United Nations Emergency Force, were treated as a special account and assessed on the basis of the scale for regular expenses of the Organization, with reductions granted to states with a limited capacity to pay. Unlike the resolutions on UNEF'S finances, however, the Assembly on December 20, explicitly stated that the 1960 costs of the Congo Force were to "constitute expenses of the Organization within the meaning of Article 17" and that assessments for the ad hoc account were to create "binding legal obligations". This principle of obligation was thus definitely established, and an amount to finance the Congo operations was authorized by the Assembly for 1960.[21] Debates on the best way to finance UN forces in field operations preceded the 19th session of the Assembly which took a comprehensive view of the whole question of peace-keeping operations in all their aspects.

Solution Based on Consensus

After a lengthy debate, the Assembly during the nineteenth session came to a decision by a general consensus. Of course they had voted on December 21, 1961, to ask the International Court of Justice for an advisory opinion:

> Do the expenditures authorized in General Assembly resolutions . . . relating to the United Nations operations in the Congo . . . and the expenditures authorized in General Assembly resolutions . . . relating to the Operations of the United Nations Emergency Force . . . constitute expenses of the Organization within the meaning of Article 17, paragraph 2, of the Charter of the United Nations?

Article 17 gives the Assembly authority to consider and approve the United Nations budget and declares that the expenses of the Organization shall be borne by the member states as apportioned by the General Assembly. In submitting the question to the Court, many members hoped, no doubt, for an affirmative answer which might encourage delinquent states to pay their UNEF and UNOC assessments. They desired a ruling that the expenses of the current peace-keeping operations were apportionable by the Assembly. On July 21, 1962, the International Court of Justice rendered its opinion. The expenses occasioned by the United Nations operations in the Middle East and in the Congo were "expenses of the Organization" within the meaning of Article 17, paragraph 2 of the Charter of the United Nations.[21] The Court rejected the idea that Article 17 referred only to "regular" or "administrative" budgetary items. Each year, from 1947 to 1959, "unforeseen and extraordinary expenses" arising in connection with the maintenance of peace and security had been included in the annual budget. This had been done without dissenting votes, except for the years 1952, 1954 and 1963 when controversial expenditures for the United Nations Korean war decorations were included. Paragraph 2 of Article 17 used the term "expenses" to mean all expenses rather than such items as might be called "regular expenses".

> The Court does not perceive any basis for challenging the legality of the settled practice of including such expenses as these in the budgetary amounts which the General Assembly apportions among the Members in accordance with the authority which is given to it by Article 17, paragraph 2.[22]

The fiscal situation was a complex one, and the attitudes of member states toward UNEF's finances involved a number of intricate questions. To explain their conduct, some states, although admitting their legal responsibility to respond to assessments, voiced dissatisfaction with what they considered an inequitable system of financing. For example, Cuba was of the opinion that, while all members should contribute to the cost of maintaining the Force, it was not fair to distribute those costs according to the proportion which members contribute to the budget of the Organization. A more satisfactory system of financing should be found that would not over-burden the budgets of countries in the process of economic development. The Force could, for example, be financed by means of a special emergency fund for the maintenance of peace, which could be raised by voluntary contributions.[23]

Such an attitude poses a practical problem: the legal obligation to contribute is not denied, but the execution of the obligation may remain incomplete. Those states which reserved their rights or *a fortiori*, and those which refused to finance the UNEF in principle, created by their behaviour on the contrary the complex problem of legal obligation. In the case of governments which reserved their rights, contribution depended on their acceptance of the particular Assembly resolution not on its financial rules. They regarded each distinct resolution solely as a recommendation and not as a legal obligation. Finally, those states which refused in principle to contribute to the UNEF's costs adopted the most radical attitude on the matter bringing into sharp focus the entire question of obligation. They declared firmly that this obligation was non-existent and they were not bound by the Assembly's resolutions on the matter.

This position was essentially the viewpoint of the Soviet Union and the Soviet-associated states.[24] Stressing always that the "aggressors" must pay and that the United Nations could only raise and use armed forces under Chapter VII, Article II (the end of paragraph 2) and Article 43 of the Charter (i.e. in accordance with a decision of the Council), the USSR stood directly opposed to the United States on this question. For the United States, Article 17 was clear: "The expenses of the Organization shall be borne by the members as apportioned by the General Assembly". No distinction is made in this article, according to the American view, between the various categories of expenses, be they administrative or operational; expenses for peace and security operations, such as UNEF and UNOC are "expenses of the Organization" and "shall be borne by the Members".[25] Furthermore, the US insisted that the sanction of Article 19 was automatic, not needing the approval of two-thirds vote before it became operative; the procedure adopted in the previous session, where the Assembly President had stated that a defaulting Haiti would lose the right to vote, indicated that the invocation of Article 19 was automatic. With the exception of France, Western Powers including Britain, Holland supported the US position. But the USSR-associated states were of the opinion that if this interpretation of Article 17 were accepted, there would be a contradiction between that Article and Article 10, which provided that "the General Assembly . . . may (only) make recommendations". If the General Assembly can in no event make decisions binding upon member states, it might be asked how it can compel these states to bear the cost of applying a recommendation. Such a contradiction, the Soviets maintained, created a difficulty which could be solved only by interpreting Article 17 in relation to all the Articles of the Charter and to its fundamental principles, that is, by taking it to refer solely to the ordinary or administrative expenses of the Organization and to no others.[26] Furthermore, Russia denied that she would not leave the UN if deprived of voting rights, and asserted that the US was trying to break up the Organization. Russia and her Allies maintained that the issue was an "important question" within the meaning of Article 8, and required a two-third majority.

However, the Arab League Council came out in support of Russia. India asserted that the invocation of Article 19 was not automatic. France continued to argue that payments for peace-keeping operations were optional; she had refused to pay for UNOC with the argument that a sovereign state could be "taxed" against her will for an operation of which she did not approve. The weakness of the French argument was that she ignored the fact that by becoming a party to the Charter, she was covenanted in advance to delegate certain financial powers to the Assembly. The position of the French-speaking African states, the Arabs, and some defaulting Latin Americans also made it unclear whether Article 19 could pass the test of two-thirds majority.

The foregoing examination reveals that the peace initiative of Ghana in the nineteenth session of the General Assembly of the United Nations succeeded in the sense that not only the International Court of Justice but the Secretary-General and a great majority of member governments believed that all member states were legally obliged to participate in the financing of the Emergency Force. The United Nations Emergency Force, they contended, was fundamentally the responsibility of the entire Organization and, as a result, the expenses of the Special Account must be considered as coming under Article 17 of the Charter. Previously, the creation of a number of other subsidiary bodies was also cause for protest by certain states, e.g. during the time of the creation of the Trusteeship Council, which moreover is a principal organ of the United Nations, the Soviet Union protested its constitution on the basis of the agreements adopted by the Assembly under Article 79.[27] The Committee on Non-Self-Governing Territories, established by the Assembly on December 14, 1946 had been considered illegal by the administering powers. The Soviet bloc did not recognize the Assembly's Interim Committee, established in 1948, or the Collective Measures Committee, created on November 3, 1950. Nevertheless, no defaults on budgetary payments, no rejection of legal obligation to contribute, were ever made by these states because of their objection to the body in question. The finances of all other United Nations organs have, however, been integrated into the regular budget of the Organization.

Certainly the 19th session of the United Nations General Assembly achieved a considerable degree of consensus in its deliberations. For example, during this session which adjourned for two periods, it was necessary to take certain decisions, such as the filling of a vacancy on the Security Council and the authorization of the establishment of UNCTAD as a UN body. Alex Quaison-Sackey, the Assembly President avoided the need for a vote — and hence a showdown — on these questions by inviting all delegates to his own office to indicate their preference to him privately. This device enabled him to pronounce that decisions had been reached by acclamation or universal agreement, without a vote.[28]

Representation at the United Nations of the Peoples Republic of China

Distinct from the problem of admitting new members to the United Nations is that of determining the representation of states that are already members. As far as effective participation in the Organization is concerned, the decision of an organ denying the right of a delegation to represent a state may have the same practical consequences as a decision not to admit a state to membership. In the case of China, for example, the Chinese people who inhabit mainland China and who are under the effective control of the Peking Government were for approximately thirty years effectively debarred from any participation through their representatives in the United Nations as if the Republic of China was not already a member, unless of course the real interests of the Chinese people on the mainland were represented by the National Government in Taiwan.

When there are — as it happened in this case — rival authorities which claim to be the government of a state, there is bound to arise the necessity of making a choice to represent the country involved. This problem arose at the time of the San Francisco Conference when Poland, though a signatory to the Declaration by the United Nations of January 1, 1942, was not invited to participate in the San Francisco Conference called to draft the Charter because the sponsoring governments were unable to agree on the government which they would recognize as representing Poland. The Chinese problem was highlighted in November 1949, when in a cablegram to the President of the General Assembly, the Foreign Minister of the Government of the People's Republic of China (i.e., the Communist regime from the mainland) stated that his Government repudiated the legal status of the delegation headed by T. F. Tsian, appointed by the National Government seated on Taiwan, and held that it could not represent China and had no right to speak on behalf of the Chinese People in the United Nations. This stand was repeated in a cablegram to the governments of members of the Security Council on January 8, 1950. It was supported by the Soviet Union and when the Council refused to accept it, the Soviet representative withdrew.[29] At this time, the great majority of members of the United Nations, including the United States, France, and the Latin

American republics, recognized the National Government as the Government of China. The Communist members, the United Kingdom, and India were among the members that recognized the Peking Government.[30]

After the initial consideration of the question by the Security Council, the Secretary General requested the preparation of a confidential memorandum on legal aspects of the problem and subsequently made it public. This memorandum argued that the question of representation had been improperly linked with the question of recognition by member governments. It argued that the proper principles could be derived, however, from Article 4 of the Charter relating to membership. The obligations of membership could be fulfilled only by governments which in fact possessed the power to do so. When a revolutionary government presented itself as representing a state, in rivalry to an existing government, the question at issue should be: which of these two governments in fact is in a position to employ the resources and direct the people of the state in fulfilment of the obligations of membership? In essence, this required an inquiry as to whether the new government exercised effective authority within the territory of the state and was habitually obeyed by the bulk of the population. If these facts were established, United Nations organs should accord to the new government the right of representation even though individual members might refuse to accord recognition for political reasons which they considered valid.

Upon admission to the United Nations, the Republic of China took a position similar to that of the Secretary General's memorandum, that for purposes of representation in the United Nations, that government should be recognized which was in effective control of all, or nearly all, the state's territory and which had the allegiance of the overwhelming majority of the population. A majority of the General Assembly then, under the leadership of the United States, evaded the main issue and recommended that the question of representation, wherever it arose, was to be considered "In the light of the Purposes and Principles of the Charter and the circumstances of each case", that the question should first be considered by the General Assembly and that the attitude adopted by the Assembly should be taken into account by other organs and by the specialized agencies.

For a considerable period, there was no change in the position of the United Nations organs and the specialized agencies on the question of Chinese representation. Two factors were important in producing this result: (1) the attitude of the United States Government, reflecting the bitter opposition to the Communist regime in China which pervaded the country and Congress; and (2) the military intervention of the People's Republic of China in Korea which strengthened United States opposition as well as the opposition of other member states of the United Nations to the seating of the representatives of the People's Republic of China. By the time Ghana joined the United Nations, it was reasonably clear that the opposition of the United States was all that stood in the way of the reversal of the Assembly's position. In his address to the United Nations General Assembly on September 23, 1960, Nkrumah made it clear that the Government of Ghana had always supported the view that the People's Republic of China should be admitted to the United Nations so that the representation of China in the Assembly will be more realistic and more effective and useful. He declared:

> We believe that the People's Republic of China, representing some six hundred and thirty million people, and with the vast economic, scientific, and technological resources that she is rapidly developing, can have a useful and constructive contribution to make towards the maintenance of peace and the advancement of civilization in our time. The issue of whether China should be admitted to the United Nations or not should, I submit, be determined on the basis of principle rather than of expediency. It would be unfortunate to underestimate the force of the socialist revolution that has taken place in China, and Ghana is convinced anyhow that any attempt to impose a form of tactical isolation on the People's Republic of China is bound to prove abortive in the long run.[31]

Opposition to the admission of the representatives of the Peking Government meant that the government which was in effective control of China, representing a substantial part of the world's population and an important sector of the world's surface, was refused from participation in the work of the United Nations, even though the Republic of China was a member. But since the opposition was largely based on domestic political attitudes in the United States, the lessening of it was not likely to have resulted from arguments such as had been adduced in the Secretary General's memorandum or in the Assembly debates. It had to come from change in opinion in the United States. Thus, the People's Republic of China was prevented from participation in UN activities throughout the period under review.

It is clear, therefore, that throughout the period under review, the People's Republic of China was effectively debarred from participation and representation in the activities of the United Nations. Of the 59 members of the UN, only 16 recognized the Peking regime while 43 recognized Taiwan.

The Nationalist Government of Taiwan was prepared to withdraw from the United Nations either when Peking had been recognized by a majority of the member Governments or when the United States had recognized Communist China. But America was not prepared at that time to recognize Communist China. According to Secretary of State, Dean C. Acheson "the whole Peking regime was an improvization that scarcely knew what it was doing or what repercussions its acts had internationally."[32] Besides, the Chinese had seized American properties and closed down its consular offices. Even though five members of the Security Council — the USSR, Norway, Yugoslavia, the United Kingdom and India — had recognized Peking, the number was not sufficient to gain American acquiescence in the recognition of the Peking regime.

The question of who should represent China became one of procedure, being in the final analysis a matter of credentials. The central difficulty arose from the unfortunate linkage of the matter of representation with that of recognition by member governments. According to a memorandum prepared by Dr. Ivan Kerno and Dr. A.H. Feller for Secretary General of the UN, Trygve Lie, membership of a state in the United Nations and representation of a state in its organs were clearly determined by collective acts: membership, by vote of the General Assembly on the recommendation of the Security Council: representation, by vote of each competent organ on the credentials of the purported representatives.[33]

Recognition, however, of a state or government was an individual act and should not be made a condition for representation in the United Nations. For example, Yemen and Burma were admitted by a unanimous vote of the General Assembly when they had been recognized by only a handful of member states. And in the Security Council, a number of members voting for admission of Transjordan and Nepal had not recognized them as states.

The Chinese case was, however, unique in the history of the United Nations — it was the first time two rival governments competed for recognition and admission into the United Nations. What principle was to be followed in choosing between the two rivals? The only principle that was just could be derived from Article 4 of the UN Charter requiring that an applicant be able and willing to carry out the obligations for membership. The question then was which of these two rival governments in fact was in a position to carry out the obligations of membership. An inquiry into which of the two governments exercised effective authority within the territory of the state and was habitually obeyed by the bulk of the population would reveal that the People's Republic of China had the right to represent China, even though individual members of the Organization refused to accord it recognition for reasons of their national policies. The People's Republic of China occupied a clearly defined territory, had a permanent population, a government which was habitually obeyed and was able to enter into relations with foreign countries.

But the Security Council members refused to budge from their earlier positions. France who could have welcomed Peking had been angered by the latter's support of the Viet Minh Movement which opposed the French-supported government in Indo-China. And the Americans too were adamant in their refusal to admit China to the UN body.

The UN had to be the meeting place between the East and West to bring about world peace and prevent war breaking out between the two power blocs. Isolating the People's Republic of China was politically, economically and morally untenable because (1) it meant excluding nearly one billion people of the world from decision-making affecting the destiny of the world; (2) it meant economic ruin for a vast number of the people of the world as they would have no legitimate trading partners and (3) it rendered the people morally as lepers, to be shunned by the rest of the world.

Isolating China was to make the Chinese people insecure. This insecurity could lead to foreign adventures, as in the case of Korea, and thus disturb the peace of the world. And when there is war, the African continent which needs peace to develop would suffer most.

This is why Dr. Nkrumah urged China's inclusion in the UN and why he also sent delegations upon delegations to China to urge them to co-operate with the US to bring about peace and stability in the world and the importance of taking their seat in the UN, joining the Security Council and opening diplomatic relations with America. This policy of Ghana was justified a decade later by Henry Kissinger, the American Secretary of State (1973–1977) flying all over to China to persuade the Chinese to take their rightful place in the United Nations Organization and for America to normalize relations with China.

NOTES AND REFERENCES

1. Nkrumah, Kwame 1970. *Africa Must Unite*. London: 194.
2. *Ibid.*, pp. 50–51.
3. Tunkin, C.I. 1974. *Theory of International Law*. Cambridge: Mass., pp. 348–440.
4. Obeng, S. 1972. *Selected Speeches of Dr. Kwame Nkrumah*. The Advance Press, p.71.
5. Speech of Welcome at conference to discuss Positive Action and Security in Africa, Accra, April 7, 1960. Obeng, p.52.
6. Homer, Jack A. 1963. "Nonalignment and a Testban agreement: The role of the nonaligned states". *Journal of Arms Control*, October 1, 1963, pp. 636–46.
7. An international preparatory committee assisted in its preparations. The Committee included Ritchie Calder (as he then was), Frank Boaten, a senior and outstanding diplomatist, was seconded to administer the office. Over a hundred delegates, amongst them some of the most distinguished members of the International Community — along with ten experts, including Dr. Oskar Lange and James Walsworth — *see* Thompson, Scot 1969. Ghana Foreign Policy 1957–1966, pp.196–197; *see* also Accra Assembly, "Selections from the papers of the Accra Assembly", Accra, 1962.
8. Nkrumah, Kwame 1973. *I Speak of Freedom: A Statement of African Ideology*. London: p.215.
9. Burton, J. W. 1960. Non-Alignment, London: 119.
10. H. Hveem and P. Willetts in Horizon of African Diplomacy (ed. Y. Tandom). Nairobi:3.
11. Mazrui, Ali 1968. *On Heroes and Uhuru-Worship*. London:203.
12. Speech at Tenth Anniversary of the CPP: Accra, January 8, 1960; Obeng, 1972, pp. 6–7.
13. Thiam, Doudou 1965. *The Foreign Policy of African States, passim*. New York.
14. *Ibid.*
15. *Ghana Today*, Vol.6 No.18, November 6, 1962, p.1. London: Ghana High Commission.
16. *Ibid.*

17. *Ibid.*
18. Official Records of the General Assembly. 1964 Session 1329th Meeting A/PV, November 15, 1964 – December 1, 1964.
19. Stoesinger, John C. 1961. Financing the United Nations. *International Conciliation* No.535 (November, 1961), pp. 23–32.
20. 52 nations voted for the resolution. 32 abstained, the Soviet Union and France voted against the measure, and 9 delegates were absent from the meeting. France declared that the Assembly could only request a Member State to pay its assessments, not require it to do so, for recognition of a requirement would transform the UN into a "world government". The USSR delegates denounced the bond issue as "illegal" and reaffirmed their government's intention not to recognize any opinion rendered by the ICJ. See the *New York Times*, December 21, 1961.
21. The Court rendered its opinion by a majority of nine votes to five. International Court of Justice, Certain Expenses of the United Nations (Article 17, paragraph 2 of the Charter) Advisory Opinion of July, 1962: *ICJ Reports, 1962*.
22. *Ibid.*
23. General Assembly *Official Records, Special Political Committee, 13th Session, 98th Meeting,* October 31, 1958, pp. 56–57.
24. They have stated their position in Plenary Sessions on November 26, 1956; November 22, 1957; November 14, 1958, in the Fifth Committee on December 3, 1956; December 6, 1957; December 2, 1958; December 3, 1958; November 29, 1959; December 16, 1960; and October 5–December 22, 1961; and in the Special Political Committee on October 29, 1958 and October 31, 1958.
25. See for example, remarks by Albert F. Bender in the Fifth Committee UN *Doc. A/C.5/ SR.895,* December 8, 1961, p.10.
26. Discussion by the delegate from Bulgaria, *ibid.,* pp. 10–11.
27. Goodrich and Hambro 1960. *The Charter of the United Nations,* pp. 437–440.
28. *The World Today,* The Royal Institute of International Affairs, Vol.21, No.1, January 1965, p.94; *Official Records of the General Assembly,* 19th Session, 1331st Meeting — September 1, 1965, p.9.
29. *Security Council Official Report Fifth Year,* 459th Meeting (January 10, 1950).
30. The Nationalist Government was recognized by 43 Members and the Communist Government by 16.
31. Obeng 1972, p.180.
32. Lie Trygve 1964. *In the Cause of Peace.* New York: 255.
33. *Ibid.,* p.256.

Chapter 7

MAJOR ISSUES OF WORLD POLITICS

We shall now discuss the involvement of Ghana in international peace initiatives outside the activities in the corridors of the United Nations Organization.

The Problem of Refugees and Freedom Fighters

Certain principles relating to the question of asylum were included in the United Nations Convention on the Status of Refugees of 1951. The notion of a right of asylum and the changing views on it have played an important part in the practices of immigration and extradition (as well as raising problems where fugitives seek protection in foreign legations or on foreign vessels). This has been the subject of much debate. Three articles of the 1951 Convention are of particular interest in connection with the right of asylum: Articles 31 (Refugees Unlawfully in the Country of Refuge); 32 (Expulsion); and 33(Prohibition of Expulsion or Return [Refoulement]).

Article 31(1) provides that:

> The Contracting States shall not impose penalties, on account of his illegal entry or presence, on a refugee who enters or who is present in their territory without authorization, and who presents himself without delay to the authorities and shows good cause for his illegal entry or presence.

> The Contracting States shall not apply to such refugees restrictions of movement other than those which are necessary and such restrictions shall only be applied until his status in the country is regularized or he obtains admission into another country. The Contracting States shall allow such refugee a reasonable period and all the necessary facilities to obtain admission into another country'.

It is in keeping with the notion of asylum to exempt from penalties a refugee who is escaping from persecution but who, after entering the country clandestinely, presents himself as soon as possible to the authorities of the country of asylum and shows good reason for his unauthorized entry. In the discussion of Article 31, it was admitted that the right of asylum was implicit in the Convention as a whole even if it was not explicitly proclaimed in it, since the very existence of refugees depend on the right. The exemption of refugees from penalties imposed on them for illegal entry into a country was a corollary of the right of asylum.[1]

Article 33 provides that:

> No Contracting State shall expel or return[2] a refugee in any manner whatsoever to the frontiers of territories where his life or freedom would be threatened on account of his race, religion, nationality or political opinion.

It was realized that the 'turning back of a refugee to the frontiers of a country where his life or freedom would be threatened on account of his race, religion, nationality or political opinion' would be tantamount to delivering him into the hands of his persecutors. For the purpose of bringing this Article (33) into line with the definition of Article 1 of the Convention, it is necessary to add that a refugee should not be expelled or returned for reasons of his membership of a particular social group. The Refugee Committee finally observed that in the text, reference was made 'not only to the country of origin, but also to other countries where the life of freedom of the refugees would be threatened for the reasons mentioned'.

No sooner had Ghana become independent and admitted to the United Nations Organization than she adopted the principles of the World Organization to protect and defend the human rights of repressed people of colonial territories in general and of freedom fighters in particular. As it is in the older democracies, e.g., the United Kingdom and France, the principle that the individual had rights which his government must respect was fully accepted and enforced by Ghana; and a body of domestic law had been developed by constitutional enactment, by legislation, and by decisions of the courts and the administrative agencies for giving effect to this principle. However, although the sympathy and support for oppressed peoples and liberation movements were firmly established in the Charter or Constitution of the Organization of African Unity[3], the manner of implementing the recommendations of that organization with regard to the problem remained erratic and controversial. It is now well known that the Ghana foreign policy of humanitarian support and protection of refugees and freedom fighters in accordance with the Constitution of OAU turned out to be not only misunderstood but totally unacceptable to neighbouring states. This problem became important in Nigeria-Ghana relations after some leaders of the then Action Group went into exile in 1962. Ikoku was appointed a lecturer at the Winneba Ideological Institute and was on the editorial staff of *The Spark*; Adebanjo was employed by Radio Ghana, and James Aluko worked with the Ghana Trade Union Congress. However, political refugees in Ghana were not limited to Nigerians. There were also Djibo Bakary, Leader of the Sawaba Party of Niger; W. Massaga and Ernest Ouandie of the Union des Populations du Cameroon; Amadou E. Diarra, leader of the Volta Workers and Peasants Party; Fattoh Elleingand Ehanaud Biley and Kadio Attie of the Sanwi National Movement, a group of political refugees from Ivory Coast, and many others. The Nigerians of Action Group persuasion, Ivory Coast citizens of the Sanwi National Movement, the Cameroonians who were members of the UPC, the members of the Sawaba Party of Niger, and the opposition members from Upper Volta and Togo were all alleged to be undergoing training in Ghana. It was rumoured that these people were trained to return to their respective countries e.g., Nigeria, Niger, Upper Volta, Togo and Cameroon to overthrow their governments. In 1965, the issue threatened to disrupt the OAU Conference to be held in Ghana. Paradoxically, it was to the Nigerian Government that the Ghana Government turned for help to arrest the situation. The then Ghanaian Foreign Minister, Alex Quaison-Sackey, was despatched with a message to the Nigerian Prime Minister, Sir Abubakar Tafawa Balewa, promising to guarantee the safety of all Heads of State during the Accra Conference, and urging the Nigerian Prime Minister to use his influence to dissuade those Heads of State who planned to boycott the conference.[4] Balewa cabled Diallo Telli, the Secretary General of the OAU requesting an extraordinary session of the Council of Ministers of the OAU to discuss the proposed boycott in Lagos in May 1965. Balewa's proposal received the required two-third majority and the conference began in Lagos on 19 June, 1965. Opening the Conference, Balewa said that the meeting was not competent to change the Accra venue of the OAU Conference since that was a decision reached by the Heads of State. He said the duty of the Conference was to take note of the threat of boycott and to recommend measures which would satisfy all concerned. He ended by urging the delegates that "you are assembled here not to destroy but to build while examining the problems before you in a frank and responsible manner, you should be extremely careful to do so in a spirit of brotherhood and with due respect to the sovereign equality of all states".[5]

The delegates of Ivory Coast, Upper Volta and Niger repeated their charge, that Ghana was a base of subversion against their countries. The Ghanaian delegation, led by Kojo Botsio, denied these charges and said that the refugees had express orders to refrain from subversion. "We categorically deny that there are any camps in Ghana against any independent African state".[6] The French-speaking states told the conference that they wanted Ghana to return wanted refugees to their countries of origin. In accordance with her determination to follow the requirements of the UN Convention on the Status of Refugees, Ghana refused to return these refugees to their home countries. The Ghana Government was not only guided by the UN Convention on refugees, it was also sympathetic to the plight of the refugees on purely humanitarian grounds. Ghana, however, compromised in sending refugees away from Accra for the duration of the conference.

While the OAU Conference in Accra considered the issue and condemned the use of refugees by member states of the organization to subvert one another. President Tubman of Liberia opposed any convention that would prevent African states from granting political asylum to refugees because international law allowed it in the sense that it is the prerogative of every state "to allow a persecuted alien to enter and to remain on its territory under its protection and thereby to grant an asylum to him".[7] Tubman pointed out that the OAU Charter already contained provisions making subversion of one state by another state

illegal and suggested that nothing more should be done about it. The Nigerian Prime Minister made a distinction between "wanted political offenders and refugees, and called on the Conference to issue a declaration that the former category should not be given political asylum."[8] Even Sekou Toure called on the Conference to agree on measures that would prevent the establishment of political exiles from independent African states in other African states. Once the conference was over, the Ghana Government allowed the refugees to come back to Accra. The reason for this step was that the Government considered it as part of its international obligation to protect the liberty of refugees.

Ghana and the Soviet Union

The first duty of Ghana after independence was to exercise the right of legation according to which every independent state has a right in international law to send and receive diplomatic envoys. This is to say that the duty of every state of the international community is to listen in ordinary circumstances to a message from another state brought by a diplomatic envoy, a practice consistent with its very membership of the family of nations; and this duty corresponds to the right of every member to send such envoys. Ghana was no exception to this rule.

In the exercise of this power of legation, Ghana adopted an open policy which accommodated almost every country in accordance with her resources. The rapid growth of Ghana's foreign service during the 1957–1966 period was indicative of the general trend in the expansion of the post-independence activities in the newly-independent territories. The establishment of diplomatic relations between Ghana and the Soviet Union came at a rather late date, i.e., Ghana had become independent in March 1957, but it was not until April 1959 that agreement was reached between Ghana and the Soviet Union to establish diplomatic relations. Early in 1960, the Ghana Government sent an advance party to Moscow to open Ghana's embassy. The Soviet objective in Ghana was twofold: (1) to spread the political and economic influence of the Soviet Union in consonance with its status as a world power; and (2) to counter the ideological and political challenge of the People's Republic of China. On the other hand, Ghana's aim of establishing diplomatic relations with the Soviet Union was to create a diplomatic posture whereby, at appropriate moments, Ghana would be well placed to understand East-West relations and be able, together with other non-aligned states, to interpose between East and West; and to create the necessary atmosphere for trade with the Soviet Union. As Geoffrey Bing observed:

> The immediate result of this diplomatic exchange was the sale of considerable quantities

of Ghanaian cocoa beans to the Soviet Union and its allies. In fact at the time of the Ghanaian independence the Soviet Union was not only a small cocoa importer. But by 1964, it had become the third largest in the world, next after the United States and West Germany; and the cocoa bought was largely Ghanaian. This trade, was by way of long-term contracts on bilateral basis.[9]

Ghana's economy is a mono-crop and the Government heavily depended upon cocoa for at least 60 per cent of its foreign exchange earnings.

Ghana cherished her independence and diplomatic freedom; her relationship with the Soviet Union, and the other East European countries was not an expression of ideological solidarity with the Warsaw pact countries in disregard of the ideological cleavage between the Soviet Union and China. Thus, at the invitation of the Ghana Government, Premier Chou-En-Lai of China paid a visit to Accra in 1962 and 1964. Nkrumah observed that:

Ghana is too new and too small a country to presume to judge between the Great Powers on an ideological basis.[10]

What Ghana had in common with the Soviet Union and the other Eastern European countries was the one party state. But unlike Russia, the Ghanaian one party system of government, during the period under review, had nothing to do with the dogma of Communism. It was based upon African traditional system of society according to which the chief being democratically selected and legally enstooled by the elders, enjoys the constitutional power to rule in council with his elders and advisers without opposition.

The one party system of Ghana was not identical with the one party system of the Soviet Union: there were in fact essential differences: in the Soviet Union, the government was controlled by a communist party committed to marxist ideology. In Ghana, the regime was under the Convention People's Party (CPP), an amorphous organization open to all without ideological qualifications. Its value depended on its internal mechanism in achieving compromise between the most varied approaches to the social and economic problems continually being thrown up in a developing society.

The Will of the Electorate under Colonial Government

It was the wish of the Colonial Government to introduce a multi-party system in Ghana. However, the disappearance of the two-party system in Ghana was not informed by any scientific theory but was in accordance with the will of the people. Within a period of thirteen years, the electorate of Ghana had gone through three national elections (1951, 1954 and 1956) and two referenda. The ostensible purpose was to test the popularity of the Convention People's Party at the polls; or to test their claim to popular representation. All these general elections were handled by the colonial government. Nonetheless, the results showed that in spite of the colonial government's imposition of repeated elections — with the electorate going through the motions of the periodic ballots — no effective opposition in an institutionalized form emerged. Since the one party system of Ghana did not represent the interests of a single group, a tribal section or an economic class in the population, it was, in the opinion of the majority of the Ghanaian electorate, democratic. This procedure conformed with the concept of popular consensus derived from the tradition of the African village meeting. The decision-making process in these meetings is based upon discussion, which because of its length and fullness, gives every one concerned a chance to express his opinion. The consensus finally reached is shared by all those present, thus obviating the necessity of a vote which would leave the community sharply divided.[11] Foreign observers, and many Africans as well, argued that the single party system was inevitable at this stage of African development. Thus, the International Commission of Jurists wrote that "the inception of a One-Party system had sometimes been prompted by a political situation in which a ruling party with massive popular support was opposed by a party or parties with only a small minority backing. In such a situation, choice had become meaningless since the ruling party candidate was almost invariably returned."[12]

Consequently, although the 1956 election had returned Dr. Kwame Nkrumah's Convention People's Party with a comfortable majority (72 per cent) of seats in Parliament and left the opposition in a minority (28 per cent), it soon turned out that since there were no arguments between Government and the Opposition regarding the evident and imperative needs and goals of economic development, parties representing different points of view were superfluous. No sooner had Parliament resumed the session than many members of the Opposition considered it meaningless to oppose the large majority of the Government and, therefore, crossed carpet to join the government which (cross-carpet) almost caused a seating crisis on Government benches.[13] So few members were left on the opposition bench that they became the representatives of only a small minority.

Accusations of Communist Influence

It is true that Nkrumah and his party were repeatedly condemned by outside commentators as Communists who followed none but the dictates of Moscow. In 1966, Dr. Fritz Schatten, the Head of the Foreign Department of the West German Broadcasting System and a man who, according to his publishers, "has a wide reputation in Germany and Switzerland for his many studies of African problems in books and in the press" wrote a general study of the continent entitled *Communism in Africa* and assured his audience that "Ghana or Mali might ultimately play the role of a Soviet bridgehead distribution centre for agitation and propaganda and for a base for infiltration in West Africa. Taking the long view, such fears, though they seem exaggerated at the moment, are by no means without foundation."[14] The writer agrees with the suggestion of Geoffrey Bing — Attorney General in the Nkrumah Government — that while Dr. Fritz Schatten was "prepared to charge Nkrumah with communism, his real complaint against him was his attempt to organize the African continent against neo-colonialism." Dr. Nkrumah had replaced Dr. Schatten's slogan "Workers of the World Unite" by the slogan "Peoples of Africa Unite". This new slogan, Dr. Schatten pointed out, "embraces the peoples of all colonial territories".[15]

During the Nii Bonne (Nii Kwabena Bonne III of Osu and again Nana Owusu Akenten III, Oyokohene of Techiman in Ashanti) riots of 1948, Governor Sir Gerald Creasey, successor of Sir Alan Burns announced in a broadcast that a communist conspiracy had occurred but that the government had arrested the leading communists. It certainly was the measure of the colonial government's lack of understanding of African political development that the so-called 'communists' arrested by the Governor were the 'Big Six' of the United Gold Coast Convention (UGCC), namely, Dr. J. B. Danquah, Edward Akufo Addo, William Ofori Atta, Ako Adjei, Obetsebi Lamptey and Kwame Nkrumah. At the time of their arrest, the only two of the six whose names were known outside Ghana (then Gold Coast) were Dr. J. B. Danquah and Dr. Kwame Nkrumah — both of whom were, at the time, at a meeting in a provincial town about 100 kilometres from Accra. Such were Sir Gerald Creasy's communists and strange to say the Governor's communists theory was at first accepted without question by the Labour Ministers and the Colonial Office. When the question of the disturbances was raised in the House of Commons, Lord Ogmore, then Parliamentary Under-Secretary, was convinced that the riots had originated from a communist plot. Willie Callagher, communist Member for West Fife, had asked whether he would consider sending "a deputation of responsible trade union officials to investigate." "We will not send such a deputation", replied the Minister. "A full investigation will be carried out — a formal inquiry by the Government — and then the facts will come to light and I will guarantee that when they come to light, Mr. Callagher will not like them". Indeed, he appeared almost to be endorsing the suppositions of Lord Winterton, by then the sole survivor in the House of those Conservative members who had been returned as supporters of Joseph Chamberlain's tariff reform and empire development. "Are we to understand", Earl Winterton had asked, "that when a full investigation has been made into the political causes, the Minister will place a statement in the Library so that we may know whether or not it is due to the Communist dupes of the Third International, including the Communist Party of this country?" And the Minister replied, "there was almost certainly communist incitement in this case. I will place a full statement in the Library when it arrives". When ultimately the full statement arrived and was placed in the Library, Lord Ogmore's guarantee was unfulfilled and it was not Mr. Callagher but the Colonial Office establishment, who did not like the findings.

The formal inquiry promised, known as the Watson Commission, after its Chairman, the late Andrew Aiken Watson, K. C., had two other members, Dr. Keith Murray, then the Rector of Lincoln College, Oxford, and the late Andrew Dalgleish, an officer of the Transport and General Workers Union. Their Report was an outstanding analysis of colonialism not only in the Gold Coast but also, by necessary implication, in the whole British Colonial Empire. The basic argument was that the Colonial Administration held in sacred trust the rights of all the people in the Gold Coast, and it was incumbent upon them to safeguard the position of a section of the population, albeit a minority, which might be opposed to the existing colonial government.

> The moral justification for Britain remaining in the Gold Coast lies in this: out of a population of approximately four and a half million Africans, on a fair assessment, barely ten per cent is literate. We have no reason to suppose that power in the hands of a small literate minority would not tend to be used to exploit the illiterate majority in accordance with the universal pattern of what has happened elsewhere in the past throughout the world. His Majesty's Government therefore has a moral duty to remain until ... some corresponding degree of cultural, political and economic achievement has been attained by all three areas now part of the Gold Coast (i.e., The Colony, Ashanti and the Northern Territories).[16]

Although they unanimously frowned upon the assumption by government of emergency powers restricting the physical liberty of the subject in time of peace (which could be justified only by the gravest of national emergencies) yet they justified the assumption by the Governor of wide emergency powers in the territory because they were in no doubt "an emergency of the gravest character existed at all times in the Gold Coast". However, they resiled from the damaging effect of some of these colonial emergency powers. For example, they were "gravely concerned" with the Removal Orders (Emergency Powers) of the Governor against the six members of the United Gold Coast Convention — a political organization of a very large membership — based (upon numerous allegations, some of which are of a somewhat nebulous character'.

Furthermore, they were of the opinion that in so far as Regulation 29 of the Emergency (General) Regulations 1948 (Order No.29 of 1948) purported to deprive His Majesty's judges in the Gold Coast of jurisdiction to entertain an application by a subject, detained otherwise than pursuant to a warrant issuing out of a court of competent jurisdiction, the 'assumption of such a power was excessive ... and unhesitatingly' condemned. The rest of the

Regulations were jettisoned because the Commissioners had already promised the existence of an emergency 'at all times in the Gold Coast'.

The Removal Order (F. N. K. Nkrumah) Order 1948 (Order No.29 of 1948) found it expedient for securing the public safety and the maintenance of public order, to remove Francis Nwia Kofie Nkrumah under the provisions of Regulation 29 of the Emergency (General) Regulations 1948 (inserted in such Regulations by the Emergency (General) (Amendment) (No.2) Regulation 1948) to such place in the Gold Coast as and when directed by the Governor. So long as the Order remained in force Kwame Nkrumah was to "remain and live in, and not leave or be absent from, the place so appointed . . . and to comply in all respects with the directions and requirements" of the Governor.

Removal Orders in identical terms were made on behalf of Edward Akufo Addo, Ebenezer Ako Adjei, William Ofori Atta, Dr. Joseph Boakye Danquah and Emmanuel Odarquaye Lamptey (*alias* Obetsebi-Lamptey).

The Commissioners admitted some confusion of thought as to their precise function in the complaint against the detained men above. They were not charged with any criminal offence to be tried by the Commission. Furthermore, by the time they came before the Commission, the foregoing Removal Orders whereof they were complaining had been revoked. Consequently, the sole duty of the Commission remained the ascertainment whether in all the circumstances the Governor acted reasonably in relation to the members of the United Gold Coast Convention (UGCC). In making the Removal Orders against them, the government based its action upon numerous allegations which were later found to be rather nebulous in character, and obviously incapable of surviving a rigorous legal test or for that matter incapable of surviving the strict rules of evidence. It was not uncommon for colonial Governors throughout the Empire to arrest citizens without warrant and have them incarcerated at the Governor's pleasure: without any attempt to establish by strictly admissible evidence, the matters alleged against them.

Notwithstanding the 'somewhat nebulous character' of the allegations against the six men and/or the illegality of the charge against them, the Commissioners came out in support of the Governor and his administration in the sense that they were satisfied that in making the Removal Orders against the six men on March 11, 1948, the Governor honestly believed that by removing them from the scene, confusion would overtake the ranks not only of those who contemplated further violence but also those 'who hoped to reap a political harvest from the violence' and thus 'centered their hopes on the six men as their real leaders'.

Misconception of the Extent of Communism in the Gold Coast

A common misconception of the Commissioners was their preoccupation with a view according to which the political developments of the country and the disturbance in particular served as a battleground of ideas in which the western way of life was engaged in a life-and-death struggle with that of Russia for the souls of the emerging and reawakening people of the Gold Coast. The Soviet Union and China, it was said, were carrying the gospel of communism to politically-inexperienced people of the Gold Coast, whose older customs, traditions, and faiths appeared to the Commissioners as collapsing and who were in their view seeking new ideology and new ways of life to fill the resulting void. The Commissioners considered as communistic, the attempt by Africans to set up political party organizations modelled, not on those of a European communist party, but essentially on the democratic party structure in the United Kingdom.[17] They saw, clearly, a new social system was necessary in the Gold Coast. However, by their preoccupation with organizational politics, they avoided any consideration of the philosophy by which the new social order could be achieved.[18] The one thing in common which united the emerging and reawakening people of the Gold Coast was the passionate desire for political independence, which, though, was sometimes compromised, in the Colony, Ashanti and the Northern Territories, by sentiments of tribalism and regional kinship, applied without exception to their attitude to the outside world, both West and East.

Where communist parties linked with Russia, but beyond the reach of Russian troops, had gone beyond giving assistance to nationalist movements and endeavoured to interfere in a contrary sense, they had been quickly halted and sometimes suppressed altogether. Such episodes have, in the past, generally, brought disfavour on the Soviet Union and they tended to rebound to the advantage of the West whose freedom of speech, pattern of life and behaviour are almost synonymous with African traditional society.

In fact, communism was not the issue in the Gold Coast. Indeed, the scope of communist philosophy in the Gold Coast was greatly exaggerated, its nature widely misconceived, and its future prospects in Ghanaian politics greatly overestimated. It is true Kwame Nkrumah looked favourably on the Marxist interpretation of colonialism. His pamphlet Towards Colonial Freedom written two years before the Watson Commission was evidence of his acceptance of the Marxist interpretation of colonialism. On this basis, the Commissioners had evidence upon which to argue that Nkrumah was inspired by communist ideology.

For example, their Report spoke of Nkrumah's 'avowed aims for a Union of West African Soviet Socialist Republics' and to substantiate this they printed, in an appendix, the constitution of a propaganda organization called 'The Circle' though they admitted 'there is no evidence it ever became a live body'. Its inclusion in the body of the Report was a physiological slip significant of their attitude of mind.[19] From that document it was clear that what was being advocated, in theory by Kwame Nkrumah was not 'A Union of West African Soviet Socialist Republics' but 'West African Unity and National Independence'. To describe a locally self-inspired political institution of the Gold Coast which had for its objective a union of all West African colonies, as the precursor of a Union of West African Soviet Socialist Republics was no less than a distortion of reality intended to arouse in the minds of western readers an emotional attitude of disapproval toward the objective of immediate self-government for the people of the Gold Coast.

The Commission went on to say that "In a working programme circulated just before the disturbance we have been inquiring into, Nkrumah boldly proposes a programme which is all too familiar to those who have studied the technique of counties which have fallen the victims of Communist enslavement".

Once again, to prove their point, they printed two paragraphs from the working programme. The first of these was a restatement, almost word for word, of the plan proposed by Earl Attlee when he first became Leader of the Labour Opposition in the period between the First and Second World Wars. The second paragraph of Dr. Nkrumah's suggestion cited as "all too familiar to those who have studied Communist techniques" might well have come from another contemporary document, the 'Maxwell Fyfe Report on Conservative Party' Organization. Indeed Dr. Nkrumah was not attacked for his Marxist analysis of imperialism. Towards Colonial Freedom was not even referred to in the Commission's Report. He was dubbed a communist because he advocated that a Western type political machine should be adopted by the United Gold Coast Convention, a conservatively-oriented nationalist organization.[20] The above analysis leads to the inevitable conclusion that the Watson Commission was an outstanding source of the internal self-government in the Gold Coast. However, it avoided the realities of the situation which were infinitely more complex and confused. Consequently, it contributed to the delay of independence for the territory for a period of ten years. Similar isolated events were taken out of context by contemporary writers to prove that Nkrumah was a communist.

It is, however, very significant that one of the most brilliant and outstanding Prime Ministers of Britain, the late Rt. Hon. Sir Harold Wilson, disagreed completely on the charges of "Communism" against Ghana and Nkrumah. Sir Harold saw the problem differently. In his book titled The War on World Poverty" published in 1953, view:

> For the vast majority of mankind the most urgent problem is NOT War, or Communism or the cost of living, or taxation. It is HUNGER. Over 1,500,000,000 (1.5 billion) people, something like two-thirds of the World's population, are living in conditions of acute hunger, defined in terms of identifiable nutritional disease. This is at the same time the effect and cause of pverty, squalar and misery in which they live.

Ghana-Soviet Trade Relations

The most striking feature of the Soviet-Ghanaian relationship was the comparatively small amount of exports originating in the Eastern Trading Area. Communist planners are generally biased in favour of self-sufficient national economies, avoiding international specialization of production. They restrict imports to goods that are deemed vital to the fulfilment of their national plan and consider exports as the means to pay for imports. Consequently, the foreign trade of the communist countries is a smaller fraction of their domestic output than is true of the market economies of the West.

Thus, Ghanaian-Soviet trade was comparatively small. In the last years of Nkrumah's Government, that is, during 1964–1966, Ghana took only 18.5 per cent of her imports from the communist bloc; but in 1967, a year after Nkrumah's Government was overthrown, this figure dropped to 7.6 per cent.[21] Conversely, the market economies of the West traded more with Ghana. The year 1953 marked the end of the Stalin era of dogmatic self-sufficiency and discouragement of Soviet trade relations with the world. Moreover, 'De-Stalinization' was not extended to the Soviet economic system until 1965; the Stalinist central planning mechanism remained intact in all essential respects not only during the Malenkov-Bulganin-Kruschev transition (1953–1957) but also throughout the Kruschev era (1957–1964).[22] The Kruschev's ascendancy in 1957 altered none of the 'basic institutions and operating principles of the Soviet Economic System', nor did it involve 'decentralization' in any useful allocative sense.[23] But under Kruschev, the Soviet leadership began to promote trade with the non-aligned countries of the Third World. More developing countries initiated measures towards co-operation with the Council for Mutual Economic Assistance (COMECON), an international economic organization embracing the socialist countries. Early in 1962, the COMECON member countries provided economic and technical assistance to many developing nations, including some African states. The COMECON member countries made great progress in their social and economic developments. The more than thirty years of COMECON's existence had been shown that co-operation within the framework of this organization boosted the economic growth and prosperity of each member country.[24]

In following the example of previous critics, writers like Scott Thompson described Nkrumah's official visit to the Soviet Union as a "pilgrimage to the East"[25], i.e., implying that Nkrumah was a devotee of communism visiting the shrine of international communism under the external leadership of Moscow in the manner of a muslim's ritual of pilgrimage to Mecca; an important ritual which must be made by the believer in his lifetime, although one may send a proxy. It is true that, in 1961, Nkrumah was invited by, and paid official visits to, the East European countries including the Soviet Union. But those visits were made in the interest of peace and understanding. The visit were also to boost trade and economic co-operation between the COMECON countries and Ghana. The need for economic and technical assistance by the socialist states for the developing states was also addressed during the visit. As far as the Ghana Government was concerned, trade was a sedative or solvent for the ideological conflict.

The new African states, caught between two major economic systems in competition with each other, two ideologies struggling for converts among the newly-liberated states, had to take the alternative of trying to economically understand and benefit from the two power blocs. The emphasis in the earlier post independent days was on military disengagement, non-alignment by the 1960s for Nkrumah, was in part a doctrine of economic liberation. To break the cold war impasse, the Third World countries, including Ghana, had to have contact with and understand both East and West. Ghana's understanding of Western countries and their leaders was adequate. This was buttressed by long association coupled with diplomatic, economic, educational and trade relations. But Ghana's contact with the Eastern countries was minimal. To be able to create the necessary balance and bring about understanding which would make settlement of disputes meaningful, it was vital that Ghana have a clear comprehension of the issues involved and have them discussed with both power blocs. This was the best way to weigh and strike a balance for peace.

More often than not, Nkrumah was accused of being a communist. It was a weapon used by vested interests to discredit his Government, and undermine his political influence and control in the territory of Ghana. The picture in the minds of the majority of his critics was entirely misleading. On the contrary, Nkrumah's African nationalism was highly eclectic in terms of ideology. "Communism", said Nkrumah, "was no danger in Ghana, our better institutions . . . do not allow the ideology to have any fruitful set up in our country".[26] Indeed, the strength of Ghanaian nationalism, against which Marxism and/or communism was to contend, lay in the differences in social ideology. Nkrumah's nationalism was strongly imbued with ideas of black consciousness, Pan-Africanism, and the 'African Personality', all of which tended to exclude or limit communism and the impact of non-African concepts or ideologies. His brand of socialism had been shaped for domestic use with no great regard for the orthodoxies or Eastern and Western interpretations of socialism. Even the radical socialists among Ghanaian nationalists initially insisted on describing their ideas as 'African socialism',[27] in order to emphasize the cultural differences between themselves and the internationalist socialists. In support of the Ghanaian position, George Padmore (one of the first black nationalists from the West Indies who flirted with communism and then groped for ways of Pan-African socialism) in his book *Pan-Africanism or*

Communism? The Coming Struggle in Africa (Dobson 1956), argued that the first principle which Africans should learn from Lenin was Lenin's pragmatism; and that Africans must be free to Africanize Marxism, if they wished, just as Lenin had Russianized it. In fact, "Marxism", said Nkrumah, "is not a DOGMA but a guide to action".[28]

According to Padmore, Marxism in African countries should not only be Africanized but should further be adapted to suit the peculiar African conditions.

> Lenin, the architect of the first socialist state, and his party, did not blindly follow Marxism in creating the instruments best suited to Russian conditions. Similarly, the African approach to socialism must be based on a policy of adaptation, while keeping constantly in mind our goal — the peaceful advance of African socialism.[29]

But it was not only Nkrumah or Padmore who subscribed to pragmatic approach to Marxism. The need for ideological flexibility was first recognized by Fredrick Engels, himself in a letter to Karl Marx written in 1882 when he was commenting on the fate of socialist revolutions in the colonial world. Lenin was later to develop this need to such a point that he was always ready to adapt Marx's ideas to changing situations and called other inflexible Marxists like Bernstein, Kautsky and Plekhanov as renegades.[30]

In fact, Nkrumah's approach to Marxism was not only pragmatic, but it also achieved an African naturalization and came to terms with African philosophy of the extended family; and the three components of Africa's historical personality: Judeo-Christianity, Islam and her own basic traditional personality. As one of Ghana's traditional rulers or chiefs, Nkrumah's traditionalism acquired impeccable credentials and established a sense of belonging to black nationalism incarnate. "Africa" said Nkrumah, "has to come to terms with these three personalities". These components became an aspect of the quest for continental unification.[31]

Ghana and the People's Republic of China

During the colonial period, Ghanaian policies towards foreign countries were determined by the colonial Governor — the representative of Her Majesty of the United Kingdom in the Colony — under the instructions of the Colonial Office in the United Kingdom. Such policies were more often than not determined by the ruling political party — Conservative or Labour.

Upon independence, Ghana pursued an independent foreign policy in spite of her diplomatic and trade ties with the super and great powers. In spite of their ideological differences, both East and West developed trade between themselves and sought economic and technical co-operation from wherever they were able to find it without strings that limited their freedom. The importance of Africa in Chinese foreign policy manifested itself in the visits of

Premier Chou-En-Lai and Foreign Minister Chen Yi to the continent. The Chinese Premier and his Foreign Minister paid a five-day visit to Accra in November, 1962. At the end of his visit to Ghana, he said that the convening of an Afro-Asian/Latin American People's Conference was desirable and that the possibility for such a conference would be explored. During this stay in Ghana, Premier Chou-En-Lai (accompanied by Marshal Cehn Yi, Vice Premier of the State Council and Minister of Foreign Affairs, together with other officials of the People's Republic of China) made a tour of interesting places in Ghana, including Tema Harbour and the industrial centres in the vicinity of Accra. He expressed a great satisfaction with the developments in Ghana and expressed great appreciation for the outstanding achievements of the Republic of Ghana in safeguarding national independence and developing the national economy.[32] The motive of Chou-En-Lai's visit to Ghana was clearly to enlist the support of Ghana against the position of the Soviet Union in Africa; it was also to strengthen the bonds of friendship between China and Ghana. But the Ghana Government had a wider interest as regards the visit. The visit of the Chinese was an opportunity for the Ghana Government to impress upon Premier Chou-En-Lai, the importance of China taking her seat at the United Nations and opening up diplomatic relations with the United States in order to foster world peace. Ghana's concern was that China's absence from the UN constituted a serious communication risk in world politics. The occasion of Chou-En-Lai's visit was used to discuss more economic assistance from China and trade expansion between the two countries. There were, however, other areas of mutual concern as revealed by the discussions between the Chinese and the Ghanaian delegations.

The exchange of opinions in their discussions revealed a community of views on such problems as general disarmament, the complete prohibition of nuclear weapons, the settlement of international issues through peaceful negotiations and the strengthening of Afro-Asian peoples' solidarity. It was noted that the greatest danger facing mankind at the time was lack of understanding between nations. It was also considered that an Afro-Asian Conference was necessary and that active preparations should be made to convene it. The communique issued at the end of the visit condemned the colonial rule of the South African authorities and their policy of racial discrimination and, in common with progressive mankind, supported the struggle of the South African peoples for equal rights and national liberation. Both parties called on all countries to terminate any existing relations, particularly economic relations, with the gruesome regime of South Africa. As regards relations with African countries, Premier Chou-En-Lai solemnly had declared: (1) that China supports the African peoples in their struggle to fight old and new colonialism and win and safeguard national independence; (2) that China supports the governments of African countries in pursuing a policy of peace, neutrality and non-alignment; (3) that China supports the African peoples in their desire to bring about solidarity and unity in the manner of their own choice; (4) that China supports the African countries in their efforts to settle their disputes through peaceful consultation; (5) that China holds that the sovereignty of African countries should be respected by all other countries and that encroachment and interference from any quarter should be opposed.

The two parties also discussed, at length, the efforts of the African peoples to attain African unity, which efforts had culminated in the establishment of the Organization of African Unity at the summit conference of African states in Addis Ababa, in 1963. The Chinese delegation expressed its support for the efforts of African unity and solidarity aimed at sovereignty, territorial integrity and independence. This was essential in eradicating all forms of colonialism from Africa; ensuring the economic and cultural development of the African peoples and achieving for them a better life. The Chinese party appreciated the Ghanaian active efforts to help to achieve liberation and unity in Africa. The Ghanaian party expressed its appreciation of the sincere sympathy which the People's Republic of China had always maintained for the African people in their struggle towards liberation and unity.

General Disarmament

On disarmament, the two parties affirmed their support for genuine general disarmament and the complete prohibition and thorough destruction of nuclear weapons. The Chinese side reaffirmed its support for the resolution of the summit conference of African states on general disarmament and the establishment of a nuclear-free zone in Africa. Indeed, at a meeting at Addis Ababa on May 22–25, 1963, the Conference of Independent African States unanimously agreed to co-ordinate efforts "to declare and accept Africa as a denuclearized zone" and to support "the banning of nuclear weapons and thermonuclear tests and the banning of the manufacture of nuclear weapons."[33] Leftwing, pro-Western, and traditional regimes in Africa had thus joined in endeavouring to keep the entire African continent from the arena of nuclear competition. By 1963, this idea had begun to gain converts in Latin America, where five states — Bolivia, Chile, Ecuador, and Brazil — proposed a comparable scheme for the 'denuclearization' of the Caribbean and Central and South America. Not unexpectedly, the Soviet Union had consistently endorsed such proposals. The United States either openly opposed them or was lukewarm towards them, on the grounds that the scheme infringed the rights of individual states to provide for their own defence, and that a continent could not be 'isolated' from world wide military tendencies and developments.[34]

The foregoing brief appraisal of the role of the non-aligned states in disarmament negotiations supports the view that Prime Minister Chou-En-Lai and President Nkrumah were correct in believing that Ghana and the non-aligned states furnished the impetus for limited progress in resolving some of the vexatious issues surrounding the problem of arms control. The signing of the nuclear-test-ban accord of 1963 by some non-aligned states including Ghana indicates that peace is also the concern of the third world states. Moreover, the behaviour of the non-aligned states at Geneva was in altering the Administration's (if not always legislative and public) viewpoints in the United States about the implications of non-alignment as a global force. The Geneva forum was regarded as one of the best available methods of prevailing upon the Soviet Union to accept its responsibility to heed the conscience and aspirations of the world community. American policy-makers also commented on the increasing realism shown by non-aligned participants in approaching the complexities inherent in the problem of disarmament.[35]

The Sino-Indian Border Dispute

The Chinese delegation and Ghana Government representatives discussed, at length, the state of the Sino-Indian border dispute since the Colombo Conference of six non-aligned states. Ghana had called on Afro-Asian countries to send a peace mission to India and China with the object of arranging acceptable terms for a cease-fire between the two countries. The fighting on the mutual border of these countries constituted a serious threat to world peace, if not actually disruptive of the non-aligned movement. Indeed, the Sino-Indian border dispute threatened Afro-Asian solidarity. In the instructions to the Ghana Permanent Representative at the United Nations, the Government called on the Afro-Asian countries in December 1962:

(1) to "send a peace mission to New Delhi and Peking with the object of arranging acceptable terms for a ceasefire on both sides, which will enable direct negotiations to take place between India and China";

(2) to stress "in this connection that while the border clashes continue with the daily loss of lives to both sides, the UN runs the risk of being exposed to ridicule if it fails to contribute immediately to the efforts being made to secure peace in Asia".

(3) to suggest that "a peace mission of the non-aligned powers...be appointed immediately to go to New Delhi and Peking to seek an early termination of hostilities and the resumption of negotiations between India and China on the boundaries in dispute."[36]

The Ghana Government was afraid that aid to one side in this Sino-Indian dispute might all too easily result in aid being given to the other side by someone else — with all the risk of escalation. Indeed, the Sino-Indian conflict provided a testing ground for non-alignment — not alone in challenging the sincerity of India's devotion to the principle of non-alignment, but also in testing the ability of other non-aligned states to apply their professed principles to a situation involving one of their own leading members. In this conflict, non-aligned states were placed in a dilemma between their overwhelming sympathy for India as the victim of aggression and their realization that no other nation, or group of nations was in a position to extinguish a blaze that might well precipitate a world conflagration. The United States quite obviously was unable to do so, due to the extreme animosity that had long characterized Sino-American relations. The Soviet Union was not in a position to do so, because of her defence ties with the People's Republic of China and professed friendship with India and other non-aligned states. The United Nations was not in a position to do so, because the People's Republic of China did not yet belong to the United Nations, neither did it indicate willingness to accept its jurisdiction. Besides, United Nations Secretary General, U. Thant, publicly denied the United Nation's usefulness in the Sino-Indian dispute. This left the non-aligned states helpless. In spite of their support for the Indian position, they accepted the responsibility for seeking a détente in the dispute.

The Peace Mission in India and China

The Afro-Asian non-aligned states could not ignore the conflict between China and India; they had to try and do something towards a solution, and they had to do so without taking sides or passing moral judgement. Mrs. Bandaranaike, Prime Minister of Sri Lanka, led the delegation including Mr. Kofi Asante Ofori-Atta, Ghana's Minister of Justice to India to explain to that government the proposals of the Colombo Conference on the Sino-Indian border dispute. Ignoring the fact that India and China had been discussing this issue, in the most minute detail, over a period not of weeks or months but of years, the delegation, nevertheless, implored the two countries to resume their discussions. Mr. Ofori-Atta asserted President Nkrumah's belief both in India and China, that the sole purpose of the conference had been for peaceful direct negotiations between the two parties. The other general principle of action agreed upon in Colombo was that the unilateral ceasefire declared by the Chinese on the November 21 was to be confirmed and sustained.

Ghana took the initiative in forming the Committee of Non-aligned States which produced the compromise that stopped what had virtually become an open Sino-Indian War.[37] Ghana was also the author of detailed proposals at the opening session of the Colombo Conference. The proposals were as follows: India and China must accept a ceasefire; they must withdraw their forces from a zone of disengagement between them, which would be neutralized and maintained only by unarmed police on both sides; this area must be determined as soon as possible through direct negotiations; if these failed, India and China must agree to the conference determining the area of disengagement.

The Government of Ghana was not overawed by the immensity of the task. In February and March of 1964, Chou-En-Lai visited Burma, Sri-Lanka, Ghana and the United Arab Republic. The proposals were discussed with the leaders of all those countries, but only the talks in Colombo produced any result. After Chou-En-Lai's visit, the delegation informed India that the new Chinese position was that they were prepared to withdraw their civilian posts in the demilitarized zone in the western sector, if India agreed to discussions. In Parliament on the April 13, 1964, the Prime Minister of India, abandoning Indian insistence that the proposals must first be accepted in toto, stated that India would be prepared to enter into negotiations, if China agreed to withdraw her posts first. This withdrawal would convert the demilitarized zone into a no man's land, an idea that had been considered and rejected by the Colombo Conference. The Ghana Government had, a year preceding the Colombo Conference, mooted the idea.

The point of interest here is the premise guiding non-aligned mediation activities. In one non-aligned capital after another, there was agreement with the Egyptian contention that China's attack was "a blow to the concept of non-alignment." "If the blow was not to become irreparable", said the Cairo daily *Al Akhbar*, "non-aligned states were required to narrow the dispute to the smallest possible dimensions". The future of non-alignment itself obliged these countries to check and settle the Indian-Chinese dispute. The Prime Minister of Sri Lanka observed that if non-aligned states had endeavoured to play a positive role, for the cause of preserving world peace with respect to cold war issues; what could be the duty of non-aligned states when they faced each other in a dispute was to endeavour to have it settled themselves. The Ghanaian delegation came to the conclusion that high on the list of China's objectives was the desire to prove that the very concept of non-alignment was a political sham, and that a non-aligned third force in reality did not exist. This increased the determination of Ghana to demonstrate the value of positive neutralism in a strife-torn international environment.

Although more than seventy nations publicly expressed sympathy with India's position in its conflict with China, it was agreed that if they were to discharge their mediatory role successfully, the six non-aligned nations represented at Colombo in 1962 (Sri-Lanka, Egypt, Ghana, Burma, Indonesia and Cambodia) had to be guided by a maxim of Kwame Nkrumah. The Colombo non-aligned states, maintained Nkrumah, could not behave toward the People's Republic of China as though they were condemning her unheard, nor could they endeavour to impose an unacceptable solution upon India and China. The goal of the delegation was to help create an atmosphere conducive to the opening of negotiations between India and China. Throughout the course of their mediatory activities, the delegation was mindful that success depended upon one permanent consideration, namely, the extent to which they would succeed in involving a cease-fire formula compatible with the minimum security interests of both belligerents. Despite its initial scepticism about non-aligned mediation, India ultimately accepted the Colombo proposals.

The People's Republic of China eventually co-operated, at least minimally, with the non-aligned mediation, for a variety of reasons. She urgently desired peace because she was passionately concerned with the problem of economic improvement. She wished to be left in peace to develop normal relations with other countries. However, although China assured the non-aligned nations that no attack would come from her, she was afraid that neighbouring countries could be used to attack her. Consequently, it was important for her to know the intentions of neighbouring countries; the Geneva Agreement particularly, the clause providing that in Indo-China, no outside interference would be allowed, guaranteed China's security. The Chinese, having discovered rich mineral resources in Sinkiang, now intended to make that region a highly-developed industrial area. For China, economic development came first; political problems were a minor issue.

As a tide of sympathy for India's cause swept through the Afro-Arab world, and as the six Colombo non-aligned states made it clear that they did not propose to advance suggestions prejudicial to Indian security, Chinese policy-makers contemplated the consequences of risking a total alienation of non-aligned opinion. Their drive to establish China as the dominant power in Asia had led them to call for a second Bandung Conference (without the Soviet Union), — a plea that had received some non-aligned support, notably in Indonesia. Rejection of the Colombo proposals would almost certainly have induced a majority of the non-aligned states to favour a new conference of non-aligned nations to which neither the Soviet Union nor China would be invited. Such a development was bound to enhance the Soviet Union's position in its dispute with China, because it would imply the exclusion of the Government of the People's Republic of China from a summit meeting of the Afro-Asian world. China's response, therefore, was to accept the Colombo proposals in principle, while rejecting them in fact by repeated and equivocal demands for clarification from India and from the Colombo non-aligned representation.

On the basis of these developments, the joint Ghana-China communique, after Chou En-Lai's visit in 1964, admitted that the situation in the Sino-Indian border dispute had relaxed, and the parties expressed full confidence and hope over the possibility of a peaceful settlement of the dispute. The Chinese side appreciated the peaceful efforts made by Ghana and the other Colombo powers. The two parties expressed their determination to continue to support such peaceful efforts aimed at bringing about direct Sino-Indian negotiations.

This dispute became also a test case on the interpretations of the Commonwealth relationship. Britain had granted military aid to Nehru's Government to fight the Chinese invasion of Indian territory. Mr. Macmillan's interpretation of Commonwealth 'ties' seemed to imply an almost automatic rallying to India's defence. But the Government of Ghana took a different view. President Nkrumah immediately wrote to Mr. Macmillan (the British Prime Minister) in the following terms:

> Are you sure that by giving support, whatever this is, to one side against the other, you will be able to increase the chances of bringing an end to hostilities? Assistance by way of arms and equipment to any country engaged in a conflict with another, in my view, is likely merely to occasion a counter offer of assistance to the other party to the dispute. The balance of military strength therefore remains the same but the dispute is made much more difficult of solution through the involvement of outside powers.[38]

In his reply, Mr. Macmillan said that he found it difficult to understand Dr. Nkrumah's objection to British sympathy and support for India. Mr. Macmillan argued that when the territory of a Commonwealth people was invaded, it was surely right and natural that Britain should be sympathetic and helpful. Mr. Macmillan was here virtually suggesting that Britain had a duty to help India militarily because India was a fellow-member of the Commonwealth. It appears that the logic of Macmillan's stand implied that the Commonwealth was a kind of *de facto* military alliance. This it was when the independent Commonwealth consisted of Britain and the older dominions only, and even after it, by virtue of the doctrine of the indivisibility of the Crown. Indeed, until the Status, of Westminster of 1931, the Commonwealth was still regarded by some as a single state. After the Statute, it remained an alliance in fact, though no longer in strict law in so far as the independent members were concerned. This was the case until, paradoxically, India acceded to independence — and turned the Commonwealth not only multi-racial but also multi-ideological in its foreign policies. The question which arose in the Sino-Indian dispute of 1962 was whether this new Commonwealth had truly ceased to have a military side to it following India's invention of non-alignment a decade earlier. The Ghana Government gave an affirmative answer to that question as follows:

> The Commonwealth is not a military alliance and it would be most detrimental to its progress if the impression were created that Commonwealth members did not judge each issue independently on its merits, but instead automatically sided with a fellow Commonwealth country when that country was engaged in a dispute with an outside power.[39]

The obvious conclusion is that, for the Government of Ghana, the lessening of world tensions at large was more important than involving the

Commonwealth in the conflict and make its solution more difficult. There was fear that military aid to one side in the dispute might all too easily result in aid being given to the other side by someone else — with all the risks of escalation. Ghana felt that if everyone were to commit himself strongly on the rights and wrongs of the dispute (Sino-Indian), the chances of impartial mediation would diminish. Thus, Ghanaian position in the instance giving opinion not on who was right in the dispute, but on what was best from the point of view of settling it.

The joint Ghanaian-China communique of January 11, 1964, during the second visit of Premier Chou En-Lai, addressed the state of the Sino-Indian border dispute since the Colombo Conference of six non-aligned states. The question of importance is what did non-aligned mediation efforts accomplish? In the Sino-Indian crisis, as in other diplomatic conflicts involving the risk of a cold war confrontation and perhaps of a nuclear war, the non-aligned states served as catalytic agents facilitating a *détente*. They showed ample awareness that any acceptable solution had to take into account clashing national interests and security needs; their proposals grew out of a search for points at which India's and China's diplomatic interests coincided. Thus, if it demonstrated nothing, else, the Colombo mediation attempt proved that the diplomatic activities of non-aligned states rested upon more durable foundations than *naivete*, lack of diplomatic realism, indifference toward global issues, or other simplistic explanations sometimes advanced to explain nations were not frightened out of their diplomatic credo by China's aggressiveness or attack.

In the communique, both parties declared that the foundation of good relations among all nations should be the observance of basic principles of international life, namely, mutual respect for territorial integrity and sovereignty, non-aggression, non-interference in the internal affairs of other countries, equality and mutual benefit and the solution of all international issues by negotiation.

According to Chinese policy-makers, needy countries ought to hesitate before accepting the Soviet Union's largess, since "in their (the Soviet blocs) economic exchanges with Asian and African countries, there are often cases in which they have no respect for their independence and sovereignty and flagrantly interfere in their internal affairs".[40] According to China, the Soviet Union asked for raw materials in exchange for aid, and Soviet officials, it was charged, did not trade fairly; they cut import prices while raising those of exports. Similarly, in providing equipment, the Russians withhold technical advice, so as to make Asian and African countries economically dependent. China's indictment was authoritative — based on its own experience with the abrupt termination of Soviet aid and the withdrawal of technicians in 1960. And by the mid 1960s, even American officials conceded that many of their earlier fears were groundless. In taking stock of intensive communist military and economic aid programmes in Africa, State Department officials in 1964 found that the communist bloc was, in many cases, unable to maintain scheduled deliveries of goods and keep up a steady flow of certain commodities (like oil) required by African countries; in other cases, the goods supplied were totally unsuited to African needs for example, heavy equipment not designed for use in the tropics.

Ghana and the United States of America

Most of the new nations have come into existence by virtue of a formal proclamation of independence, either in the form of a decree by the former sovereign or, in the case of a mandate of trust territory, the joint action of the United Nations and the mandatory power; or, as the result of some kind of international agreement, whether bilateral or multilateral, usually ending a period of strife between the aspiring new nation and the former ruler. Ghana came to independence under a regime which had the blessing of the departing colonial power. There was no violent switch of economic, social or political policy and both internally and externally Ghana had, from independence onwards, ostentatiously dissociated itself from the world's ideological conflicts. The Ghana Government, it is true, had proclaimed socialism as its aim but it was a socialism of the Scandinavian model. Its economic policy allowed the old commercial pattern of colonial days to continue almost unchanged. Europeans were not expelled. Indeed, more of them came to live in Ghana after independence than before it. There was no nationalization, let alone expropriation of Western-owned properties. Quite the reverse in fact.

The mode of the American recognition of the Ghanaian independence and republican status was by express declaration in both cases, and the exchange of diplomatic representatives in the first instance. The method involved announcements in the USA, the sending of international messages, the dispatching of a delegation and representatives to Accra, the capital of Ghana, and the elevation of the American consulate therein to the status of Embassy. On February 14, 1957, the State Department announced the appointment of an official delegation that was to accompany Vice-President Nixon to the independent celebrations from March 3 to March 10 — marking the independence of Ghana. The US Consul-General in Accra was designated to serve as adviser to this official delegation. On leaving for Accra, the Vice-President, Nixon, stated that "the United States by sending this delegation to the ceremonies is indicating its support and its friendship for this new nation as it enters into the activities in which it will engage in the years ahead as an independent member of the British Commonwealth".

On March 5, 1957, one day prior to the attainment of formal independence, the State Department announced that the US Government "has officially recognized the new state of Ghana, which becomes independent and a member of the British Commonwealth on 6 March".[41] This recognition of Ghana's independence was enhanced by (1) the Senate's confirmation of Wilson C. Flake as US Ambassador to Ghana on May 20, 1957,[42] (2) the United States' support of Ghanaian' application for membership of the United Nations,[43] and (3) two congressional and one state legislative resolutions congratulating Ghana on the attainment of independence.

On July 1, 1960, Ghana became a Republic. On the occasion of the celebration of this change and of the inauguration of Dr. Kwame Nkrumah as President of the new Republic of Ghana, President Eisenhower sent a message to President Nkrumah, extending his "most cordial greetings and felicitations on the accession of Ghana to the status of Republic."[44]

The US and the Volta Hydro-Electric Scheme of Ghana

In the period under review there was a deep and pervasive scepticism about diplomatic non-alignment which characterized public and official attitudes in the United States. An uneasiness and apprehension with regard to non-alignment expressed itself in a variety of ways — ranging from contemptuous references by State Department officials to 'so-called neutralism' and in some cases to outright condemnations of pro-communist non-alignment to blunt warnings to the Government of Morocco, for example, concerning its proposed purchase of Soviet aircraft, the prolonged hesitation in the United States before offering American assistance for Ghana's Volta River Project, the unmistakable chagrin among officials in the Kennedy Administration about the Belgrade Conference of non-alignment. Doubtless American opposition to non-alignment can be traced to several sources. A factor that pervaded a greater number of them was the widespread American failure to understand the concept of diplomatic non-alignment correctly.[45] In its crudest manifestations, American opposition to non-alignment appeared to stem from a distorted conception of what the doctrine involved and in some cases rested upon expected patterns of non-aligned behaviour that proponents of the ideology have never accepted.

In so far as the First Republic of Ghana could be accused of favouring any Western country, it was the United States and in so far as any of the Ghanaian development projects were of a neo-colonialist nature, the Volta Hydro-Electric Scheme best fitted the pattern. It involved, as Mr. Tony Killick had pointed out, an extraordinarily generous agreement with two United States firms, the Kaiser Aluminium and Chemical Corporation and the Reynolds Metal Company. The project was originally planned at a time of aluminium shortage in the sterling area and as a scheme to develop the very large bauxite deposits in Ghana. Aluminium production proceeds in three distinct and separate stages. The least profitable is the first stage — the mining by open cast methods of the raw material, bauxite. The second stage is the conversion of this bauxite into pure aluminium oxide or 'alumina' as it is called. The third stage is the reduction of this alumina in a smelter into metal by a process which consumes such large quantities of electricity that aluminium has been described as 'packaged power'.

The original idea for producing aluminium metal locally had come from Sir Gordon Guggisberg. He had proposed an integrated aluminium industry based on hydro-electric power from the Volta. Local bauxite would be processed near where it is mined and the alumina so produced would be reduced in a smelter in the territory into the final product, aluminium metal. The post-war British Government proposal for a Gold Coast aluminium industry was likewise based on the whole manufacture taking place in Ghana. The Volta River Project, as finally established, however, was of quite a different character. It was unconnected with any processing of local bauxite. Valco, the aluminium company established in Ghana by the two American firms, merely undertook to erect a reduction plant which would reduce to alumina powder produced by the two firms in the United States from bauxite mined in Jamaica. The only obligations of the American firms to Ghana were first to build a smelter and secondly to pay annually in foreign exchange a sum for a quantity of power from the Volta Hydro-Electric station, rising from £542,000 in 1967 to £2,464,000 in 1973 and thereafter.[46] In order to supply this power, the Ghana Government had to undertake to construct a dam behind which was from the Volta lake, 400 kilometres long and with an area of 8,384 square kilometres.

To pay for this immense hydro-electric complex, Ghana had to expend £40.4 million in foreign exchange and £27.6 million in local currency. Of the foreign exchange needed, it was only possible for Ghana to borrow £9.6 million of this total at the 'soft' rate of 3 1 per cent over a period of 30 years. The Government had to find £5 million from their own depleted reserves of foreign exchange and obtain the remainder from the United States Export and Import Bank and the United Kingdom Export Credits Department at the 'hard' rates of 5 ¾ per cent to 6 per cent repayable within 25 years. On top of this Mr. Killick estimated that Ghana had to meet further costs of some £7 million, much of it in foreign exchange, in ancillary work. Further, Tema Harbour, essential to the scheme cost £27 million.[47]

The relations between Ghana and the United States started downhill after September 1960, when Secretary of State Herter (somewhat unwisely) described Dr. Kwame Nkrumah "very definitely as moving towards the Soviet bloc"[48] and when neither Herter nor Eisenhower received Dr. Nkrumah who visited New York for the United Nations in 1960. By the time President J. F. Kennedy's Ambassador arrived in Ghana at the end of January, the Ghanaian Cabinet met to consider whether he should be allowed to present his credentials at all. The murder of Lumumba in 1960 brought a well-organized outburst of anti-American rioting in Ghana, following which Dr. Nkrumah served as the host for Leonid Brezhnev, the President of the Soviet Union. But there was the Volta River Project, originally conceived by the British colonial administration, with a dam on the Volta River. This dam was not only capable of creating a great lake to help meet internal needs for irrigation, fish and transport, but equally capable of generating hydro-electric power and making possible the installation of a smelter to convert Ghana's economic future. The British and Canadian aluminium industry had considered aiding the Volta Dam until the increase in the British bank rate in 1958 made participation too costly. The Government of Ghana then appealed to the United States where as we have noted above Douglas Dillon called the project to the attention of Edgar Kaiser and Chad Calhoun of Kaiser Industries. After study, the Kaiser people pronounced the dam economically feasible. In course of 1960, the United States Government held out for a moment the possibility of participation, and Kaiser and Calhoun tried to put together a consortium of aluminium companies to back the project. But as US relations with Ghana grew worse, most of the group except Reynolds Metals withdrew leaving Kaiser with ninety per cent of the consortium. In the beginning of 1961, there still remained the hope of getting support from the new administration. Meanwhile the President of Ghana had engaged on his fact-finding trip to the East European and socialist countries in 1961. From the view of his Western critics, each statement in each new communist capital drew him further from a position of non-alignment.

His tour of the communist countries with the resulting communique — read equally in the United States — raised new questions about the Volta River Dam at a time when good offices had almost brought the agreement to the point of signature. President J. F. K. Kennedy (who had been prevailed upon by friends to intervene on behalf of Ghana in the tough negotiations) now began to wonder whether it was appropriate to invest a large share of the limited funds set aside for Africa in a single project in a single country — above all, in a country which was not providing what was considered a sterling example either of liberalism at home or 'non-alignment' in the world. Congress of the United States was increasingly unhappy; Albert Gore and Kennedy's African sub-committee were hostile to American support for the dam. Public opinion was critical; Robert Kennedy was opposed; even Adlai Stevenson suggested that aid to the project be suspended. Only Chayes, Bowles, Williams and Fredericks at State Department were solidly in favour. On the other hand, Kaiser and Calhoun, whom President Kennedy had sent to Accra in October for tough talks with Dr. Kwame Nkrumah, returned with his cordial assurances that Ghana would stay on a course of true neutrality; and a circular inquiry to other African embassies friendly to the United States showed that most African governments, including some of Dr. Nkrumah's political enemies, hoped the United States would go ahead with the project. In any case, President Kennedy believed that this project would preserve a positive American presence within Ghana and that the Government of Ghana's nationalism would in the end prevail over their leanings towards the communist countries of the East. He, therefore, made the final decision to go ahead in November.

President Kennedy exercised great foresight in sanctioning American aid for the Volta River Project. If the project had been rejected on grounds of Nkrumah's visit to the East, it would have been a big blunder. What the United States did not know was that one of the most important reasons for Nkrumah's visit to the East was the ardent desire of the Ghana Government that China should have a normal diplomatic relations with the United States; and that socialist countries must do all in their power to lessen the cold war which was clearly at its apex at the time of the visit. Nkrumah, therefore, set out to break the concept of the bi-polar balance of power between US and Russia; he thought that it was too risky a situation, and that a misunderstanding or a mistake could precipitate a nuclear war which could bring about the extinction of the world; and Africa could only develop when there was peace. The Ghana Government saw China's admission to the UN and a diplomatic relationship between China and US as the basis for bringing about the tri-polar balance of power. In pursuit of this, the Ghana Government sent delegations to Peking and wide discussions were held with Premier Chou-En-Lai in order to break the impasse between China and the US.[49]

NOTES AND REFERENCES

1. The principle limitation on the Status of Refugees Convention, that it only covered events prior to January 1, 1951 (*See* Modlefi v Principal Legal Adviser (1971) AC 182 (1970) 3) All ER 724), has been remedied by the availability of an additional Protocol of 1967 (See. 606 UN Threaty Series 267).
2. UN Doc.E/1850, Article 28. The meaning of the terms 'expulsion' and 'return' ('refoulment') in this article and the following interpretation was recorded; that the word 'expulsion' related to a refugee already admitted into a country whereas the word 'return' ('refoulment') related to a refugee already within the territory but not yet resident there.
3. The Charter of the Organization of African Unity (1963) Article II.
4. Akinyemi, A. B. 1974. *Foreign Policy and Federalism*. University of Ibadan Press, p.93.
5. *Daily Times*, April 28, 1965.
6. *Ibid.*
7. Lauterpacht, Oppenheim 1953. *International Law*, 7th edn. London: p.618.
8. *Daily Times*, October 25, 1965.
9. Bing, Geoffrey 1968. *Reap the Whirlwind*, p.378.
10. Nkrumah, Kwame 1957. Speech to Parliament (Accra), August 29, 1957.

11. Cowan, Gray L. 1968. *The Dilemmas of African Independence*, p.8. New York.
12. International Commission of Jurists, Human Rights in a One-Party State (London) (1978), pp. 110–111.
13. Armah, Kwesi 1965. *Africa's Golden Road.* London: 67–68.
14. Bing 1967, p.35 and p.434.
15. *Ibid.*
16. Report of the Commission of Enquiry Into Disturbances in the Gold Coast (1948) Colonial No.231 (Colonial Office) London, H. Stationery Office, (1948) p.26.
17. Bing 1968, *op. cit.*, p.106.
18. *Ibid.*
19. *Ibid.*
20. *Ibid.*
21. Willets, B. and P. Willets 1974. The practice of non-alignment. In *Horizon of African Diplomacy* (ed. Y. A. Tanden & D. Chanarama) (Nairobi) 1974, p.15.
22. Wright Arthur W. 1960. Soviet economic planning and performance. In *The Soviet Union since Stalin* (ed. Stephen F. Cohen, Alexander Rabinowitch and Robert Sharlet). London: The Macmillan Press Ltd., p.117.
23. Hoeffding, Oleg 1959. The Soviet industrial reorganization of 1951. *American Economic Review* 49, p.65.
24. *Weekly Spectator* (Ghana) Saturday, June 21, 1980, p.5.
25. Wright 1980, pp. 124–125.
26. Thompson, Scott 1969. *Ghana's Foreign Policy, 1957–1966.* London: p.43.
27. For further details see the Minister of Defence, Hon. Kofi Baako's address on 'Nkrumahism — African Socialism' to the Conference of Ghana Envoys in Accra, January 1962. *Report of Conference of Ghana Envoys.* Vol.II 1962, pp. 118–124.
28. Nkrumah's address 'On Ideology" at the *First Seminar at Winneba, Ideological School (Ghana)* February 3 1962, passim.
29. Padmore, George 1964. A guide to Pan-African socialism', written in 1959 just before his death, and published as Appendix 1. In *African Socialism,* (eds. William H. Friedland and Carl C. Roseberg Jr.). Standford: Standford University Press, p.230.
30. *West Africa* "Nkrumahism and the Rebuilding of Ghana". January 5, 1981, p.20.
31. Kofi Awoonor, 'Kwame Nkrumah: Symbol of emergent Africa". *Africa Report,* June, 1972. p.23.
32. Ghana Today, Vol.6, No.20, December 5, 1962. London: 3.
33. See the text of the resolutions adopted by this conference in *Ghana Today,* Vol 7, June 5, 1963. London: Ghana High Commission, pp. 4–5.
34. See the discussions of the American viewpoint in Egyptian Gazette, November 10, 1961, and Egyptian Mail, November 25, 1961.
35. See State Department report on the first phase of the Geneva disarmament talks, in *Documents on American Foreign Relations* (1962) (New York, Harper & Row, 1963), pp.80–81; the remarks of Secretary Rusk in *Hearings Nuclear Test Ban Treaty.* US Senate Committee on Foreign Relations, 88th Cong., 1st Session (Washington DC: Government Printing Office, 1963), p.55; *The United States in World Affairs:* (1962) (New York: Harper & Row, 1963), p.71; *The New York Times,* November 10, 1963.
36. *Ghana Today* Vol.6 No.20, December 5, 1962, p.1.
37. Bing 1968, p.432; Armah, pp. 194–195; and Thompson 1969. See also Jansen, G. H. 1966. *Afro-Asian and Non Alignment,* p.338; Van Eckelen, W. F. 1964. *Indian Foreign Policy and the Border Dispute with China.* The Hague, p.121.
38. For full text of Dr. Nkrumah's letters, see *Ghana Today,* November 7, 1962. *See also Africa Report.* August, 1962, Vol.7, No.8,

39. *Ghana Today,* November 7, 1962.
40. *The New York Times,* June 22 and July 6, 1964.
41. Department of State press release No.113, dated 5 March, 1957 (Announcement of U.S. Recognition), as reproduced in *Department of State Bulletin* 36, p.389–390. Also reproduced in the same Bulletin the message from President Eisenhower to the Government and people of Ghana (White House Press Release, dated 6 March, 1957).
42. *Ibid.*
43. *Ibid.* Henry Cabot Lodge, U.S. Representative to the United Nations General Assembly, made the following statements: 'The United States will vote here in the General Assembly for the admission of Ghana to the United Nations as we did in the Security Council.
44. *Department of State Bulletin* 43 (1960), p.147.
45. *Ibid.*
46. Geoffrey Bing has given us an effective breakdown of the project according to which 'power as the smelter might require had to be sold by the Volta Hydro-Electric Authority at a fixed price of 2.625 nukks, which is equivalent to just under 1d a unit'. All the same it was cheaper than power could have been obtained by the companies elsewhere. In the United States it would have cost them up to 4 mills, in Western Europe between 4 and 6 mills and even in Japan, where power is cheap, between 2.7 mills and 4 mills. (Bing 1968), pp. 392.
47. *Ibid.*
48. Schelesinger, Jr., A. M. 1965. *A Thousand Days (John F. Kennedy in the White House.* Washington D.C.: 497.
49. Kwesi Armah, 1977. Looking Back to the Days of Nkrumah and the Government of the CPP. *New African Development* (London), March 1977, p.186.

Chapter 8

CONCLUSION

In this we may now summarize Ghana's pursuit of peace without the use of military and economic power from 1957 to 1966 — from independence to the first military coup d'etat.

It may be recalled that the importance of the problem examined lies in the fact that in the period under review, small and newly-independent states of the Third World considerably influenced the international behaviour of the Great Powers. The role of small and non-nuclear states in the mediation of the rivalry of Great Powers not to use nuclear weapons was a peculiar one. Indeed, small states like Ghana were threatened by the cold war between nuclear powers who were infinitely powerful and capable of imposing their will upon the small states and putting an end to their newly-gained independence. But this was rendered impossible by conflicting interests of the Great Powers themselves. Thus, the small states stood between the Great Powers, with the result that each nuclear Power preferred the maintenance of the newly-independent states to the extinction of their independence at the hands of the rival Power.

But however necessary the reliance of Ghanaian foreign policy on the prevention of nuclear warfare among the Great Powers, the real tests of Ghanaian foreign policy lay in the attempt to preserve and develop Ghanaian independence. This was expressed in (1) opposition to colonialism and neo-colonialism, (2) support for African freedom and unity, (3) the adoption of a common pan-African foreign policy, (4) an overall economic planning on a united-African basis including a more equitable system of international trade, (5) the creation of a joint-African military command, (6) the establishment of a 'Third Force' — a grouping of non-aligned states independent of the East and West and capable of a concerted policy of its own, (7) the international legal equality of all independent states and (8) co-operation between the industrialized states and the poorer states which comprise the great bulk of mankind.

The obstacles to a speedy adoption of these policies were the profound internal differences between the party in power (CPP) and the party in opposition (UP); between those in charge of the five influential and related departments of the Government: the Ministry of Foreign Affairs, the Bureau of African Affairs, the African Affairs Secretariat, the African Affairs Centre and the Civil Service; between the Government and public opinion; and between the politicians and soldiers. Thus, there developed major differences of approach which have been examined in Chapter 1. The inevitable result was that some of the differences caused annoying constitutional problems which had not been foreseen and about which nothing had been said in the Constitution of the First Republic. But subsequently, constitutional developments settled most of these problems which were made possible by the character of the existing Government, and Ghana's Government in this period was Government of the Convention Peoples Party. The power to conduct foreign policy or to maintain diplomatic relations with other states was vested in the President as a necessary part of his special powers under Article 55 of the first republican Constitution. According to Article 55(2), Parliament had no power to control the foreign policy prerogatives of the President. On the contrary, it was affirmed that whenever the President considered it to be in the national interest to do so, he could give directions by legislative instrument. However, in exercising this power to execute foreign policy, the President remained flexible. Changes and adaptations were in many cases made by the Foreign Ministry, the African Affairs Secretariat and the Bureau of African Affairs.

Ghana's foreign policy within the international community could not have been based on the external policy tradition of the colonial administration. In her capacity as the governing power of the then Gold Coast Colony, the United Kingdom Government had dictated the degree of freedom to be allowed the colonial administration with regard to external activities. The colonial structure was firmly controlled by Britain as the governing power of the Gold Coast Colony (Ghana). The colonization of the Gold Coast meant the loss on the part of the pre-colonial polities of their power to enter into foreign relations: the existing independent political entities within the territory of the Gold Coast became submerged under the sovereignty of the metropolitan Power. Thus, the pre-colonial modes of international intercourse with kingdoms like Ashanti were closed to those indigenous states and kingdoms. The new external relations became identified with those of Great Britain until the attainment of independence in 1957.

The Government of Ghana was no longer satisfied with an internal administration of the country only. On the contrary, they demanded concrete opportunities to demonstrate their independence. Thus, they were suspicious of rules which limited that independence. They regarded the first major political hurdle as de-colonization, and the consolidation of the newly-acquired independence against the forces of neo-colonization. They continuously remained opposed to all remaining forms of colonialism and/or neo-colonialism anywhere on the African continent or indeed in any part of the world. The Government was determined to resist old relationships according to which certain countries (colonies) remained producers of raw materials for the benefit of highly-industrialized countries (metropolitan powers) on other continents. But the Colonial Office believed in a centralized colonial structure firmly controlled by the United Kingdom Government which assured uniformity of colonial administration throughout the British Empire. For an independent Ghana, this exercise imposed a distorted economic, social and cultural patterns far beyond the territory. It diverted the foreign trade of the country from its natural direction, i.e., to neighbouring African states, almost invariably overseas to the metropolitan power and foreign industrialized states through the metropolitan power. The biting effects of such colonial operation were particularly evident in the field of inter-African communications: this lack of inter-communication between territories on the African continent posed one of the greatest obstacles to African unity and intra-continental developments.

That obstacle was only capable of being removed when independent African states were free to plan their communication systems in concert. This was only possible by the eradication of colonialism; for as long as colonialism still existed in any part of the African continent, it was impossible either to plan African development on a continental basis, or make the fullest use of African resources for the benefit of the people. Thus, the First Republican Government of Ghana placed this pan-continentalism as the cornerstone of the foreign policy of independent Ghana, which reflected a vision stretching beyond the territorial limits or frontiers of Ghana.

With the decline of colonial rule, there emerged pressures for the formation of new political units that were more closely representative of the economic, historical, and cultural affinities and diversities of the people in the country. The Government was at once faced with conflicting demands for both territorial integration and for regionalism in the sense of federation. They have to reconcile the need, on the one hand, for relatively large economic and political units (in order to facilitate rapid economic development and to sustain genuine regional independence), with on the other hand the desire for a centralized unitary government. These opposing pressures were confounded by the legacy of the colonial rule, which created within the artificial units of colonial administration in the country new loyalties and interests cutting across those of pre-existing cultural and traditional communities. Thus, the focal issue in nation-building became conflicting demands for unification and separation. Unitary government was the choice of the ruling party (CPP). Indeed, the apparently predominant trend against liberal democratic institutions, the propensity for active or executive presidential form of government, one party system, the emphasis upon rapid economic growth and national consolidation and solidarity, and the shortage of trained civil servants to manage complex systems of administration, all appeared to provide a generally unfavourable climate for a federal system of government. The Government believed in a unitary structure of government for the country because it was more suited to African conditions and especially the conditions of the newly-independent Ghana, than other constitutions based upon the historical pattern of certain older nations in Europe and America.

In contradistinction, a federal form of government automatically meant that it would be impossible to concentrate the limited manpower available in the central government machine. It would have to be dispersed in regional and the federal governments and would hence be very thin on the ground. Even more serious than this, could be the power vacuum a federal form of government would have created. Once institutions started laying down what powers a federal government would have, a vast area of doubt would at once be created. Just at a time when a strong government was necessary for the country, a federal administration as an alternative would be slowing down the process of government action. From the Government point of view federalism was a luxury which Ghana could not afford. The obvious solution, therefore, was a form of political organization which allowed expression to all ethnic groups and yet maintained that essential unity which was a pre-requisite of true independence.

Ghana supported the United Nations' emphasis on the idea of self-determination from 1960 onwards. In 1960, the process of de-colonization, in fact, reached its peak with the admission to the United Nations of sixteen newly-independent African States. The time was then ripe to concentrate on what had long since been a wide-spread ideal, namely self-determination for colonial peoples. On December 14, 1960, the Afro-Asian bloc saw its draft resolution on the "Declaration on the Granting of Independence to Colonial Countries and Peoples" accepted by an overwhelming majority in the General Assembly. Thus, becoming General Assembly resolution 1514 (XV), it would figure prominently in all future United Nations' resolutions relating to the question of colonialism. Ghanaian foreign policy in the Congo crisis of 1960 supported the United Nations — even when the Ghana Government was eventually to become highly critical of the United Nations actions. Though under considerable pressure from the more radical African states, the Ghana Government refused to withdraw Ghanaian troops as other states had done and throughout insisted on a solution being found within the framework of the United Nations.

The Ghanaian concern with de-colonization and Pan-Africanism led the Government to convene not only the First Conference of Independent African States but also the All African Peoples Conference both in Accra. The Conferences were able to work out consensus on matters such as de-colonization, an African foreign policy, economic, social and cultural goals, as well as on the methods to attain these aims, namely peaceful means of liberation and only a loose inter-state co-operation. It was assumed that unity would grow as the externally-imposed barriers fell, and that future meetings would do to give it periodic form. This was followed by direct material aids to nationalists leaders and colonial peoples from all parts of Africa.

The Ghanaian foreign policy within the Commonwealth was essentially directed to the preservation of the country's integrity as a Pan-African power and to secure and strengthen her Commonwealth connections. In another respect, the relationship of the Commonwealth provided advantages for Ghana through Britain's facilities and position as a member of the Western alliance and more recently, the European Economic Community. This is not to state that there were no criticisms of the internal developments in Ghana in other Commonwealth capitals. The British Press were very unhappy about the series of measures taken by the Government of Ghana in order to establish a sort of one-party administration: in particular British Press criticisms of the trends towards what was alleged as dictatorship in Ghana were so severe as to provoke counter-attack by the Ghanaian Press. Equally the Nigerian Press was very highly critical of political developments in Ghana.

Notwithstanding these differences, the Ghanaian foreign policy took into account the bonds of Commonwealth relations. Particularly important, as regards to Ghana's membership of the Commonwealth, were Ghanaian relations with the United Kingdom Government and the other member states of the Commonwealth in the Third World. Although the advent of independence formally established Ghana as an independent state and severed the colonial tie from Great Britain, it was clear that this did not mean the end of the special relationship that existed between Great Britain and Ghana. The power of the colonial heritage was too strong and the economic ties too binding to permit their dissolution by the mere grant of independence by the United Kingdom Parliament. Quite apart from the administrative and political structures left behind by the Government of the United Kingdom, the generation of Ghanaian leaders who assumed control at independence were bound by ties of sentiment and education to Great Britain, however bitter their anti-British feelings might have been during the period of the nationalist struggle. Some had spent extended periods of time in the United Kingdom. Most of the rest had received at least part of their education in the United Kingdom and even those who had not, had their schooling in educational institutions modelled on those of Britain.

For Ghana, the close connection with the Commonwealth was most important. Consequently, and in the interest of efficiency, the Commonwealth Secretariat was proposed by Ghana at the Commonwealth Prime Minister's Conference of 1964. Supported by the Prime Minister of Trinidad and Tobago and the Presidents of Uganda and Kenya, the proposal was adopted by the Prime Ministers Conference of 1965. Arnold Smith of Canada was appointed the first Secretary General. This idea of a permanent secretariat had been proposed without success at earlier times when centralizing machinery met with lack of enthusiasm on the part of some members, and the desire to avoid an upset of the existing arrangement, namely, the "continuous consultation of Cabinets" as an informal and flexible means of maintaining contact among Commonwealth countries, was entrenched.

Ghana Government's commitment to African unity was total as expressed in the First Republican Constitution. Article 2 provided that "in the confident expectation of an early surrender of sovereignty to a union of African states and territories, the people now confer on Parliament the power to provide for the surrender of the whole or any part of the sovereignty of Ghana". Article 13 included the following fundamental principles: "that the union of Africa should be striven for by every lawful means and, when attained, should be faithfully preserved; that the independence of Ghana should not be surrendered or diminished on any grounds other than the furtherance of African unity". The pivot of this unity was to be a union government consisting of an assembly of Heads of State and Government headed by a President elected from among the Heads of State and Government of the independent African states. The executive of the union government was to be a cabinet or council of ministers with a Chancellor or Prime Minister as its head, and a House consisting of two chambers — the Senate and a House of Representatives.

Although the political union proposed was the ideal, most African states present in Addis Ababa were of the opinion that a functional approach was more profitable and realistic at the time. Some believed that the idea of forming a Union of African States was premature, too radical and perhaps too ambitious to be of any value now. As the members of the African community travelled further from the moment of independence diverse national interests inevitably became more deeply entrenched. Consequently, the advantages of political unity became increasingly less apparent. It is suggested that all Africa's leaders had long realized that there were formidable obstacles in the way of true African unification. Differences of language and cultural background and the rivalries of ancient nations and ethnic groupings remain natural barriers to African solidarity. Despite the desire of the nationalist leaders to overcome the colonial heritage, the most natural groupings of the African states appeared to be those whose colonial and especially linguistic background was similar. As the abortive unions across the continent clearly have proved, the task of devising common institutions for countries that were the products of different colonial systems might be a difficult and arduous one. It became clear in the discussions which preceded the establishment of the Organization of African Unity, that the Heads of State were not yet ready to accept the idea of a political union of African states. Thus, during the Nkrumah era (1957–1966), the relations between the various units of the community of independent African states turned, in large degree, on one or another aspect of the theme of African unity. Without exception, the leaders of the new states placed African unity in the forefront of the goals of foreign policy for their countries. Not all were prepared, however, to accept the submergence of their new-found sovereignty into the union government of Africa that was advocated by the Ghana Government in its foreign policy. But at the same time, African unity was accepted as an ideal to be pursued and all were prepared to make at least some sacrifice of their complete independence in order to gain a greater measure of unity and co-operation.

The pattern of colonial economic development did little to improve the Ghanaian economy. Under colonial rule, the country had restricted economic links with the rest of the world. Its natural resources were developed only insofar as they served the interests of the foreign investors. The colonial officials in Ghana were not concerned with the foreign policy of the country; that was a matter for the Colonial Government in London. Their objective was the maintenance of law and order and the balancing of a budget which was designed, as far as possible, to maintain the colonial status. The colonial administration also limited the export of raw materials by preventing their direct shipment to foreign markets. Immense profits were made and taken out of the country. Significant mineral deposits attracted foreign capital, but this served mainly to enrich alien investors. There was no partnership in development, simply because there was no partnership at all.

It is true, therefore, to say that major barriers to foreign economic policy and growth after independence were due to the colonial heritage. The transportation network of the country was designed primarily by the colonial administration for service within the territory. Roads and railways were built from the coast inland but not across the Ghanaian borders into the neighbouring French colonies of La Côte d'Ivoire (the the Ivory Coast), Burkina Faso (then the Upper Volta), etc. Until independence, external communications were made through the United Kingdom. To telegraph to Accra, it was necessary to route one's message via London and even letters to Ghana had to follow a similar route. The operations of the foreign companies, together with systems of protective tariff, were such that, the trade of Ghana remained largely with the metropolitan country. The economy was almost static. This factor made work easier for colonial officials since innovation and development were invariably administratively difficult. As long as the colonial economy of the Gold Coast (Ghana) was functioning "adequately", i.e. to the satisfaction of the Colonial Office in London, the colonial officials were happy to go about their daily task of administration.

Indeed, Ghana continued its open economy after independence, and maintained the traditional outlook of the pre-independence period till 1961. Importance was, however, placed on changing the structure of the economy from a lop-sided primary goods-producing economy to, at least, a balanced agricultural and light industrial economy. The main objective behind this was to attain a certain measure of economic independence by reducing the country's economic vulnerability. The economy was to make possible the creation of the institutional structures that would mobilize and direct domestic and foreign savings for industrialization and provide the basic infrastructure necessary for such action. The Government developed a mixed economy in which vigorous public and co-operative sectors operated together with the private sector. By the Investment Act 1963, the Government refrained from any expropriation of foreign ventures in the country.

The bulk of the materials needed for the industrialization and infra-structural programme — especially machinery and construction materials — had to be imported. The country was, therefore, faced with the large import bills involved, which were paid from the foreign exchange reserves. Consequently, the net foreign exchange assets of the banking system were depleted considerably by 1966. As the import bills rose with the development programme but export earnings continued to fluctuate with the unstable world prices of the commodities exported from Ghana, particularly cocoa, the Government adopted a new policy involving increased trade with the centrally-planned economies of Eastern Europe and China. These countries offered generally-stable prices which, on the average, led to higher export earnings. The first phase of the country's industrial and infra-structural development had taxed its resources so much as to compel the Government to look for credit for its imports and bilateral trade agreements.

Furthermore, Ghana's pre-independence trade was heavily biased in favour of the West. It soon became clear that the long commercial practices of the trading companies of the West were in conflict with the independent foreign economic policy of Ghana. Many commercial houses then operating in the country were incorporated in the West and dealt with Western suppliers. The latter were not prepared to enter into bilateral trade agreements that deferred cash payments for imports — at a time when Ghana's determination to create the basic infra-structure necessary for the independent economy. On the other hand, economic transactions with the East European countries and China were always with the governments. These countries were always prepared to enter into bilateral trade agreements with Ghana which did not involve cash payments for imports. The Government's anti-neo-colonist posture was also at variance with some of the agreements which it was, out of necessity, signing with some western multinational companies. The embarrassments to the Government over some of these agreements increased their aversion to government-company dealings, especially with multinational companies.

During the colonial period, advanced processing of raw materials and industrial development within the territory was discouraged, if not actually prohibited. Manufacture of consumer goods or even the processing of raw materials scarcely existed. Private capital came from abroad; it, therefore, meant that quite a substantial part of the profits accruing from production were sent there. Few industrial skills were imparted to Africans, with the exception of employees of the public services — the workshops of Public Works Departments, the railway and the electricity corporations. Overseas capital in the country was used principally for the development of primary products for export to overseas markets. Investments in the extractive industry and in public utilities were dominated by export considerations. Independence ushered in changes in the interest of national development. The Government of the First Republic, by a direct appeal to a significant number of international and national agencies who made available the necessary corps of experts, wasted no time in restructuring vital aspects of the inherited colonial economy.

After independence, the sources of outside international aid available to Ghana greatly multiplied. New European sources opened up, and countries like Britain, West Germany, Holland, Denmark, Scandinavia and many in Eastern Europe became important donors of aid to Ghana. Israel also extended technical assistance to Ghana. A wide variety of international bodies, such as the World Bank, the United Nations Technical Assistance Fund, the International Monetary Fund and many others made available loans, grants and technical personnel. The Government of Ghana was well aware that aid frequently carried with it invisible political strings. Thus, it was a constant source of concern for the Government to avoid commitment or implied political support which went with certain aid programmes. The Government made sure that Ghana was in the end, the one to decide whether or not to accept the foreign aid, and how far it should go in co-operating with the donor nation as to the use of the aid. The Government was not prepared to allow complete foreign ownership where investment was open to foreign investors. The bulk of Ghanaian industry still remained closed to complete foreign ownership. The basic policy was to foster joint ventures in which Ghanaian participation was at a percentage of equity.

The Government was aware that a major requirement for the country's development plans was the accumulation of real capital. Ghana's economy after independence had more than enough room for all the investment capital that was available from foreign investors, central and local governments as well as individual citizens. But there were a considerable number of individual Ghanaians who invested their profits abroad and outside of the country. One of the worst features of colonialism was that it produced an unbalanced economy in which there was little room for investment of the profits which were made by expatriate firms in particular. In the colonial period, it was most appropriate that profits made in the country be invested abroad. But the situation changed after independence. It was then argued that an investor who laid out his money wisely in Ghana was likely to make a larger profit than if he had invested it in a more developed country overseas. All the same, old habits of investment during the colonial period persisted and there were still a considerable number of Ghanaians who kept their savings — even after independence, in foreign investments and in properties outside of Ghana.

Exchange control was one of the means adopted by the Government to remedy this situation. While the Government maintained a liberal trade policy, it was convinced that a system of exchange control offered a ready-made weapon to combat the drain on the country's foreign exchange reserves. Furthermore, exchange control regulations rendered it impossible to avoid tax; whether in the form of a penalty, exchange rate or an exchange tax. The Government was determined to make certain that all foreign exchange received by residents of Ghana was actually surrendered to them. Under the 1963 Exchange Control Law of Ghana, it was illegal for Ghanaians to have property abroad without having declared it to the appropriate authorities. However, this aspect of the law was not always understood by the people and, therefore, the Government leaned backwards to make allowance for their ignorance and take a lenient view of the violations of the law in this respect.

Ghanaian foreign economic policy was firmly set against any type of formal link of the country with the European Economic Community. The Government believed that the association with the EEC under Article 131 of the Rome Treaty would hamper the industrialization programme of Ghana. Until the end of his regime, Dr. Nkrumah carried on a campaign against the Community with a view to dissuading other African non-associates from joining it and the associated African countries from continuing their association. The Ghanaian foreign policy viewed the EEC as not merely an attempt to effect the political, military and economic union of western Europe but as eventually an economic means of impeding progress and development of primary producing countries. Furthermore, to associate with the EEC under Part IV, Article 131 of the Rome Treaty would conflict with Ghanaian foreign policy of non-alignment. Any association, in the view of the Government, would be contrary to the principles of African unity.

On the contrary, Ghana called on all African states to unite to build an African Common Market "rather than serve as appendages to the European Common Market". Despite the fact that the structure of the economy of the African states did not make an African Common Market a very attractive proposition, Ghana believed that such an African Common Market using a common currency and operating a common external trade policy would be in the best interests of the whole of the African people. An African Common Market would also attract into the continent more foreign investment, and promote the growth of great industrial complexes in Africa. Finally, it was argued that such a Common Market of Africa would turn the continent of Africa into an economic giant as powerful as any of the existing economic giants such as the United States, the Soviet Union and West Germany. Ghana also favoured an African Common Market because it would boost inter-African trade and enable the continent of Africa to stand on its own economically as did other parts of the world.

In the opening paragraphs of our conclusions we stated that Ghanaian independence, as expressed in an effective international state practice, was against a potential nuclear holocaust. Consequently, the concern of the Government of Ghana, in international affairs, was not only with the liberation and unification of Africa but also with the struggle for world peace and security, which is indeed a vital condition for economic development in the Third World.

An important instrument of Ghana in her struggle for peace was the United Nations Organization and its specialized agencies which can be counted on effectively to promote international peace. To be effective in these international organizations, Ghana and other members of the Third World insisted upon the principle of equality. The emergence of so many new Afro-Asian independent states within a short time caused practical problems with regard to the implementation of this principle. At the UN, Ghana identified itself with projects and discussions which aimed at protecting the right of states to sovereign equality and to full and equal participation in the life of the community of nations; and in the creation and modification of rules of the international community. Ghana advocated the entitlement of the newly-independent states to every assistance on the part of the international community in making their equality effective, especially in the economic field.

Ghana was represented at the nineteenth session debate of the General Assembly of the United Nations with respect to the expenses relating to the UN forces engaged in peace-keeping operations. This debate was chaired by the Ghanaian Representative, Alex Quaison-Sackey, as President of the Assembly in this period. For the first time in history, a force of this type was necessary to work toward the peaceful settlement of dangerous international disputes. Efforts to achieve this goal had been made many times in the past: always they had failed. The issue had become increasingly complicated with the rise of similar difficulties in regard to the UN activities in the Congo. Expenses for the Congo Force, like those for the United Nations Emergency Force (UNEF), were treated as a special account and assessed on the basis of the scale for regular expenses of the Organization. A significant achievement of the 19th session of the UN General Assembly was the decision that all member states were legally obliged to participate in the financing of the UNEF. The UNEF, they agreed, was fundamentally the responsibility of the entire Organization.

Ghana opted for positive neutrality in her foreign policy. The term neutrality means the attitude of impartiality adopted in international affairs by third states towards belligerents and recognized by belligerents, such attitude creating rights and duties between the impartial states and the belligerents. In the state of the cold war which existed between the Soviet Union and the United States by the time of the First Republic of Ghana, those super powers were considered belligerents by third states including Ghana. Whether or not Ghana adopted an attitude of impartiality in that cold war was entirely a question of international politics. Under the impact of the cold war, the most important basis of non-alignment was abstention from permanent alignment with either bloc.

Outside the UN, Ghana fought, where possible, for the preservation of the continent of Africa as a non-nuclear zone. The Government obtained the co-operation of other independent African states towards the achievement of that objective. Ghana organized an eight-day ban-the-bomb conference in Accra, rallying international opinion against the use of nuclear weapons. The Accra Conference called for a positive campaign by all peoples of the world to awaken the conscience of the world and to secure the banning of atomic tests, destruction of all weapons of mass slaughter and the reduction of conventional armament. In his address to the Conference, the President of Ghana reminded all persons and organizations engaged in the struggle for the abolition of nuclear weapons that their task would be just as arduous as for those who struggled against slavery. He believed an almost exact parallel existed with the issue of war and peace in our own time. He cautioned the Conference that in ridding the world of the threat of nuclear warfare, vehement protest was an essential element to arouse man's conscience. The Conference accepted the recommendations of its commissions and endorsed the concept of a nuclear-free Africa and welcomed the initiative taken by the people of Africa. It proposed the creation of nuclear-free zones in other areas, such as South-East Asia, the Middle East and Latin America, along with a number of other proposals. The Government offered facilities for the establishment of a secretariat in Accra to implement the proposals of the Conference and to plan future conferences.

Ghana pleaded for a peaceful settlement during the Cuban missile crisis between the United States of America and the Soviet Union. The Ghanaian President addressed correspondence to both President Kennedy of the United States and Nikita Krushchev of the Soviet Union, expressing his pleasure at the restraint of the two leaders in the matter, and arguing that the whole world had been gravely disturbed by the course of events which led to the Cuban missile crisis. In his capacity as a member of the Commonwealth, the President of Ghana addressed a similar message to Mr. Harold Macmillan, the British Prime Minister.

The nine years of independence (1957–1966) gave ample opportunities to discuss other major issues of world politics e.g. general disarmament, international peace and security, the problem of refugees and displaced persons, the cold war between the United States of America and the Soviet Union, and the problems of the non-aligned states of the Third World.

On disarmament, the foreign policy of Ghana supported a genuine general disarmament and the complete prohibition and thorough destruction of nuclear weapons; especially the establishment by the super powers of a nuclear-free zone in Africa. The signing of the nuclear-test-ban accord of 1963 by Ghana and some non-aligned states indicates that, peace was also the concern of the third world states.

On these questions of disarmament and the complete prohibition of nuclear weapons Ghana's relationship with the opposing super powers, the Soviet Union and the United States of America, was defined as that of non-alignment. Her foreign policy was aimed essentially at the settlement of international issues through peaceful negotiations among states and the strengthening of the non-aligned states' solidarity. Ghana was aware that the greatest danger facing mankind then emanated from lack of understanding between nations in general and the two nuclear powers in particular. There was no cause better than that of reconciling these super powers and the elimination of the cold war between them and their respective allies. Super power military balance did not follow that existing armaments in the world could be left where they were, allowed to increase without eminent danger of world catastrophe as Ghana had always dreaded. The rivalries and differences among the great powers remained and competitive striving to maintain prestige before the rest of the world might touch off a nuclear war. Thus, world disarmament, in the foreign policy of Ghana, was not an issue to be pursued in isolation, as the experience of the League of Nations after the rise of Hitler's Nazis showed. The First Republic of Ghana, therefore, believed that a frontal attack on the level of armaments must be resolutely pursued with redoubled efforts to reduce tension.

In view of Ghana's inclination to non-alignment, the question had to be faced in respect of the implications for Ghana's economic development, which required links with the United States and the Soviet Union. It might have been argued that strict non-alignment entailed a complete severing of all such links. If Ghana alone had renounced trade with and economic aid from the two super powers, other countries in Africa would not have followed suit, and the only result would have been to weaken her still further economically and make her even more dependent. Ghana was incapable of remaining in a permanently-dependent position.

So far as the First Republic of Ghana can be accused of favouring either of the two nuclear super powers, it was the United States, and in so far as any of the Ghanaian development projects were of a neo-colonialist nature, the Volta Hydro-Electric Scheme best fitted the pattern. It involved an extraordinarily-generous agreement with two United States firms, the Kaiser Aluminium and Chemical Corporation and the Reynolds Metal Company. It was planned at a time when aluminium was short in the sterling area. It was devised as a scheme to develop the very large bauxite deposits in Ghana. President Kennedy believed that the Volta project would preserve a positive American presence within Ghana and that the Government of Ghana's nationalism would, in the end, prevail over their leanings towards the communist countries of the East. With foresight he, therefore, sanctioned American aid for the Volta River Project.

One of the most important reasons for the visit of the President of Ghana to the East was the ardent desire on his part to bring about a diplomatic relation between China and the United States. It was his desire to do all he could to lessen the cold war that existed between them. It was the foreign policy of Ghana in this period to break the bi-polar balance of power between the United States and the Soviet Union. Thus, the Government saw China's admission to the United Nations and a diplomatic relationship between China and the United States as the basis for bringing about a tri-polar balance of power. In pursuit of this, the Ghana Government sent delegations to Peking and wide discussions were held with Premier Chou-En-Lai and other Chinese leaders in order to bring peace between China and the United States.

In spite of the rapid growth of the Ghana foreign service after independence the establishment of diplomatic relations with the Soviet Union came at a later date; Ghana had become independent in March 1957, but it was not until April, 1959 that agreement was reached between Ghana and the Soviet Union to establish diplomatic relations, and for a Soviet Ambassador to be in Accra. Early in 1960, the Ghana Government sent an advance party to Moscow to open Ghana's Embassy. The immediate result of that diplomatic exchange was the sale of considerable quantities of Ghanaian cocoa beans to the Soviet Union and its allies. This trade was by way of long-term contracts on a bilateral basis. The relationship between Ghana and the Soviet Union and the other East European countries was in disregard of the ideological cleavage between the Soviet Union and China and the United States of America. Thus, in the same period and at the invitation of the Ghana Government, Premier Chou En-Lai of China paid a visit to Ghana in 1962 and 1964.

Ghana also engaged in other peace moves in addition to her attempts to bring the United States and the Soviet Union together. For example, Ghana took the initiative in forming the Committee of Non-aligned States which produced the compromise that helped to contain the Sino-Indian conflict in 1962. Indeed, that conflict provided a testing ground for non-alignment — not only in challenging the sincerity of India's devotion to the principle of non-alignment, but also in testing the ability of other non-aligned states to apply their professed principles to a situation involving one of their own leading spokesmen. In this conflict, Ghana and the non-aligned states were placed in a dilemma between their overwhelming sympathy for India and their realization that no other nation, or group of nations, was in a position to extinguish a blaze that might well ignite a world war. The United States quite obviously was unable to do so, due to the extreme animosity that had long characterized Sino-American relations. The Soviet Union was not in a position to do so, because of its defence ties with the People's Republic of China then, its acute embarrassment over China's aggressiveness, and its professed friendship with India and other non-aligned states. The United Nations was not in a position to do so, because the People's Republic of China did not yet belong to the Organization and showed no willingness to accept its jurisdiction. Besides, United Nations Secretary General U. Thant publicly doubted the United Nations usefulness in the Sino-Indian dispute. This left the non-aligned states helpless. They sent a peace mission to India and China. The delegation included the Prime Minister of Sri Lanka and Ghana's Minister of Justice, to explain to both disputants the sole purpose of the Conference, which was to establish the conditions for peaceful direct negotiations between the parties. The People's Republic of China eventually co-operated, at least minimally, with the non-aligned mediation, for a variety of reasons.

On July 30, 1981, Dr. Henry Kissinger, former American Secretary of State for Foreign Affairs, speaking in the *The Times* on "A unique opportunity to re-forge the alliance with an America no longer in trauma," said "Many of us tend to think of developing countries in the way we did of Europe at the time of the Marshall Plan. That is to say we have thought there was an automatic connection between economic progress and political stability. In fact, in many developing countries, the process of economic development is bound to produce the opposite. This is not an argument against economic development, but it is an argument about being thoughtful about what it is we can work for and how we should go if, I would argue, for example that the primary cause of the collapse of the pro Western government in Iran was a rate of economic growth of 10 per cent a year."[1]

This view of Kissinger, an influential foreign policy maker of the world's most powerful nation, could be said to be representative of Western governments and financial institutions like the IMF and the World Bank. He warns them to be careful about assisting developing countries to develop, because as was in Iran, economic progress brings political chaos. If possible, developing countries should be kept underdeveloped. The rich nations must continue to dominate the world and dictate economic policies. Hence "globalization" a euphemism for world government in which the Western world and international financial cartels, led by the IMF and the World Bank, play a leading role. The structural adjustment programmes and privatization policies of the IMF/World Bank are all part of the grand design to keep Africa and its people underdeveloped. Africa is being asked to open up its economy to foreign investors, if the continent is to develop. But will it?

As Sir Thomas Moore puts it, "Where wealth is successfully employed its increase is in proportion to its amount; great capitalists become like pikes in a fish pond, who devour the weaker fish; and it is but too certain that the poverty of the one part of the people seems to increase in the same ratio as the riches of another."[2]

Unless globalization caters adequately for the needs of the Third World such as transfer of technology and information, fair trade not free trade, and debt cancellation, it will lead to the neo-colonization of the world, with Africa suffering the most.

What must Africa do to extricate itself from the creeping clutches of neo-colonialism? The challenge facing Africa is to go back, to revisit Nkrumah's arguments for economic independence. They must integrate their individual economies into a continental one, to create the necessary institutional structures to mobilize direct domestic and foreign savings for industrialization. Industrialization is the key to Africa's development and all efforts must be geared towards that goal. We must rethink our reliance on primary products as the main source of foreign exchange earnings. The economy must be diversified to place emphasis on the development of the non-traditional export sector and industrialization.

African nations need to develop their communication networks between themselves as a means of bringing them closer together and making their common intercourse easier and more fruitful. Foreign investment must be welcomed in a spirit of partnership, i.e., foreign investment allow local ownership participation in some industries or investment projects. In other words, there must never be one hundred per cent foreign ownership in the economy.

Above all, there must be an African union government to plan the economic development of the continent. When Nkrumah was asking for an African union government, the West, afraid of losing their vested interests, accused him of over-ambition and lack of realism. Unfortunately, other African leaders supported the Western view and sabotaged Nkrumah's plan for Africa's emancipation. But while the West were actively undermining Nkrumah to ensure the failure of his scheme, they were "nicodemously" planning their own integration. And today the Europeans are more united than Africans. Now what is good for the goose must be good for the gander. If integration is good for Europeans why should it be bad for Africans?

Unless Africa goes back to Nkrumah's ideas, the continent will continue to wallow in the quagmire of neo-colonialism. And the consequences of neo-colonialism can be pretty grim not only for the neo-colonized but also for the neo-colonizers. Without wishing to sound like the prophet of doom, the next generation would not stomach what the present generation is swallowing: economic recovery programmes, structural adjustment and globalization policies of the IMF/World Bank. If the globalization policies continue to widen the gap between the rich and poor nations, political instability, civil strife and wars will erupt in the latter nations and create problems for the former.

We are not saying that we do not need the financial support of the IMF and the World Bank. No. What we are saying is that their policies must be fashioned to work for us and not to destroy us. The linkage of economic reforms with democracy is a policy fraught with danger, unless democracy can also be funded because the economy cannot sustain democracy as it is an expensive exercise. The danger is that a democracy that is not funded leads to a *de facto* one party state. The incumbent takes advantage of its incumbency to organize elections with state funds and win hands down. So unless the state funds all registered political parties to create a level playing field, the incumbent political party will continue to win elections after elections, despite its incompetence, to the anger and frustrations of other parties who think they must also rule. This creates tension, political instability and *coups d'etat.*

For as Tsatsu Tsikata, a Senior Lecturer, University of Ghana, Legon and Adviser to the defunct Provisional National Defence Council, Accra, and former Chief Executive, Ghana National Petroleum Corporation, said:

> Without an automatic compensatory financial device, the volatility of commodity prices poses severe danger to reform programmes, of the kind Ghana is undertaking, for just as the programmes get underway, adverse terms of trade wipe off the value of increased production . . . that is why the policies of stabilization is often also the policies of destabilization, as a Government determined to effect these transformations will face attempts to overthrow it. Ghana has had its full share of such destabilization effects and perhaps the best testimony to the role of the vested interests in these attempts had been the extent of external financial resources as well as external political backing they have received even from quarters in which the economic reforms have been applauded. It is possible such "reforms" could be carried out in a manner that restores the pre-eminence of the vested interests which would firmly sustain the neo-colonial order. But quite simply, in our view, unless the neo-colonial state is transformed or is transforming, there can be little hope for sustained recovery for Africa's economies much less hope of attaining developments.[3]

This view appears to be one of the best assessments of the IMF/World Bank policies on the economies of Africa. If these policies persist, the future will not augur well for both Africa and the developed world. Africa, therefore, presents both a window of opportunity and disaster. Opportunity, in that, if the policies of the West work for Africa, there will be peace and security in the world and if they fail there will be disaster. As people are denied education, health, employment and food, they become restless. They take to the streets in demonstrations as is evident on the campuses and work places. A sign that we are sitting on a tinderbox and only a spark is needed to ignite it into an inferno.

Of special concern is the increasing outflow of Africa's resources to the developed countries. The activities of Trans National Corporations(TNCs) are responsible for this outflow of capital. "The industrial profits of TNCs have long since surpassed their capital investment. In the period 1970–1982 alone, the repatriation of these profits from Africa equalled US$24 billion whereas the overall sum of direct investment as of the end of 1981 was no more than US$15.5 billion."⁴ This means that TNCs put less capital in the economy and take more from it.

African countries are also being plundered at the level of external trade. The prices of export commodities continue to fall while those of imports continue to rise. "In 1986 when export prices literally collapsed, Africa's export earnings declined from US$60.6 billion in 1985 to US$44.3 billion."⁵ And the foreign debt burden to the capitalist states and banks amounted to nearly US$200 billion in 1986, which is twice as much as Africa's average annual export revenues. These adverse developments actually deprive African countries of the much-needed capital to sustain development.

All these go to show that only the implementation of Nkrumah's arguments for African unity and African economic integration and the establishment of the African High Command can save Africa from total collapse. Given the present policies of the IMF and the World Bank, there is not much hope that things will change for the better in the future. The process of structural and technological changes in the economies of the advanced countries will continue to have an adverse impact on developing countries, structural changes entailing a steady decline in the demand for raw materials of the developing countries. Faced with these adverse developments, Africa can only survive by embracing and implementing Nkrumah's ideas for the continent.

While it would be a mistake to exaggerate Ghana's impact on the international political relations of the great powers, this study does perhaps show that despite the fact that Ghana between 1957 and 1966 was a small, weak, poor and new and untried state, its role in world affairs was by no means insignificant. In the UN, in the Commonwealth, in the Non-Aligned Movement and above all in African affairs, Ghana was able to play an important role — partly because of circumstances and partly because of effective leadership.

NOTES AND REFERENCES

1. Henry, Kissinger, 1981. "A unique opportunity to reforge the alliance with America no longer in trauma", *The Times*, July 30, 1981.
2. Moore, Sir Thomas 1963. *After Imperialism*, by M.B. Brown, CASS, 1963, p.viii.
3. Tsikata, Tsatsu 1990. "Ghana" *The Human Dimension of Africa's Persistent Economic Crisis*, (ed. Adebayo Adedeji, Sadig Rasheed and Melody Morison), London: Han Zell Publishers, pp. 143–161.
4. Sorokine, A. A. 1971. The Challenge of African Economic Recovery and the concept of the International Economic security. *The Challenge of African Economic Recovery and Development*, (ed. Adebayo Adedeji, Owodunni Teriba and Patrick Bugeme). Exeter: Frank CASS: London: pp. 271–284.
5. *Ibid.*

Appendix 1

Export of Domestic Produce 1957–1966
Percentage Distribution of Commodities

Commodities	1957	1958	1959	1960	1961	1962	1963	1964	1965	1966
Cocoa Beans	55.9	60.0	61.0	58.0	61.6	60.0	63.7	60.2	61.1	0.6
Cocoa Paste	–	–	1.0	0.9	0.9	0.8	0.2	0.2	0.4	0.6
Cocoa Butter	–	–	–	–	0.4	2.5	3.2	3.9	5.1	6.2
Timber (Logs)	5.9	6.0	7.1	9.1	8.0	5.2	6.7	7.1	5.9	5.9
Timber (Sawn)	5.0	4.6	4.7	4.8	5.5	5.8	5.4	5.9	5.1	5.4
Bauxite	–	–	0.3	0.5	0.4	0.6	0.5	0.6	0.6	0.8
Manganese	9.9	8.3	6.0	5.6	5.4	4.9	3.7	3.8	4.3	6.5
Diamonds	9.9	8.3	7.7	8.6	6.3	6.7	3.1	5.4	6.1	5.8
Gold	10.8	10.2	9.9	9.7	9.5	10.1	10.7	9.1	8.5	9.2
Kola Nuts	–	–	0.7	1.1	0.9	1.3	0.8	0.3	0.3	0.7
Others	2.6	2.6	1.7	1.7	1.6	2.1	2.0	3.5	2.6	3.4
Total	100.0	100.0	100.0	100.0	100.0	100.0	100.0	100.0	100.0	100.0
Value of Domestic Produce Exported (N¢' mill)	181.9	207.6	225.5	228.8	225.1	223.4	213.7	226.4	223.4	185.8
Value of Total Exports (N¢' mill)	183.2	209.1	226.7	232.0	229.0	230.1	217.6	229.3	226.9	191.4
% of Domestic Produce Exported to Total Exports	99.3	99.3	99.5	98.6	98.3	97.6	98.2	98.7	98.5	97.1

Source: Ghana Central Bureau of Statistics Economic Surveys, 1958, 1960, 1964 and 1966.

Appendix 2

Imports by End Use (Percentage of Total Value)

End use	1956	1957	1958	1959	1960	1961	1962	1963	1964	1965	1966
Non-durable consumer goods	44.0	47.4	44.9	42.1	41.3	41.2	41.9	33.1	29.5	28.7	27.2
Durable consumer goods	10.2	9.4	9.6	8.2	8.6	8.2	6.3	6.3	4.1	5.5	3.8
Raw and Semi-finished Materials	25.7	24.1	25.0	26.0	23.9	27.7	28.0	30.4	34.0	31.5	34.3
Capital Equipment	15.1	12.9	13.9	18.8	21.6	18.7	18.2	24.7	26.7	30.2	30.6
Fuel and Lubricants	5.0	6.2	6.6	4.9	4.6	4.2	5.6	5.5	5.7	4.0	4.1
Total Imports	100.0	100.0	100.0	100.0	100.0	100.0	100.0	100.0	100.0	100.0	100.0

Source: Ghana Central Bureau of Statistics Economic Surveys, 1960, 1964 and 1966.

Appendix 3

Net Foreign Exchange Assets of the Banking System (£G' mill)

Period	With Bank of Ghana	With other Banking Institutions	Total
1957	–	–	–
1958	31.1	14.4	45.4
1959	43.4	10.8	54.2
1960	53.8	6.5	60.3
1961	45.4	3.1	48.5
1962	47.9	−2.3	45.6
1963	35.5	−6.0	29.5
1964	27.5	−3.8	23.7
1965	0.3	−9.0	−8.7
1966	9.5	−11.3	−1.8

Source: Ghana Central Bureau of Statistics Economic Surveys, 1964 and 1966.

Appendix 4

Ghana's Medium-Term Debt Burden as at June 1996 by Country

A. IMF Members Countries

Country	Debt	% to IMF Total	% to Grand Total
United Kingdom	110.17	41.4	33.0
West Germany	42.57	16.0	12.7
Netherlands	25.45	9.6	7.6
Yugoslavia	18.54	6.9	5.5
Italy	15.99	6.0	4.8
France	16.42	6.2	4.9
Japan	15.69	5.9	4.7
Spain	7.66	2.8	2.3
Norway	8.92	3.4	2.7
Israel	2.67	1.0	0.8
Belgium	1.30	0.4	0.3
USA	0.72	0.3	0.2
USSR	0.16	0.1	0.0
Canada	0.07	0.0	0.0
Australia	0.06	0.0	0.0
Total IMF Member Countries	266.39	100.0	79.7

B. NON-IMF COUNTRIES

Country	Debt	% to IMF Total	% to Grand Total
Czechoslovakia	13.27	19.6	4.0
Rumania	1.54	2.3	0.5
USSR	30.99	45.7	9.3
China	6.72	9.9	2.1
East Germany	0.89	1.3	0.3
Poland	10.63	15.7	3.2
Hungary	2.41	3.5	0.7
Bulgaria	1.39	2.0	0.4
Total Non-IMF Countries	67.85	100.0	20.3
C: GRAND TOTAL ALL COUNTRIES (A + B)	334.24		100.0

Source: J. H. Mensah 1970. *The State of the Economy and the External Debts Problem.* Accra:15.

Appendix 5

Direction of Trade (% Share)

Source of import	1957 Impt	1957 Expt	1958 Impt	1958 Expt	1959 Impt	1959 Expt	1960 Impt	1960 Expt	1961 Impt	1961 Expt	1962 Impt	1962 Expt	1963 Impt	1963 Expt	1964 Impt	1964 Expt	1965 Impt	1965 Expt	1966 Impt	1966 Expt
Sterling Areas	42.2	42.2	43.3	36.2	46.4	34.8	41.7	36.0	41.0	32.8	38.8	35.2	38.8	31.9	35.4	26.4	28.9	23.8	30.9	28.6
UK alone	–	–	–	–	40.1	30.8	36.7	31.3	36.3	28.7	34.6	31.5	32.8	28.2	27.4	23.1	25.8	20.8	28.8	25.0
African Countries	–	–	–	–	3.2	1.7	1.6	2.0	0.6	1.3	0.5	1.0	2.2	0.7	3.6	0.7	1.6	1.0	1.0	0.9
EEC	19.1	29.4	29.0	18.1	22.3	37.8	25.6	35.1	21.7	31.9	22.3	28.0	25.3	38.6	23.0	29.4	21.4	27.8	21.2	22.0
Dollar Areas	5.8	16.8	6.0	19.8	8.8	19.8	8.3	15.9	11.0	24.7	11.3	19.6	8.8	16.9	11.6	22.9	10.5	18.6	17.5	17.0
Centrally Planned Economics (China, USSR and other East European Countries)	1.5	6.8	1.6	0.4	3.3	1.9	4.1	6.9	5.4	4.7	7.5	8.9	11.0	13.7	15.8	11.8	26.3	21.3	15.2	21.0
African Countries (excluding those in Sterling Area)	–	–	–	–	4.0	0.4	5.2	1.6	6.7	1.5	6.2	2.5	4.5	1.1	5.8	1.3	2.8	0.9	3.3	1.0
Japan	10.7	–	8.0	–	7.6	0.5	8.3	0.8	7.7	1.4	6.6	2.1	6.2	3.4	5.4	3.5	4.3	2.3	5.3	4.9
Others	20.7	42.8	12.1	25.5	6.2	4.8	5.4	3.7	5.1	2.9	6.3	3.7	4.9	4.4	2.4	4.7	5.4	5.3	6.4	5.3
Parcel Post	–	–	–	–	1.4	0.0	1.4	0.0	1.4	0.1	1.0	0.0	1.0	0.0	0.6	0.0	0.4	0.0	0.2	0.0
TOTAL	100.0	100.0	100.0	100.0	100.0	100.0	100.0	100.0	100.0	100.0	100.0	100.0	100.0	100.0	100.0	100.0	100.0	100.0	100.0	100.0

Source: Ghana Central Bureau of Statistics Economic Surveys, 1962, 1964, 1966.

BIBLIOGRAPHY

Abraham, P. 1954. Last word on Nkrumah. *West African Review*, xxv, p.913.
Abraham, W. E. 1967. *The Mind of Africa*, London.
Adedeji, Adebayo, et al., (ed.) 1990. *The Human Dimension of Africa's Persistent Economic Crisis*. London: Hans Zell.
Adedeji, Adebayo, et al., (ed.) 1971. *The Challenge of Africa Economic Recovery and Development*. London: CASS.
Adu. A. L. 1965. *The Civil Service in New African States*, London.
Akinyemi, A. B. 1974. *Foreign Policy and Federalism*. Ibadan: University of Ibadan Press.
Aluko, Olajide 1976. *Ghana and Nigeria: A Study in Inter-African Discord*. London.
Armah, Kwesi 1965. *Africa's Golden Road*, London: Hernemann.
Armah, Kwesi 1974. *Ghana: Nkrumah's Legacy*, London: Paul Mall Press.
Armah, Kwesi 1977. Looking Back to Days of Nkrumah and the Government of CPP, *New African Development*, March 1977. London.
Aron, Raymond 1966. *Peace and War: A Theory of International Relations*, (Translated by Richard Howard and Annette Baker Fox). New York
Austin, Denis 1961. *The Province of Jurisprudence*. London.
Awoonor. Kofi 1972. Kwame Nkrumah: Symbol of Emergent Africa. *Africa Report*, June, 1972.
Bauer. P. T. 1954. *West African Trade*. London: Routeledge and Kegan Paul.
Benemy, F. W. G. 1965. *The Elected Monarch — The Development of the Powers of the Prime Minister*, London.
Bing, Geoffrey 1967. *Reap The Whirlwind*: A UN Case History. London.
Birmingham, W. 1966. The economic development in Ghana. In *Planning and Growth of Rich and Poor Countries* (ed. W. Birmingham and A. G. Ford). London.
Birmingham, W. and Ford, A.G.V 1966. *Planning and Growth in rich and Poor Countries*. London.
Bretton, H. L. 1966. *The Rise and Fall of Kwame Nkrumah*. London: Paji Mall.
Burton, J. W. 1960. *Non-Alignment*. London.
Cohen, S. F., Rabinowitch, A. and Sharlet, R. (ed.) 1960. *The Soviet Union Since Stalin*. London: The Macmillan Press.
Coldicott, T. 1964. *Post-Graduate Seminar Paper: Ghana's External Relations*, London: Institute of Commonwealth Studies.
Cowan, Gray L. 1968. *The Dilemmas of African Independence*. New York: Walter and Company.
Crossman, R. H. G. 1963. *Introduction to Bgehot. The English Constitution* (new edn). London.
Dei-Anang, M. F. 1975. *The Administration of Ghana's Foreign Relations, 1957–1965: A Personal Memoir*. London.
Dobson. 1956. *The Coming Struggle in Africa*.
Douglas-Home, Lord, 1978. *The Way the Wind Blows. An Autobiography*. London:
Du Bois, W. E. B. 1921. A second journey to Pan-Africa. *New Republic*. December 7, 1921.
Eekelen, Van W. F. 1964. *Indian Foreign Policy and Border Dispute with China*. The Hague.
Frankel, Joseph 1963. *The Making of Foreign Policy: An Analysis of Decision-Making*. Oxford:
Friedland William, H. and Roseberg, Carl, C. (ed.) 1964. *African Socialism*. Standford: Stanford University Press.
Goodrich, L. M. 160. *The United Nations*. London.
Goodrich, L. M. and Hambro 1960. The Charter of the United Nations. London.
Greig, D. W. 1970. *International Law*. London.
Hatch, John 1974. *Africa Emergent*. London.

Hertslet, Sir Edward 1896. *Map of Africa by Treaty.* London.
Hoeffding, Oleg 1959. The Soviet Industrial Reorganization of 1951. *American Economic Review* 49; 2 May, p.65.
Homer, Jack A. 1963. Non-Alignment and Testban Agreement: The Role of the Non-aligned States. *Journal of Arms Control,* October, 1963, pp. 636–646.
Hveem, H. and Willetts, P. 1974. *Horizon of African Diplomacy* (ed. Y. Tand and D. Chanarama). Nairobi.
Ingram, Derek 1977. *The Imperfect Commonwealth.* London.
Jansen, G. H. 1966. *Afro-Asian and Non-Alignment.* London.
Jones-Quartey, K. A. B. 1974. A Summary of History of the Ghana Press, 1822–1960.
Killick, Tony 1978. *Development Economics in Action: A Study of Economic Policies in Ghana.* London.
Kirk-Greene, A. H. M. 1974. *The Formation of Foreign Service Cadres in Nigeria, Kenya and Uganda.* London: (Institute of Commonwealth Studies Series 81). London: the Institute.
Kissinger, Henry, 1981. "A unique Opportunity to Re-forge the alliance with the America no longer in trauma". The Times of London.
Knorr, Klaus 1975. *The Power of Nations: The Political Economy of International Relations.* New York.
Krafona, Kwesi 1986. The Pan-African Movement: Ghana's Contribution. London: Afroworla Publishing Co.
Lauterpacht, Oppenheim 1953. *International Law*, 7. London.
Legum, Colin 1962. *Pan-Africanism: A Short Political Guide.* London.
Lie, Trygve 1964. *In the Cause of Peace.* New York: Macmillan Co.
Mackintosh, John 1962. *The British Cabinet.* London.
Mansergh, Nicholas 1963. *Documents and Speeches on Commonwealth Affairs, 1952–62.* London: Oxford University Press.
Mazrui, Ali 1963. African Attitudes to the European Community" In *International Affairs.* London, January 1963, p.34.
Mazrui, Ali 1963. Consent, Colonisation, and Sovereignty. *Political Studies*, xi, 1963, pp. 50–51.
Mazrui, Ali 1968. *On Hereos and Uhuru-Worship.* London.
Mazrui, Ali 1969. *Towards a Pan African: A Study of Ideology and Ambition.* London.
Mazrui, Ali 1977. *Africa's International Relations, The Diplomacy of Dependency and Change.* London.
Mensah, J. H. 1970. *The State of the Economy and the External Debts Problem.* Accra.
Menzies, Sir Robert 1967. *Afternoon Light: Some Memories of Men and Events.* London.
Moore, Sir Thomas 1963. *After Imperialism* by M.B. Brown London: CASS.
Mulhall, J. A. 1952. *Note for the Guidance of Members of the Public Service Commissioners in Overseas Territories.* London: Colonial Office.
Nkrumah, Kwame 1962. *Towards Colonial Freedom.* London.
Nkrumah, Kwame 1963. *Africa Must Unite.* London: Heinemann.
Nkrumah, Kwame 1965. *Neocolonialism, the Last Stage of Imperialism.* London: Thomas Nelson.
Nkrumah, Kwame 1967. *Challenge of the Congo.* London.
Nkrumah, Kwame 1970. *Africa Must Unite.* London: Panaf.
Nkrumah, Kwame 1973. *I Speak of Freedom.* London: Panaf.
Nkrumah, Kwame 1973. *Revolutionary Path.* London.
Nyerere, Julius K. 1967. *Freedom and Unity: A Selection from Writings and Speeches, 1962–1965.* London: Oxford University Press.
Nyerere, J. K., The Entrenchment of Privilege. *South Africa*, 2.

Obeng, Samuel 1972. *Selected Speeches of Dr. Kwame Nkrumah*. Accra: The Advance Press Limited.
O'Brien, Conor Cruise 1962. *To Katanga and Back. A UN Case History*. London.
Padmore, George 1964. A Guide to Pan-African Socialism. In *African Socialism* (ed. William H. Friedland and Carl G. Rosberg Jr.) Stanford: Standford University Press.
Padmore, George 1964. *Pan-Africanism or Communism?*
Schlesinger, J. Arthur M. 1965. *A Thousand Days (John F. Kennedy in the White House)*. London.
Sorokine, A. A. 1971. In *The Challenge of African Economic Recorvery and Development (ed. Adebayo Adedeji et al.)*. London: CASS.
Stevens, Chris 1974. In Search of the Economic Kingdom: The Development of Economic Relations between Ghana and Russia. *The Journal of Development Areas* October, 1974, p.5.
Stoessinger, John G. 1961 Financing the United Nations. *International Conciliation*, No.535, November, 1961. pp. 23–32.
Tandem, Y. A. and Chanaroma, D. (ed.) 1974. *Horizon of African Diplomacy*. Nairobi.
Thiam, Doudu 1965. *The Foreign Policy of African States*. New York: Praeger.
Thompson, Scott 1969. *Ghana's Foreign Policy, 1957–1966*. Princeton.
Tsikata, Tsatsu 1990.
Tunkin, C. I. 1974. *Theory of International Law*. Cambridge, Mass: Harvard University Press.
Wallerstein, Immanuel 1968. *Africa: The Politics of Unity*. London: Pall Mall Press.
Walker, Patrick Gordon 1970. *The Cabinet*. London.
Waltz, Kenneth N.1967. *Foreign Policy and Democratic Politics*. London.
Willets, B. and Willets. P. 1974. The practice of non-alignment. In *Horison of African Diplomacy* (ed. Y. A. Tandem and D. Chanarama). Nairobi.
Wilson, Harod 1976. *The Governance of Britain*. London.
Wolfers, Arnold 1944. In Defence of Small Countries *Yale Review*, Winter, 1944, pp. 201–220.
Wright, Arthur W. 1960. *Soviet Economic Planning: The Soviet Union Since Stalin*. London.

INDEX

Abrahams, Peter, 60
accelerated education plan, 26
Adjei, Ako, 20, 99
Adu, A. L. 25, 27, 36
Africa Must Unite, 20
African Affairs Committee, 22
African Affairs Secretariat, 17, 21–22, 29, 30, 38
African Common Market, 127–129, 196
African High Command, 55–56
African Liberation Committee, 76
African Unity, 9, 10, 105, 106, 107
Afrifa, A. A., 40
All-African Peoples' Conference (1958), 51, 58–59, 61, 62, 63, 95, 190
Amonoo, Harry, 17, 21, 22, 29
Anlo Youth Association, 7
Apartheid, 77
Armah, Kwesi, 38
Asante, K. B., 21, 29
Atiyah, Patrick, 70
Balewa, Sir Abubakar, 160
ban-the-bomb conference, 136–137, 198
Banda, Dr., 82, 83
Barden, A. K., 22, 29
Basner, Harry, 17
Belgrade Conference (1961), 136, 139–140
Bing, Geoffrey, 8, 40, 65, 71, 111, 161–162, 164
Boateng, Kweku, 28
Bonne, Nii, 164
Bosomtwe-Sam, David, 23, 29, 38
Bostio, Kojo, 20, 25–26, 29, 30, 38
Brazzaville Group, 99–100, 101
British Monarchy, 84–85
Bureau of African Affairs, 22, 23, 27, 29, 38
Burkina Faso, 93–94
Calhoun, Chad, 183
Capital Investment Act (1963), 112, 113
Casablanca Conference (1961), 56–57
Casablanca Group, 100–102, 103, 104
China, 152, 153, 154, 155, 156, 172, 173, 174
Chou-En-Lai, 172, 173–174, 176, 200
Civil Service, 23, 26, 28
Cocoa Marketing Board Scholarship, 26
Colonial boundary agreements, 13–14

Colonial Laws Validity Act (1865), 15
Colonization, 45–46
Committee of African Organizations (CAO), 106, 107
Commonwealth of Nations, 64, 71, 72, 73, 74, 75, 190, 191
Commonwealth Secretariat, 87, 191
Conference of Independent African States (1963), 173, 190
Congo (The), 51
Congo Co-ordinating Committee, 28
Congo crisis, 41, 53, 54–57
  Belgian interventions in, 75–76
Constitution(s)
  Republican (1960), 39–40, 41, 91, 191–192
Convention of Association, 125
Cross, Ulric, 70
Crossman, Richard, 33
Council for Mutual Economic Assistance (COMECON), 169, 170
Cuba, 145, 146, 198
Daily Telegraph, 65, 66
Daniels, Ekow, 23
Dei-Anang, Michael, 17, 21, 27, 28, 29, 30, 35, 37, 38
Development Fund for Overseas Countries and Territories (DFOCT), 125
Diagne, M. Blaise, 59–60
Diefenbaker, J. C., 73
Douglas-Home, Sir Alec, 70, 75, 87
Du Bois, 60
East and Central African leaders Conference, 95–96
European Economic Community (ECC), 125, 126–127, 196
Federalism, 47, 48
Freedom Fighters, 16–17
Foreign Ministry (Ghana), 16, 21, 30
  policy formulation, 18–20
Founding Conference of the Organization of African Unity, 76
France
  nuclear test, 137–138
Front de Liberation Nationale (FLN), 95
Gaulle, Charle de, 137, 138
Ghana, 2, 3

commitment to African Unity, 90–93, 97, 98
Exchange Control, 123, 124, 195–196
independence, 180–181
inflow of foreign capital, 120–121
refugees in, 159–160, 161
relations with Britain, 34, 35, 85, 86
relations with China, 171–173
relations with the Soviet Union, 161–162, 169–170, 200
relations with the USA, 180–184, 199
trade with Eastern European countries, 113–114
Ghana Action Party, 7
Ghana, Guinea-Mali Union, 93, 96
Ghana Independence Act (1957), 15
Ghanaian foreign policy, principles of, 15–16
Gower, L. C. B., 70
Gray-Cowan, 108
Guggisberg, Sir Gordon, 182
International Corps of Volunteers, 61, 62
International Monetary Fund (IMF), 202
and World Bank policies, 203, 204
Jantuah, Kwame, 34
Kaiser Aluminuim Chemical Corporation, 199
Kaiser, Edger, 183
Kasavubu, 55, 57, 103
Katanga, 52, 57
Kennedy, J. F. K., 145, 146, 183–184
Kirk-Greene, A. H., 25
Kissinger, Dr. Henry, 201
Krushchev, Nikiti, 145, 146, 147, 169
Lang, John, 70–71
Lumumba, Patrice, 51, 53, 54, 55, 56, 57, 103
Macmillan, Mr., 178
Mazrui, Ali, 3–4, 141
Mboya, Tom, 58
Mensah, J. H., 115
Menzies, R. C., 73
Mohammed V, King, 56
Monkton Commission, 81
Monrovia group, 101–102, 103, 104
Moore, Thomas, 201
Morocco, 56
Muslim Association Party (MAP), 7

National Congress of British West Africa (NCBWA), 60
National Liberation Movement, 7, 117
Nkrumah, Kwame, 2, 3, 4, 14–15, 17, 20, 21, 22, 31, 32, 34, 47, 48, 49, 50, 55, 56, 60, 61, 63, 65, 66, 67, 68–69, 70, 72, 74, 77, 78, 83–84, 86, 87, 90, 97, 98, 99, 106, 119, 125–126, 127, 135, 136, 138, 142, 145, 146, 178, 202
approach to Marxism, 171
British and Nigerian press and, 65
role in foreign policy formulation, 31, 32, 33, 38
Non-alighnment, 1, 139, 140–145
Non-alignment Movement, 143
Northern Peoples Party (NPP), 7
Nyerere, President, 72–73, 140
OAU Heads of State Conference (1965), 36–37, 38, 98
Ogmore, Lord, 164
Padmore, George, 27, 171
Pan-African Congress
(1921), 59
(1945), 60
Pan-Africanism, 8, 9, 10
Pioneer Industries and Companies Act (1959), 112
Public Service Commission, 24
Quaison-Sackey, Alex, 20–21, 30, 160, 197
Racism, 68
Rassemblement Democratique Africain (RDA), 94
Rhodesia, 78, 79, 80–81, 82
Sanniquellie Declaration, 97
Schatten, Dr. Fritz, 163–164
Sino-India Conflict, 174–180, 200–201
South Africa, 68, 69, 70–71, 72, 73, 74, 77, 78, 82
Southern Rhodesia see Rhodesia
Soviet Union, 147, 161, 162, 200
Taiwan, 154
Thiam, Doudou, 142, 143
Thompson, Scott, 24, 33, 169
Togoland Congress, 7
Trans National Corporation (TNCs), 203–204
Tshombe, 57
Tsikata, Tsatsu, 203
Unitary government, 83

Index 217

United Nations, 50, 190
United Nations Convention on the Status of Refuges, 158, 159
United Nations Emergency Force (UNEF), 148, 149, 150, 197
United States of America, 180–184
Universal Declaration of Independence (UDI), 34
University of Ghana, 25

Valco, 182
Volta Hydro-Electric Scheme, 181
Volta River Project, 182, 183
Watson Commission, 165–168
West African National Secretariat (WANS), 60
West African Pilot, 66–67
Wilson, Harold, 168
Wolfers, Arnold, 5

www.ingramcontent.com/pod-product-compliance
Lightning Source LLC
Chambersburg PA
CBHW072108010526
44111CB00037B/2046